**SECTION SIX —
EQUATIONS &
CALCULATIONS**

Balancing Equations
Relative Formula Mass ....
Two Formula Mass Calculations ....
Calculating Masses in Reactions ....
Atom Economy ....
Percentage Yield ....
Revision Summary for Section Six 73

**SECTION SEVEN —
INDUSTRIAL
CHEMISTRY**

Rates of Reaction 74
Measuring Rates of Reaction 75
Collision Theory 76
Catalysts 77
Energy Transfer in Reactions 78
Reversible Reactions and Ammonia 79
Minimising the Cost of Production 80
Acids and Bases 81
Acids Reacting with Metals 82
Neutralisation Reactions 83
Making Salts 84
Electrolysis 85
Crude Oil 86
Alkanes and Alkenes 87
Vegetable Oils 88
Plastics 89
Chemical Production 91
Washing-up Liquids and Detergents 92
Water Purity 93
Revision Summary for Section Seven 95

**SECTION EIGHT —
FORCES AND
MOTION**

Speed and Velocity 96
Acceleration 97
Mass, Weight and Gravity 98
Friction Forces and Terminal Speed 99
Forces and Acceleration 100
Stopping Distances 102
Momentum and Collisions 103
Car Safety 104
Work and Potential Energy 105
Kinetic Energy and Roller Coasters 106
Power 107
Revision Summary for Section Eight 108

**SECTION NINE —
ELECTRICITY**

Static Electricity 109
Uses of Static Electricity 111
Circuits — The Basics 112
Measuring AC 113
Resistance and $V = I \times R$ 114
Circuit Symbols and Devices 115
Series Circuits 116
Parallel Circuits 117
Fuses and Safe Plugs 118
Energy and Power in Circuits 119
Revision Summary for Section Nine 120

**SECTION TEN —
NUCLEAR PHYSICS**

Atoms and Isotopes 121
Ionising Radiation 122
Radioactive Decay 123
Background Radiation 124
Radioactive Safety 125
Half-Life 126
Uses of Ionising Radiation 127
Radioactive Dating 129
Nuclear Fission and Fusion 130
Revision Summary for Section Ten 131

EXAM SKILLS

Thinking in Exams 132
Answering Experiment Questions 133
Index 137
Answers 140

Published by Coordination Group Publications Ltd.

From original material by Richard Parsons.

Editors:
Ellen Bowness, Gemma Hallam, Sharon Keeley, Andy Park, Kate Redmond, Alan Rix,
Ami Snelling, Claire Thompson, Julie Wakeling.

Contributors:
John Duffy, Sandy Gardner, James Foster, Jason Howell, Lucy Muncaster, John Myers,
Adrian Schmit, Claire Stebbing, Mike Thompson.

ISBN: 978 1 84146 753 5

With thanks to Glenn Rogers for the proofreading.

Data used to construct stopping distance diagram on page 102 from the Highway Code.
Reproduced under the terms of the Click-Use Licence.

Groovy website: www.cgpbooks.co.uk

Printed by Elanders Hindson Ltd, Newcastle upon Tyne.
Jolly bits of clipart from CorelDRAW®

Cells

In Physics you often start off with <u>forces</u>, in Chemistry it's usually <u>elements</u>, and in Biology it's the <u>cell</u>. Not very <u>original</u>, but nice and <u>familiar</u> at least. So away we go — a-one, a-two, a-one, two, three, four...

Plant and Animal Cells Have Similarities and Differences

Most <u>human cells</u>, like most <u>animal</u> cells, have the following parts — make sure you know them all:

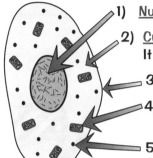

1) <u>Nucleus</u> — contains <u>genetic material</u> that controls the activities of the cell.

2) <u>Cytoplasm</u> — gel-like substance where most of the <u>chemical reactions</u> happen. It contains <u>enzymes</u> (see page 4) that control these chemical reactions.

3) <u>Cell membrane</u> — holds the cell together and controls what goes <u>in</u> and <u>out</u>.

4) <u>Mitochondria</u> — these are where most of the reactions for <u>respiration</u> take place (see page 23). Respiration releases <u>energy</u> that the cell needs to work.

5) <u>Ribosomes</u> — these are where <u>proteins</u> are made in the cell.

Plant cells usually have <u>all the bits</u> that <u>animal</u> cells have, plus a few <u>extra</u> bits:

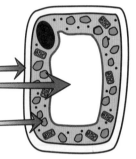

1) Rigid <u>cell wall</u> — made of <u>cellulose</u>. It <u>supports</u> the cell and strengthens it.
2) <u>Permanent vacuole</u> — contains <u>cell sap</u>, a weak solution of sugar and salts.
3) <u>Chloroplasts</u> — these are where <u>photosynthesis</u> occurs, which makes food for the plant (see page 34). They contain a <u>green</u> substance called <u>chlorophyll</u>.

Most Cells are Specialised for Their Function

Similar cells are grouped together to make a <u>tissue</u>, and different tissues work together as an <u>organ</u>. Most cells are <u>specialised</u> for their function within a <u>tissue</u> or <u>organ</u>. In the exam you might have to explain <u>how</u> a particular cell is adapted for its function. Here are a couple of plant examples:

1) Palisade Leaf Cells are Adapted for Photosynthesis

1) They're packed with <u>chloroplasts</u> for <u>photosynthesis</u>.
2) Their <u>tall</u> shape means a lot of <u>surface area</u> is exposed down the side for <u>absorbing CO$_2$</u> from the air in the leaf.
3) They're <u>thin</u>, so you can pack loads of them in at the top of a leaf.

Lots of palisade cells make <u>palisade tissue</u> where most of the <u>photosynthesis</u> happens.

2) Guard Cells are Adapted to Open and Close Pores

1) They have a special shape which <u>opens</u> and <u>closes</u> pores (<u>stomata</u>) in a leaf.
2) When the plant has <u>plenty</u> of water the guard cells fill with it and go plump. This makes the stomata <u>open</u> so <u>gases</u> can be exchanged for <u>photosynthesis</u>.
3) When the plant is <u>short</u> of water, the guard cells lose water and go floppy, making the stomata <u>close</u>. This helps stop too much water vapour <u>escaping</u>.
4) They're <u>sensitive to light</u> so they <u>close at night</u> to save water.

For some examples of specialised animal cells, see red and white blood cells (page 26) and sperm (page 13).

There's quite a bit to learn in Biology — but that's life, I guess...

At the top of the page are <u>typical cells</u> with all the typical bits you need to know. But cells <u>aren't</u> all the same — they have different <u>structures</u> and <u>produce</u> different substances depending on the <u>job</u> they do.

2

DNA

Ah... DNA. The molecule of life. Trouble is, it's so darn complicated.

Chromosomes _are Really Long Molecules of_ DNA

1) DNA stands for deoxyribose nucleic acid.
2) It contains all the instructions to put an organism together and make it work.
3) It's found in the nucleus of animal and plant cells, in really long molecules called chromosomes.

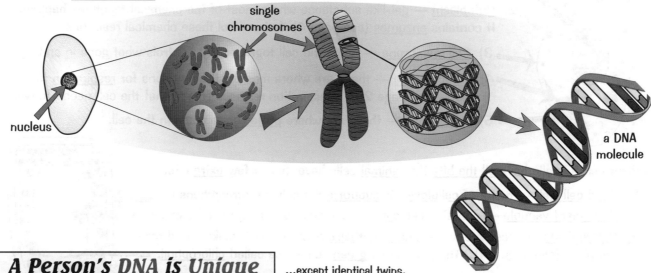

A Person's DNA _is Unique_   ...except identical twins.

Your DNA is unique, unless you're an identical twin (then the two of you have identical DNA) or a clone.

DNA fingerprinting (or genetic fingerprinting) is a way of cutting up a person's DNA into small sections and then separating them. Every person's genetic fingerprint has a unique pattern (unless they're identical twins or clones, of course). This means you can tell people apart by comparing samples of their DNA.

DNA fingerprinting is used in...

1) Forensic science — DNA (from hair, skin flakes, blood, semen etc.) taken from a crime scene is compared with a DNA sample taken from a suspect. In the diagram, suspect 1's DNA has the same pattern as the DNA from the crime scene — so suspect 1 was probably at the crime scene.

2) Paternity testing — to see if a man is the father of a particular child.

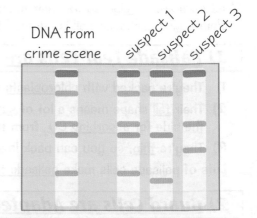

Some people would like there to be a national genetic database of everyone in the country. That way, DNA from a crime scene could be checked against everyone in the country to see whose it was. But others think this is a big invasion of privacy, and they worry about how safe the data would be and what else it might be used for. There are also scientific problems — false positives can occur if errors are made in the procedure or if the data is misinterpreted.

So the trick is — frame your twin and they'll never get you...

In the exam you might have to interpret data on DNA fingerprinting for identification. They'd probably give you a diagram similar to the one at the bottom of this page, and you'd have to say which of the known samples (if any) matched the unknown sample. Pretty easy — it's the one that looks the same.

DNA — Making Proteins

Your DNA is basically a long list of instructions on how and when to make <u>all the proteins</u> in your body.

DNA — a Double Helix of Paired Bases

1) A DNA molecule has <u>two strands</u> coiled together in the shape of a <u>double helix</u> (two spirals), as shown in the diagram.

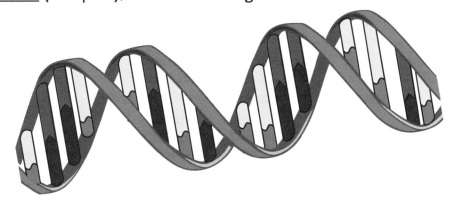

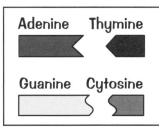

Adenine   Thymine

Guanine   Cytosine

2) The two strands are held together by chemicals called <u>bases</u>. There are <u>four</u> different bases (shown in the diagram as different colours) — <u>adenine</u> (A), <u>cytosine</u> (C), <u>guanine</u> (G) and <u>thymine</u> (T).

3) The bases are <u>paired</u>, and they always pair up in the same way — it's always **A-T** and **C-G**. This is called <u>base-pairing</u>.

A Gene Codes for a Specific Protein

1) A <u>gene</u> is a <u>section</u> of DNA. It contains the <u>instructions</u> to make a <u>specific protein</u>.

2) Cells make <u>proteins</u> by stringing <u>amino acids</u> together in a particular order.

3) Only <u>20</u> different amino acids are used to make up <u>thousands</u> of different <u>proteins</u>.

4) The <u>order of the bases</u> in a gene simply tells cells <u>in what order</u> to put the amino acids together:

> Each set of <u>three bases</u> (called a <u>triplet</u>) <u>codes</u> for a <u>particular amino acid</u>.
> Here's an <u>example</u> (don't worry — you don't have to remember the specifics):
> TAT codes for tyrosine and GCA for alanine. If the order of the bases in the gene is TAT-GCA-TAT then the order of amino acids in the protein will be tyrosine-alanine-tyrosine.

5) DNA also determines which genes are <u>switched on or off</u> — and so which <u>proteins</u> the cell <u>produces</u>, e.g. haemoglobin or keratin. That in turn determines what <u>type of cell</u> it is, e.g. red blood cell, skin cell.

What do DNA and a game of rounders have in common?

...they both have four bases. The order of bases determines what amino acid is added and the order of amino acids determines the type of protein. All the <u>enzymes</u> in your body are <u>proteins</u>, as are your hair and your nails. Enzymes control many processes that make non-protein things.

Enzymes

Chemical reactions are what make you work. And enzymes are what make them work.

Enzymes are Catalysts Produced by Living Cells

1) <u>Living cells</u> have thousands of different <u>chemical reactions</u> going on inside them all the time — like <u>respiration</u>, <u>photosynthesis</u> and <u>protein synthesis</u>.

2) These reactions need to be <u>carefully controlled</u> — to get the <u>right</u> amounts of substances and keep the organism working properly.

3) You can usually make a reaction happen more quickly by <u>raising the temperature</u>. This would speed up the useful reactions but also the unwanted ones too... not good. There's also a <u>limit</u> to how far you can raise the temperature inside a living creature before its <u>cells</u> start getting <u>damaged</u>.

4) So... living cells produce <u>enzymes</u> which act as <u>biological catalysts</u>. Enzymes reduce the need for high temperatures and we <u>only</u> have enzymes to speed up the <u>useful chemical reactions</u> in the body.

An **ENZYME** is a **BIOLOGICAL CATALYST** which **INCREASES** the speed of a reaction, without being **USED UP** in the reaction.

5) Enzymes are all <u>proteins</u>, which is one reason why proteins are <u>so important</u> to living things.

6) <u>Every</u> different biological reaction has its <u>own enzyme</u> designed especially for it.

Enzymes are Very Specific

1) <u>Chemical reactions</u> usually involve things either being <u>split apart</u> or <u>joined together</u>.

2) Each enzyme has a unique <u>shape</u> that fits onto the substance(s) involved in a reaction.

3) Enzymes are really <u>picky</u> — they usually only catalyse <u>one reaction</u>. That's because, for the enzyme to work, the substance has to fit its special shape — like a key in a lock.

Enzymes Have an Optimum Temperature and pH

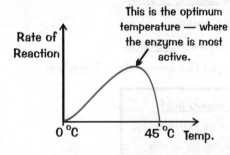

This is the optimum temperature — where the enzyme is most active.

Rate of Reaction

0 °C   45 °C   Temp.

Changing the <u>temperature</u> changes the <u>rate</u> of an enzyme-catalysed reaction.

Like with any reaction, a higher temperature <u>increases</u> the rate at first. If it gets <u>too hot</u> though, the rate rapidly <u>decreases</u>.

Each enzyme has its own <u>optimum temperature</u> when the reaction goes <u>fastest</u>. The optimum temperature for the most important <u>human</u> enzymes is about <u>37 °C</u> — the <u>same</u> temperature as our bodies. Lucky for us.

The <u>pH</u> also has an effect on enzymes.

Like with temperature, all enzymes have an <u>optimum pH</u> that they work best at. It's often around <u>neutral pH 7</u>, but <u>not always</u>.

For example, <u>pepsin</u> is an enzyme used to break down <u>proteins</u> in the <u>stomach</u>. It works best at <u>pH 2</u>, which means it's well-suited to the <u>acidic conditions</u> in the stomach.

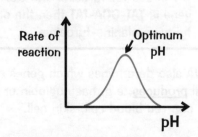

Rate of reaction   Optimum pH

pH

No horses were harmed in the making of this page...

...it's just our high-tech special effects that give that impression. Enzymes allow us to have a huge amount of control over which chemical reactions go on in our bodies. They're also useful outside the body — where we use them in things like biological washing powders.

Diffusion

Particles <u>move about randomly</u>, and after a bit they end up <u>evenly spaced</u>. It's not rocket science, is it...

Don't be Put Off by the Fancy Word

"<u>Diffusion</u>" is simple. It's just the <u>gradual movement</u> of particles from places where there are <u>lots</u> of them to places where there are <u>fewer</u> of them. That's all it is — just the <u>natural tendency</u> for stuff to <u>spread out</u>. Unfortunately you also have to learn the fancy way of saying the same thing, which is this:

> <u>DIFFUSION</u> is the <u>passive movement</u> of <u>particles</u> from an area of <u>HIGHER CONCENTRATION</u> to an area of <u>LOWER CONCENTRATION</u>

Diffusion happens in both <u>liquids</u> and <u>gases</u> — that's because the particles in these substances are free to <u>move about</u> randomly. The <u>simplest type</u> is when different <u>gases</u> diffuse through each other. This is what's happening when the smell of perfume diffuses through a room:

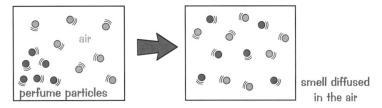

smell diffused in the air

Cell Membranes are Kind of Clever...

They're clever because they <u>hold</u> the cell together <u>but</u> they let stuff <u>in and out</u> as well. Substances can move in and out of cells by <u>diffusion</u> and <u>osmosis</u> (see page 7). Only very <u>small</u> molecules can <u>diffuse</u> through cell membranes though — things like <u>glucose</u>, <u>amino acids</u>, <u>water</u> and <u>oxygen</u>. <u>Big</u> molecules like <u>starch</u> and <u>proteins</u> can't fit through the membrane.

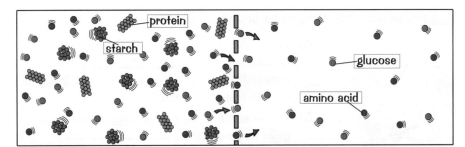

1) Just like with diffusion in air, particles flow through the cell membrane from where there's a <u>higher concentration</u> (more of them) to where there's a <u>lower concentration</u> (not such a lot of them).

2) They're only moving about <u>randomly</u> of course, so they go <u>both</u> ways — but if there are a lot <u>more</u> particles on one side of the membrane, there's a <u>net</u> (overall) movement <u>from</u> that side.

> The <u>rate</u> of diffusion is affected by the <u>CONCENTRATION DIFFERENCE (gradient)</u>:
> Substances diffuse faster if there's a <u>big difference</u> in concentration.
> If there are <u>lots more</u> particles on one side, there are more there to move across.

Revision by diffusion — you wish...

Wouldn't that be great — if all the ideas in this book would just gradually drift across into your mind, from an area of <u>higher concentration</u> (in the book) to an area of <u>lower concentration</u> (in your mind — no offence). Actually, that probably will happen if you read it again. Why don't you give it a go...

6

Diffusion in Cells

And here's how diffusion happens in our bodies. Are you sitting comfortably — then I'll begin...

Small Food Molecules Can Diffuse into the Blood

1) Food is <u>digested</u> in the gut to break it down into pieces small enough to be absorbed into the <u>blood</u> by <u>diffusion</u>.

2) The absorption happens in the <u>small intestine</u>, after big molecules like <u>starch</u> and <u>proteins</u> have been broken down into small ones like <u>glucose</u> and <u>amino acids</u>.

3) These molecules can diffuse into the blood from the small intestine because their <u>concentration</u> is <u>higher</u> than it is in the blood.

4) The concentration of these substances in body cells is <u>low</u>, so when the blood reaches cells that need them they can diffuse out easily from an area of <u>higher concentration</u> to an area of <u>lower concentration</u>.

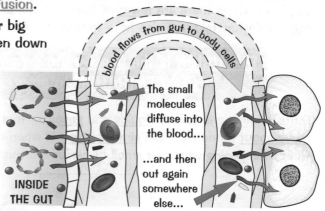

Alveoli Carry Out Gas Exchange in the Lungs

The <u>lungs</u> contain millions and millions of little air sacs called <u>alveoli</u> where <u>gas exchange</u> happens.

1) The <u>blood</u> passing next to the alveoli has just returned to the lungs from the rest of the body, so it contains <u>lots</u> of <u>carbon dioxide</u> and <u>very little oxygen</u> (see p.27).

2) <u>Oxygen</u> diffuses <u>out</u> of the <u>alveolus</u> (higher concentration) into the <u>red blood cells</u> (lower concentration).

3) <u>Carbon dioxide</u> diffuses <u>out</u> of the <u>blood</u> (higher concentration) into the <u>alveolus</u> (lower concentration) to be breathed out.

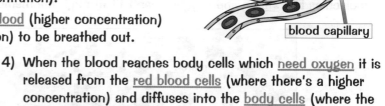

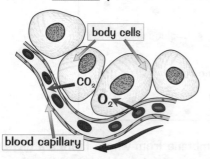

4) When the blood reaches body cells which <u>need oxygen</u> it is released from the <u>red blood cells</u> (where there's a higher concentration) and diffuses into the <u>body cells</u> (where the concentration is lower).

5) At the same time, <u>carbon dioxide</u> diffuses out of the <u>body cells</u> (where there's a higher concentration) into the <u>blood</u> (where there's a lower concentration). It's then carried back to the <u>lungs</u>.

Diffusion Also Happens in the Placenta

A <u>foetus</u> needs to be supplied with <u>food</u> and <u>oxygen</u> to survive. It also needs to get rid of <u>waste</u> products like <u>carbon dioxide</u>. In mammals, foetuses are connected to their mother by an organ called the <u>placenta</u>.

1) <u>Food</u> and <u>oxygen</u> diffuse across from the <u>mother's</u> blood to the <u>foetus's</u> when the foetus needs them, from an area of <u>higher</u> concentration to an area of <u>lower</u> concentration.

2) <u>Carbon dioxide</u> and other <u>wastes</u> diffuse across the placenta in the other direction, from <u>foetus</u> to <u>mum</u>. You can probably fill in the higher concentration to lower concentration bit yourself by now.

Don't worry — there's still diffusion in a leaf to look forward to...

...just in case you were getting upset at the thought of not hearing any more about it. So that's <u>three human examples</u> (and the leaf, see p.36). The process of diffusion is the <u>same</u> in each case.

Section One — Life and Cells

Osmosis

If you've got your head round <u>diffusion</u>, osmosis will be a <u>breeze</u>.

Osmosis *is a Special Case* of *Diffusion, That's All*

<u>OSMOSIS</u> is the <u>movement of water molecules</u> across a <u>partially permeable membrane</u> from a region of <u>higher water concentration</u> to a region of <u>lower water concentration</u>.

1) A <u>partially permeable</u> membrane is just one with very small holes in it. So small, in fact, only tiny <u>molecules</u> (like water) can pass through them, and bigger molecules (e.g. <u>sucrose</u>) can't.

2) The water molecules actually pass <u>both ways</u> through the membrane during osmosis. This happens because water molecules <u>move about randomly</u> all the time.

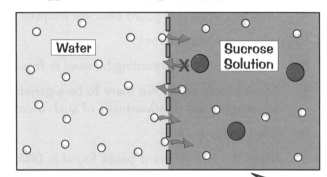

3) But because there are <u>more</u> water molecules on one side than on the other, there's a steady <u>net flow</u> of water into the region with <u>fewer</u> water molecules, i.e. into the <u>stronger</u> sugar solution.

4) This means the <u>strong</u> solution gets more <u>dilute</u>. The water acts like it's trying to "<u>even up</u>" the concentration either side of the membrane.

5) Osmosis is a type of <u>diffusion</u> — the passive movement of <u>water particles</u> from an area of <u>higher water concentration</u> to an area of <u>lower water concentration</u>.

Water Moves Into and Out of Cells *by Osmosis*

1) <u>Tissue fluid</u> surrounds the cells in the body — it's basically just <u>water</u> with <u>oxygen</u>, <u>glucose</u> and stuff dissolved in it. It's squeezed out of the <u>blood capillaries</u> to supply the cells with everything they need.

2) The tissue fluid will usually have a <u>different concentration</u> from the fluid <u>inside</u> a cell. This means that water will either move <u>into the cell</u> from the tissue fluid, or <u>out of the cell</u>, by <u>osmosis</u>.

3) If a cell is <u>short of water</u>, the solution inside it will be quite <u>concentrated</u>. This usually means the solution <u>outside</u> is more <u>dilute</u>, and so water will move <u>into</u> the cell by osmosis.

4) If a cell has <u>lots of water</u>, the solution inside it will be <u>more dilute</u>, and water will be <u>drawn out</u> of the cell and into the fluid outside by osmosis.

There's a fairly dull <u>experiment</u> you can do to show osmosis at work.

You cut up an innocent <u>potato</u> into identical cylinders, and get some beakers with <u>different sugar solutions</u> in them. One should be <u>pure water</u>, another should be a <u>very concentrated sugar solution</u> and a few others should have concentrations <u>in between</u>.

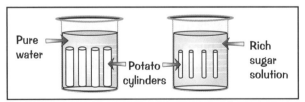

You measure the <u>length</u> of the cylinders, then leave a few cylinders in each beaker for half an hour or so. Then take them out and measure their lengths <u>again</u>. If the cylinders have drawn in water by osmosis, they'll be a bit <u>longer</u>. If water has been drawn out, they'll have <u>shrunk</u> a bit. Then you can plot a few <u>graphs</u> and things. See, told you it was dull.

And to all you cold-hearted potato murderers...

And that's why it's bad to drink seawater. The high <u>salt</u> content means you end up with a much <u>lower water concentration</u> in your blood and tissue fluid than in your cells. Lots of water is sucked out of your cells by osmosis and they <u>shrivel and die</u>. So next time you're stranded at sea, remember this page...

Revision Summary for Section One

Well, just look at this — it's your first Revision Summary page. There's one of these little fellas at the end of every section, and my, they're a right bundle of laughs. No really, they're hilarious. Just look at question one there — "Where in the cell does respiration happen?" HAAAAH HAR HAR HAR. Good one.

1) Where in the cell does respiration happen?

2) Name five parts of a cell that both plant cells and animal cells have.
   What three things do plant cells have that animal cells don't?

3) Give three ways that a palisade leaf cell is adapted for photosynthesis.

4) Give two ways that guard cells are adapted to open and close pores.

5) What are chromosomes?

6) How can DNA fingerprinting be used in forensic science?

7) Some people would like there to be a genetic database of everyone in the country. Discuss the advantages and disadvantages of such a database for use in forensic science.

8) What shape is DNA?

9) Name the four different bases found in DNA. How do they pair up?

10) What is a gene?

11) What does a triplet of three DNA bases code for?

12) What name is given to biological catalysts?

13) What does a catalyst do?

14) Give one reason why proteins are so important to living things.

15)* The graph on the right shows how the rate of an enzyme-catalysed reaction depends on pH:

   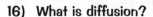
   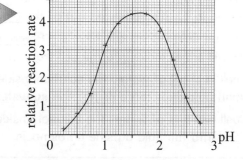

   a) State the optimum pH of the enzyme.

   b) In which part of the human digestive system would you expect to find the enzyme?

16) What is diffusion?

17) Why does oxygen enter the blood in the alveoli, and leave it when it reaches a respiring tissue?

18) How does glucose get from the small intestine to inside body cells?

19) What is osmosis?

20) A solution of pure water is separated from a concentrated sugar solution by a partially permeable membrane. In which direction will molecules flow, and what substance will these molecules be?

* Answers on page 140

Growth

This topic's about <u>growth and development</u> in plants and animals. Organisms grow using a combination of cell division, cell elongation and cell differentiation — which you'll learn all about in exquisite detail as you go through the topic. But first, here's a bit of general stuff about growth...

Growth <u>is an Increase in Size</u> or <u>Weight</u>

You can <u>measure</u> the <u>growth</u> of an organism in these three ways:

1) **Size** — You can measure its <u>height</u>, <u>length</u>, <u>width</u> or <u>circumference</u>.

2) **Wet weight** — Organisms <u>contain</u> a lot of <u>water</u>. The weight of the organism depends on how much water it has gained or lost (e.g. through drinking or sweating). The <u>wet weight</u> of the organism is its weight <u>including all the water</u> in its body — it can vary a lot from <u>one day to the next</u>.

3) **Dry weight** — The <u>dry weight</u> is the weight of an organism with <u>no water in its body</u>. This doesn't vary in the same way as wet weight, but you can only measure it once the organism's dead. The dead organism is <u>dried out</u> by leaving it in a hot oven overnight — then what's left is weighed.

<u>Organisms of the Same Species Vary in Size</u>

1) <u>Individual organisms</u> of the same species <u>vary</u> in <u>size</u> — e.g. humans aren't all the same height.

2) But each species has a <u>range of sizes</u> which <u>most individuals</u> fall within — e.g. most adult humans are between 4' 8" and 6' 8" in height. It's very unusual for a human to grow to 8 foot tall.

3) Several <u>factors</u> affect how individual organisms <u>grow</u> and what <u>size</u> they become. For example, how tall humans grow is influenced by their <u>genes</u>, <u>hormones</u> and <u>diet</u>.

Animals <u>Stop Growing</u>, Plants Can Grow <u>Continuously</u>

Plants and animals <u>grow differently</u>:

1) Animals tend to grow while they're <u>young</u>, and then they reach <u>full growth</u> and <u>stop</u> growing. Plants often grow <u>continuously</u> — even really old trees will keep putting out <u>new branches</u>.

2) In animals, growth happens by <u>cell division</u>, but in plants, growth in <u>height</u> is mainly due to <u>cell enlargement</u> (elongation) — cell <u>division</u> usually just happens in the <u>tips</u> of the <u>roots</u> and <u>shoots</u>.

<u>Some Animals are Able to Regenerate</u>

1) A few animals have the ability to <u>regrow</u> (regenerate) part of their body if it is <u>damaged</u>:

- If some types of <u>worm</u> are cut in two, the front part can grow a new 'tail'.
- If a <u>young spider</u> loses a leg, it can grow a new one (adult spiders can't, though).
- Some <u>reptiles</u>, like lizards, can regrow a lost leg or tail.

2) The ability to regenerate parts of the body is <u>pretty rare</u> though. It tends to happen in fairly simple (or very young) animals which still contain lots of <u>stem cells</u> (see p.14).

<u>Growth — birds do it, bees do it, even educated fleas do it...</u>
I wonder what it'd be like to grow an extra leg. Could help in P.E., but finding clothes might be a problem.

Growth in Humans

Growth in humans is <u>more complicated</u> than just getting <u>born</u> and then getting <u>bigger</u>.

Growth Starts Well Before Birth

Mammals give birth to live young. So, the baby grows inside its mothers womb until it reaches a stage where it can <u>survive</u> outside. This period is called <u>gestation</u> and its length <u>varies</u> in <u>different mammals</u>:

<u>Gestation length</u> is usually related to the <u>size</u> of the animal, but also to <u>how developed</u> it is at birth (e.g. kangaroo babies are born relatively <u>undeveloped</u> and so the gestation period is quite <u>short</u>).

The human body <u>doesn't</u> grow <u>evenly</u> in the mother's womb or in early life. Certain organs grow <u>faster</u> than others, and the <u>fastest-growing</u> of all is the <u>brain</u>. This is because a large and well-developed brain gives humans a big <u>survival advantage</u> — it's our best tool for finding food, avoiding predators, etc.

The graphs show that, during the first year of life, a baby's <u>head size</u> increases <u>in proportion</u> with its <u>body weight</u> (the <u>slope</u> of both graphs is about the <u>same</u>). <u>Head growth</u> is actually responsible for much of the <u>weight increase</u> in the baby.

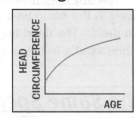

The Human Life Span Has Five Stages

During a normal life span, everyone passes through these <u>five stages</u>. Some of the stages have a <u>clearly defined</u> beginning and end, while others are a bit more vague.

STAGE	DESCRIPTION
<u>Infancy</u>	Roughly the <u>first year</u> of life. Time of rapid growth, child begins to walk.
<u>Childhood</u>	Period between <u>infancy</u> and <u>puberty</u>. Development of the brain.
<u>Adolescence</u>	Begins with <u>puberty</u> and continues until body development and growth are <u>complete</u>.
<u>Maturity/adulthood</u>	Period between <u>adolescence</u> and <u>old age</u>. Cell division for growth stops.
<u>Old age</u>	Usually considered to be between <u>age 65</u> and <u>death</u>.

Growth Factors Can be Used to Enhance Performance in Sport

1) Growth factors are chemicals which <u>stimulate</u> the <u>body</u> to <u>grow</u> and to make <u>extra muscle</u>.
2) Some athletes have used growth factor drugs to <u>improve their performance</u> at <u>sport</u>. This is <u>illegal</u> because it gives them an <u>unfair advantage</u> over other competitors. It also has health risks:

- Growth factor drugs can have <u>bad side effects</u> for health: they can <u>reduce fertility</u>, can increase the risk of <u>heart disease</u> and can sometimes trigger mental illnesses like <u>depression</u>.
- Some growth factors cause <u>women</u> to develop <u>male characteristics</u>, e.g. a deeper voice.

3) <u>Athletes</u> are given <u>random tests</u> for growth factor drugs.

I'm growing rather sick of this topic...

Listen, you think <u>you're</u> sick of reading these lame jokes? Just think how <u>I</u> feel, having to make them up.

Growth in Plants — Plant Hormones

Plants <u>don't</u> grow randomly. Plant hormones make sure they grow in a <u>useful direction</u> (e.g. towards light).

Auxins are Plant Growth Hormones

1) <u>Auxins</u> are <u>plant hormones</u> which control <u>growth</u> near the <u>tips</u> of <u>shoots</u> and <u>roots</u>.
2) Auxin is produced in the <u>tips</u> and <u>diffuses backwards</u> to stimulate the <u>cell elongation (enlargement) process</u> which occurs in the cells <u>just behind</u> the tips.
3) If the tip of a shoot is <u>removed</u>, no auxin is available and the shoot may <u>stop growing</u>.
4) Auxins are involved in the responses of plants to <u>light</u>, <u>gravity</u> and <u>water</u>.

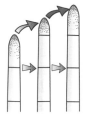

Auxins Change the Direction of Root and Shoot Growth

Extra auxin <u>promotes</u> growth in the <u>shoot</u> but actually <u>inhibits</u> growth in the <u>root</u> — but this produces the <u>desired result</u> in <u>both cases</u>.

Shoots grow towards light

1) When a <u>shoot tip</u> is exposed to <u>light</u>, <u>more auxin</u> accumulates on the side that's in the <u>shade</u> than the side that's in the light.
2) This makes the cells grow (elongate) <u>faster</u> on the <u>shaded side</u>, so the shoot bends <u>towards</u> the light.

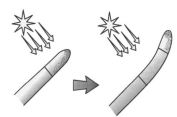

Shoots grow away from gravity

1) When a <u>shoot</u> is growing sideways, <u>gravity</u> produces an unequal distribution of auxin in the tip, with <u>more auxin</u> on the <u>lower side</u>.
2) This causes the lower side to grow <u>faster</u>, bending the shoot <u>upwards</u>.

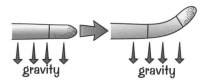

Roots grow towards gravity

1) A <u>root</u> growing sideways will also have more auxin on its <u>lower side</u>.
2) But in a root the <u>extra</u> auxin <u>inhibits</u> growth. This means the cells on <u>top</u> elongate faster, and the root bends <u>downwards</u>.

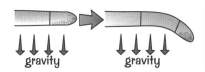

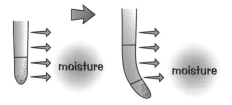

Roots grow towards water

1) An uneven amount of moisture either side of a root produces <u>more auxin</u> on the side with more <u>moisture</u>.
2) This <u>inhibits</u> growth on that side, causing the root to grow in that direction, <u>towards the moisture</u>.

Plant Hormones Can be Extracted and Used by People

1) <u>Seedless fruits</u> can be made with <u>artificial hormones</u>:

> Fruit (with seeds) normally only grows on plants that have been <u>pollinated</u>. But if <u>growth hormones</u> are applied to the <u>unpollinated flowers</u> of some types of plant, the <u>fruit will grow</u> but not the <u>seeds</u>.

2) <u>Selective weedkillers</u> have been developed from <u>plant growth hormones</u>.
3) <u>Cuttings</u> (see p.18) can grown using <u>rooting powder</u> (containing a <u>plant growth hormone</u>).
4) <u>Fruit</u> can be <u>ripened</u> on its way to the shops using a <u>ripening hormone</u>.

A plant auxin to a bar — 'ouch'...

Plants grow in places where there are <u>good growing conditions</u> — like lots of nutrients, light and CO_2.

Cell Division — Mitosis

The cells of your body <u>divide</u> to <u>produce more cells</u>. This is so that your body can grow and repair damaged cells. Of course, cell division doesn't just happen in humans — animals and plants do it too.

Mitosis Makes New Cells for Growth and Repair

1) <u>Human body cells</u> are <u>diploid</u>. This means they have <u>two versions</u> of each <u>chromosome</u> — one from the person's <u>mother</u>, and one from their <u>father</u>. This diagram shows the <u>23 pairs of chromosomes</u> in a human cell.

2) When a cell <u>divides</u> it makes <u>two</u> cells <u>identical</u> to the <u>original</u> cell — each with a <u>nucleus</u> containing the <u>same number</u> of chromosomes as the original cell.

3) This type of cell division is called <u>mitosis</u>. It's used when humans (and animals and plants) want to <u>grow</u> or to <u>replace</u> cells that have been <u>damaged</u>.

Mitosis Results in Two Identical Cells

In a cell that's not dividing, the DNA is all spread out in <u>long strings</u>.

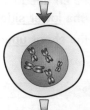

If the cell gets a signal to <u>divide</u>, it needs to <u>duplicate</u> its DNA — so there's one copy for each new cell. The DNA is copied and forms <u>X-shaped</u> chromosomes. Each 'arm' of the chromosome is an <u>exact duplicate</u> of the other.

The left arm has the same DNA as the right arm of the chromosome.

The chromosomes then <u>line up</u> at the centre of the cell and <u>cell fibres</u> pull them apart. The <u>two arms</u> of each chromosome go to <u>opposite ends</u> of the cell.

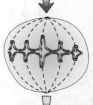

<u>Membranes</u> form around each of the sets of chromosomes. These become the <u>nuclei</u> of the two new cells.

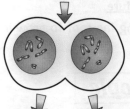

Lastly, the <u>cytoplasm</u> divides.

You now have <u>two new cells</u> containing exactly the same DNA — they're <u>identical</u>.

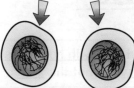

ASEXUAL REPRODUCTION Also Uses Mitosis

Some organisms also <u>reproduce</u> by mitosis, e.g. strawberry plants can form runners in this way, which become new plants. This is an example of <u>asexual</u> reproduction. The offspring have exactly the <u>same genes</u> as the parent — so there's <u>no variation</u>.

Sexual Reproduction

People can look very similar to their mum and dad, often a good mix of the two. Here's why.

The Other Type of Cell Division is Meiosis

1) Reproductive cells undergo <u>meiosis</u> to make <u>gametes</u>. These are the <u>sex cells</u> — <u>eggs</u> and <u>sperm</u>.

2) <u>Meiosis</u> is a type of cell division where the parent cell divides to form <u>four new cells</u> that are all <u>genetically different</u>.

3) <u>Sex cells</u> are <u>haploid</u>. They only have <u>one copy</u> of each chromosome, due to the way they divided. This is so that you can supply one sex cell from the <u>mum</u> (the egg) and one sex cell from the <u>dad</u> (the sperm) and <u>still</u> end up with the <u>usual number of chromosomes</u> in body cells.

Sexual Reproduction Creates Variation

> <u>SEXUAL REPRODUCTION</u> involves the fusion of male and female gametes (sex cells). Because there are <u>TWO</u> parents, the offspring contains <u>a mixture of their parents' genes</u>.

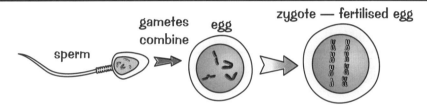

<u>Sexual reproduction</u> produces more <u>variation</u> than <u>asexual reproduction</u> (which uses mitosis). Here's why:

1) The gametes are <u>genetically different</u> from each other because the genes all get <u>shuffled up</u> during meiosis. Each gamete only gets <u>half</u> of them, selected at <u>random</u>.

2) The offspring will have a <u>mixture</u> of chromosomes from their mum and their dad, so it will inherit features from <u>both</u> parents.

Egg and Sperm Cells are Adapted for Their Function

The main functions of an <u>egg cell</u> are to carry the female DNA and to <u>nourish</u> the developing embryo in the early stages. The egg cell is <u>large</u> as it contains huge <u>food reserves</u> to feed the embryo. The <u>nucleus</u> carries the genes from the <u>mother</u>.

The function of a sperm is to <u>transport</u> the <u>male's DNA</u> to the <u>female's egg</u> so that their DNA can <u>combine</u>.

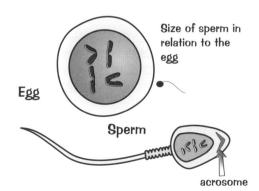

Egg

Size of sperm in relation to the egg

Sperm

acrosome

1) Sperm are <u>small</u> and have <u>long tails</u> so they can <u>swim</u> to the egg.

2) Sperm have lots of <u>mitochondria</u> (see page 1) to provide the <u>energy</u> needed to swim this distance.

3) Sperm also have an <u>acrosome</u> at the front of the 'head', where they store the <u>enzymes</u> they need to <u>digest</u> their way through the <u>membrane</u> of the egg cell.

4) They're produced in <u>large numbers</u> to <u>increase</u> the chance of fertilisation.

5) The <u>nucleus</u> carries the genes from the <u>father</u>.

Right — no sniggering in the back, please...

For many kids in year seven, the mere sight of a <u>sperm</u> is enough to convulse them in <u>giggles</u>. Those of them that don't think it's an innocent <u>tadpole</u>, anyway. But that's not the case for you lot. We hope.

Stem Cells and Differentiation

Differentiation is pretty important if you're planning on being bigger than an amoeba.

Being Multi-Cellular Has Some Important Advantages

1) There's nothing wrong with single-celled organisms — they're pretty successful. Bacteria, for example, aren't in danger of extinction any time soon. But there are some big advantages in being multi-cellular, and so some organisms have cleverly evolved that way.

2) Being multi-cellular allows for cell differentiation. Instead of being just one cell that has to do everything, you can have different types of cells that do different jobs.

3) This means multi-cellular organisms can be more complex — they can have specialised organs, different shapes and behaviours — and so can be adapted specifically to their particular environment.

Embryonic Stem Cells Can Differentiate into Any Type of Cell

1) A fertilised egg can divide by mitosis to produce a bundle of cells. This is the embryo of the new organism.

2) To start with, the cells in the embryo are all the same (undifferentiated). They are called embryonic stem cells.

3) Stem cells are able to divide as many times as they like to produce either more stem cells or different types of specialised cell (e.g. blood cells).

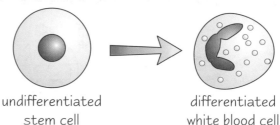

undifferentiated stem cell

differentiated white blood cell

4) The process of stem cells becoming specialised is called differentiation. It is by this process that a human embryo starts to develop a recognisably human body with organs and systems.

5) Adult humans only have stem cells in certain places like the bone marrow. These stem cells aren't as versatile as the stem cells in embryos — they can only differentiate into certain types of cell.

Stem Cells May be Able to Cure Many Diseases

1) Medicine already uses adult stem cells to cure disease. For example, people with some blood disorders (e.g. sickle cell anaemia) can be treated by bone marrow transplants. Bone marrow contains stem cells that can turn into new blood cells to replace the faulty old ones.

2) Scientists can also extract stem cells from very early human embryos and grow them.

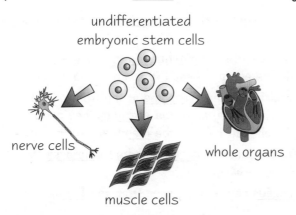

undifferentiated embryonic stem cells

nerve cells

muscle cells

whole organs

3) These embryonic stem cells could be used to replace faulty cells in sick people — you could make beating heart muscle cells for people with heart disease, insulin-producing cells for people with diabetes, nerve cells for people paralysed by spinal injuries, and so on.

4) To get cultures of one specific type of cell, researchers try to control the differentiation of the stem cells by changing the environment they're growing in. So far, it's still a bit hit-and-miss — lots more research is needed.

Stem cells — but who will buy...

The potential of stem cells is huge — but it's early days yet. For example, some researchers think it might be possible to get cells from umbilical cords to behave like embryonic stem cells.

Embryos and Termination

Some People are Against Stem Cell Research

1) Some people are against stem cell research because they feel that human embryos shouldn't be used for experiments since each one is a potential human life.

2) Others think that curing patients who already exist and who are suffering is more important than the rights of embryos.

3) One fairly convincing argument in favour of this point of view is that the embryos used in the research are usually unwanted ones from fertility clinics which, if they weren't used for research, would probably just be destroyed. But of course, campaigners for the rights of embryos usually want this banned too.

4) These campaigners feel that scientists should concentrate more on finding and developing other sources of stem cells, so people could be helped without having to use embryos.

5) In some countries stem cell research is banned, but it's allowed in the UK as long as it follows strict guidelines.

Embryos don't stay embryos for very long — they quickly start to differentiate into a foetus.

A Pregnancy Can Legally be Terminated up to 24 Weeks

1) After the 8th week of pregnancy, the embryo starts to look a bit more human and is called a foetus.

2) In Britain, a termination (induced abortion) is legal until a foetus is 24 weeks old if two doctors agree that termination is necessary.

3) An abortion can be carried out later than this if the pregnancy is putting the mother's health at serious risk or if there is a major foetal abnormality (if the baby would be severely disabled).

4) The 24-week limit came into effect in 1991, but it remains the subject of some fairly heated debate:

> 1) Some people argue that abortion at any stage of pregnancy is unethical. They argue that human life starts at fertilisation — and ending pregnancy is the same as killing a human being.
>
> 2) Other people argue that the foetus doesn't become human until it is conscious — for example, when it starts feeling pain. They argue that abortion should be allowed up until this point. But it's difficult to pinpoint exactly when the foetus becomes conscious and can feel pain.
>
> Some people argue that it's the point when pain receptors first develop at about 7 weeks.
>
> Others argue that the foetus can't feel pain until the pain receptors are connected up in the foetus' brain — which doesn't happen until about 26 weeks.
>
> 3) The legal argument in this country is based on the 'viability' of the foetus — that is, whether or not the foetus can survive outside the womb (with medical help).
>
> With advances in medicine, foetuses are becoming potentially viable earlier in the pregnancy — babies have survived from as early as 21 weeks, so some people argue that the limit should be reduced from 24 weeks to 20 weeks.
>
> But babies born so prematurely can have serious problems. Only about a quarter of babies born at 24 weeks or under survive and, of those, over a third suffer severe disabilities.

There certainly aren't any easy answers.

This page is an ethical minefield...

Topics like stem cell research and abortion often make people feel emotional. Which isn't usually the best mindset for scientific thought... Learn the various sides of the arguments and, whatever your own personal opinions, make sure you can give a balanced view.

Selective Breeding

Selective breeding is a way for humans to develop crops/herds with <u>useful characteristics</u>.

Selective Breeding is Mating the Best Organisms to Get Good Offspring

<u>Selective breeding</u> is when humans select the plants or animals that are going to breed and flourish, according to what <u>we</u> want from them. It's also called <u>artificial selection</u>.

This is the basic process involved in selective breeding:

1) From the existing stock, the organisms which have the <u>best characteristics</u> are selected.

2) They're <u>bred</u> with each other.

3) The <u>best</u> of the <u>offspring</u> are selected and <u>bred</u>.

4) This process is repeated over several generations to develop the <u>desired traits</u>.

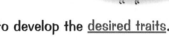

Selective Breeding is Very Useful in Farming

Farmers can improve the quality of milk from cattle

1) Cows can be selectively bred to produce offspring with particular characteristics, e.g. a <u>high milk yield</u> or <u>milk high in nutrients</u> (such as calcium or protein).

2) Cows are usually impregnated using <u>artificial insemination</u>. Semen from a <u>bull</u> whose mother had <u>good characteristics</u> (bulls don't produce milk) is used to inseminate a <u>large number of cows</u>.

3) A typical dairy cow now produces between <u>5000 and 6000 litres</u> of milk a year. This is much more than dairy cows produced a hundred years ago. This is partly because of selective breeding and partly due to <u>intensive farming methods</u> (e.g. giving cows a special diet).

Farmers can increase the number of offspring in sheep

Farmers can selectively breed <u>sheep</u> to <u>increase</u> the number of <u>lambs born</u>. Female sheep (ewes) who produce large numbers of offspring are bred with rams whose mothers had large numbers of offspring. The <u>characteristic</u> of having large numbers of offspring is <u>passed on</u> to the next generation.

Farmers can increase the yield from dwarf wheat

1) Selective breeding can be used to combine <u>two different desirable characteristics</u>.

2) <u>Tall wheat plants</u> have a good grain yield but are easily damaged by wind and rain. <u>Dwarf wheat plants</u> can resist wind and rain but have a lower grain yield.

3) These two types of wheat plant were <u>cross-bred</u>, and the best resulting plants were cross-bred again. This resulted in a <u>new variety</u> of dwarf wheat which can <u>resist bad weather</u> and has a <u>high grain yield</u>.

There are Disadvantages to Selective Breeding

1) Only some of the original population is bred from — so there's <u>less variety</u> in the <u>gene pool</u> of the organisms. All the organisms in a crop/herd will be <u>closely related</u> and have <u>similar characteristics</u> — including their <u>level of disease-resistance</u>. Some diseases might be able to <u>wipe out</u> the whole lot.

2) Some of the characteristics encouraged by selective breeding are <u>beneficial for humans</u>, but <u>not</u> for the <u>organisms</u> themselves. E.g. selective breeding to <u>increase milk yields</u> means cows produce more milk than they would need to feed a calf. They often suffer from <u>mastitis</u> (inflammation of the udders).

I use the same genes all the time too — they flatter my hips...

Selective breeding can be used to nurture all sorts of characteristics — high yield, fast growth, ability to survive in a tough environment, resistance to a particular disease...

Genetic Engineering

Genetic engineering — playing around with genes. Cool.

Genes Can be Transferred into Animals and Plants

Scientists can now move sections of DNA (genes) from one organism into another — this is called genetic engineering or genetic modification. The transfer needs to be done in the very early stages (i.e. shortly after fertilisation) of plant and animal development. It's a young science with exciting possibilities (but potential dangers too).

1) Genetically modified (GM) plants have been developed that are resistant to viruses and herbicides (chemicals used to kill weeds). And long-life tomatoes can be made by changing the gene that causes the fruit to ripen.

2) Genes can also be inserted into animal embryos so that the animal grows up to have more useful characteristics. For example, sheep have been genetically engineered to produce new substances, like drugs, in their milk that can be used to treat human disorders.

3) Genetic disorders like cystic fibrosis are caused by faulty genes. Scientists are trying to cure these diseases by inserting working genes into sufferers. This is called gene therapy.

Genetic Engineering is Great — Hopefully

You need to be able to explain some of the advantages and risks involved in genetic engineering.

1) The main advantage is that you can produce organisms with new and very useful features. There are some examples of this below — make sure you learn them.

2) The main risk is that the inserted gene might have unexpected harmful effects. For example, genes are often inserted into bacteria so they produce useful products. If these bacteria mutated and became pathogenic (disease-causing), the foreign genes might make them more harmful and unpredictable. People also worry about the engineered DNA 'escaping' — e.g. weeds could gain rogue genes from a crop that's had genes for herbicide resistance inserted into it. Then they'd be unstoppable. Eeek.

Learn These Three Examples of Genetic Engineering:

1) In some parts of the world, the population relies heavily on rice for food. In these areas, vitamin A deficiency can be a problem, because rice doesn't contain much of this vitamin, and other sources are scarce. Genetic engineering has allowed scientists to take a gene that controls beta-carotene production from carrot plants, and put it into rice plants. Humans can then change the beta-carotene into vitamin A. Problem solved.

2) The gene for human insulin production has been put into bacteria. These are cultured in a fermenter, and the human insulin is simply extracted from the medium as they produce it. Great.

3) Some plants have resistance to things like herbicides, frost damage and disease. Unfortunately, it's not always the plants we want to grow that have these features. But now, thanks to genetic engineering, we can cut out the genes responsible and stick them into any useful plant we like. Splendid.

Barry played God in the school nativity — I was a sheep...

You can do great things with genetic engineering. But some people worry that we don't know enough about it, or that some maniac is going to come along and combine Cherie Blair with a grapefruit. Possibly.

Cloning

Eeek, cloning. People get even more worked up about this than they do about genetic engineering. But embryo transplants are pretty widely used now — people don't get as upset when it's just farm animals. Learn this definition of clones:

Clones are genetically identical organisms.

Clones occur naturally in both plants and animals. Identical twins are clones of each other. These days clones are very much a part of the high-tech farming industry.

Plants Can be Cloned from Cuttings and by Tissue Culture

1) Cuttings — gardeners can take cuttings from good parent plants, and then plant them to produce genetically identical copies of the parent plant. These plants can be produced quickly and cheaply.

2) Tissue Culture — this is where a few plant cells are put in a growth medium with hormones, and they then grow into new plants — clones of the parent plant. The advantages of using tissue culture are that you can make new plants very quickly, in very little space, and you can grow new plants all year.

The disadvantage to both these methods is a 'reduced gene pool' (see below).

You Need to Know About Embryo Transplants in Cows

Normally, farmers only breed from their best cows and bulls. However, such traditional methods would only allow the prize cow to produce one new offspring each year. These days the whole process has been transformed using embryo transplants:

1) Sperm cells are taken from the prize bull. They can also be frozen and used at a later date. Egg cells are taken from prize cows. Cows are given hormones to make them produce lots of eggs. The sperm are then used to artificially fertilise the egg cells.

2) The fertilised eggs divide to give balls of genetically identical cells which develop into embryos. Their sex is checked and they're screened for genetic defects. The embryos are then split into separate cells before any cells become specialised. Each cell grows into a new embryo which is a clone of the original one.

3) The offspring are clones of each other, not clones of their parents.

4) These embryos are implanted into other cows, called 'surrogate mothers', where they grow. They can also be frozen and used at a later date.

"Nurse — the screens!"

Advantages of Embryo Transplants — Hundreds of Ideal Offspring

a) Hundreds of "ideal" offspring can be produced every year from the best bull and cow.

b) The original prize cow can keep producing prize eggs all year round.

Disadvantages — Reduced Gene Pool

The main problem is that the same alleles keep appearing (and many others are lost). So there's a greater risk of genetic disorders, and a disease could wipe out an entire population if there are no resistant alleles (see page 20).

Oh Eek!

Thank goodness they didn't do that with my little brother...

It seems strange that you can pull apart a growing embryo and not harm it. But at that stage, the cells are all the same — they haven't started to differentiate into different cells with different jobs to do. So if you can separate them gently enough that the cells aren't damaged, they keep dividing quite happily.

Cloning

Clones are organisms with <u>identical DNA</u> — identical twins are naturally occurring clones.
<u>Cloning</u> is using an organism's DNA to create a genetically identical new organism.

Cloned Mammals Can be Made by Adult Cell Cloning

<u>Dolly the sheep</u> (born in 1996) was the <u>first mammal cloned</u> from an adult cell. Here's how it was done:

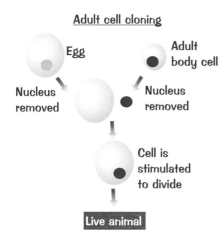

Adult cell cloning

Egg

Adult body cell

Nucleus removed

Nucleus removed

Cell is stimulated to divide

Live animal

1) Dolly was made by taking a sheep's <u>egg cell</u> and removing its <u>nucleus</u> — leaving the cell <u>without any genetic material</u>.
2) The nucleus removed from the egg cell was <u>haploid</u> (it only had half the normal number of chromosomes).
3) Another nucleus was inserted into the egg cell in its place. This was a <u>diploid nucleus</u> from a cell of the <u>parent</u> sheep — it contained the <u>full number of chromosomes</u>.
4) The cell was <u>stimulated</u> so that it started <u>dividing by mitosis</u>, as if it was a normal fertilised egg cell. It formed an <u>embryo</u>.
5) The embryo was <u>implanted</u> in the uterus of a female sheep, which carried it and <u>gave birth</u> to it.
6) The new sheep was <u>genetically identical</u> to the <u>parent sheep</u> which the nucleus was taken from (<u>not</u> the sheep that gave birth to it).

Cloned Mammals May Not Live As Long

1) Dolly the sheep <u>only lived for 6 years</u> (half as long as many sheep of her breed). She was put down because she had a serious <u>lung disease</u>, and she also had <u>arthritis</u>.
2) These diseases are more usual in <u>older sheep</u>. Because Dolly was <u>cloned</u> from an <u>older sheep</u>, it's been suggested her <u>'true' age</u> may have been much <u>older</u>. But it's possible she was <u>just unlucky</u> — and that her illnesses weren't linked to her being a clone.
3) There are many <u>risks</u> and problems associated with cloning:
   • The cloning process <u>often fails</u>. It took hundreds of attempts to produce Dolly.
   • Clones are often born with <u>genetic defects</u>.
   • Cloned animals' <u>immune systems</u> are sometimes unhealthy, so they suffer from <u>more diseases</u>.

Cloning Humans is a Possibility — with a Lot of Ethical Issues

As technology <u>improves</u>, it becomes more and more likely that <u>humans</u> could one day be <u>cloned</u>. However, there are still huge <u>difficulties</u> to overcome — including finding women willing to <u>donate</u> hundreds of <u>eggs</u>. There might have to be lots of <u>surrogate pregnancies</u>, probably with <u>high rates</u> of <u>miscarriage</u> and <u>stillbirth</u>. The problems scientists have had with other mammals have shown that the clones produced might be <u>unhealthy</u> and <u>die prematurely</u>. There are also worries in cloning humans we would be '<u>playing God</u>', and meddling with things we <u>don't fully understand</u>. And even an entirely healthy clone might be <u>psychologically damaged</u> by the knowledge that it's just a clone of <u>another</u> human being.

Star Wars II: Attack of Dolly the Sheep...

In the future, cloning might be really useful for copying animals or plants with good characteristics (e.g. good quality wool). But this would mean <u>even less variety in the gene pool</u> than with selective breeding.

Genetic Diagrams

In the exam they could ask about the inheritance of <u>any</u> characteristic that's controlled by a <u>single gene</u>, because the principle's <u>always the same</u>. So here's the <u>first</u> example ever described, to show you the basics.

Genetic Diagrams Show the Possible Genes of Offspring

1) <u>Alleles</u> are <u>different versions</u> of the <u>same gene</u>.
2) Most of the time you have <u>two copies</u> of each gene — one from each parent.
3) If they're different alleles, only one might be 'expressed' in the organism. The characteristic that appears is coded for by the <u>dominant allele</u>. The other one is <u>recessive</u>.
4) In genetic diagrams <u>letters</u> are used to represent <u>genes</u>. <u>Dominant</u> alleles are always shown with a <u>capital letter</u>, and <u>recessive</u> alleles with a <u>small letter</u>.

You Need to be Able to Interpret Genetic Diagrams

<u>Gregor Mendel</u> was an Austrian monk (back in the 1800s), famous for his genetics experiments with <u>pea plants</u>. He noted how <u>characteristics</u> in plants were passed on from one generation to the next.

In one of his experiments he studied the inheritance of height in pea plants — you can use the letter 'T' (for tall) to <u>represent</u> the gene.

The allele that causes the tall height is <u>dominant</u>, so use a <u>capital 'T'</u> for it.
Dwarf height is due to a <u>recessive allele</u>, so use a <u>small 't'</u>.

1) For an organism to show a <u>recessive</u> characteristic, <u>both</u> its alleles must be <u>recessive</u> — so a dwarf pea plant must have the alleles 'tt'.

2) However, a <u>tall pea plant</u> can have <u>two possible combinations of alleles</u>, TT or Tt, because the dominant allele <u>overrules</u> the recessive one.

First Cross

A <u>tall pea plant</u>, TT, was crossed with a <u>dwarf pea plant</u>, tt.

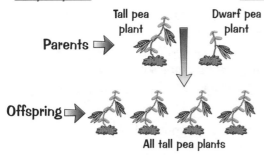

All tall pea plants

Second Cross

Two pea plants were crossed from the <u>1st set of offspring</u>.

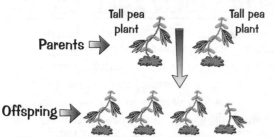

Three tall pea plants and one dwarf pea plant

These are <u>genetic diagrams</u>. They show the possible combinations of offspring from a given cross.

First Cross

Parents ⇒ TT   tt

Offspring ⇒ Tt   Tt   Tt   Tt

Second Cross

Parents ⇒ Tt   Tt

Offspring ⇒ TT   Tt   Tt   tt

Clearly, being a monk in the 1800s was a right laugh...

In Mendel's time, nobody knew anything about genes or DNA, so the significance of his work wasn't realised until after his death. Poor guy, spent all his time growing peas only to be ignored...

Genetic Disorders

Defective genes can cause serious problems — you need to know about two of them.

Cystic Fibrosis is Caused by a Recessive Allele

Cystic fibrosis is a genetic disorder of the cell membranes. It results in the body producing a lot of thick sticky mucus in the air passages and in the pancreas.

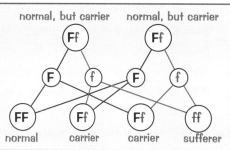

1) The allele which causes cystic fibrosis is a recessive allele, 'f', carried by about 1 person in 30.
2) Because it's recessive, people with only one copy of the allele won't have the disorder — they're known as carriers.
3) For a child to have the disorder, both parents must be either carriers or sufferers.
4) As the diagram shows there's a 1 in 4 chance of a child having the disorder if both parents are carriers.

Huntington's is Caused by a Dominant Allele

Huntington's is a genetic disorder of the nervous system that's really horrible, resulting in shaking, erratic body movements and eventually severe mental deterioration.

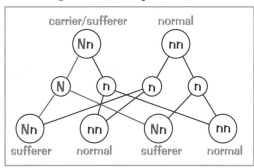

1) The disorder is caused by a dominant allele, 'N', and so can be inherited if just one parent carries the defective gene.
2) The "carrier" parent will of course be a sufferer too since the allele is dominant, but the symptoms don't start to appear until after the person is about 40. By this time the allele might already have been passed on to children and even to grandchildren.
3) As the genetic diagram shows, a person carrying the N allele has a 50% chance of passing it on to each of their children.

Embryos Can be Screened for Genetic Disorders

1) During in vitro fertilisation (IVF), embryos are fertilised in a laboratory, and then implanted into the mother's womb. More than one egg is fertilised, so there's a better chance of the IVF being successful.
2) Before being implanted, it's possible to remove a cell from each embryo and analyse its genes.
3) Many genetic disorders could be detected in this way, such as cystic fibrosis and Huntington's.
4) Embryos with 'good' genes would be implanted into the mother — the ones with 'bad' genes destroyed.

There is a huge debate raging about embryonic screening. Here are some arguments for and against it.

Against Embryonic Screening
1) There may come a point where everyone wants to screen their embryos so they can pick the most 'desirable' one, e.g. they may want a blue eyed, blonde haired, intelligent boy.
2) The rejected embryos are destroyed — they could have developed into humans.
3) It implies that people with genetic problems are 'undesirable' — this could increase prejudice.

For Embryonic Screening
1) It will help to stop people suffering.
2) There are laws to stop it going too far. At the moment parents cannot even select the sex of their baby (unless it's for health reasons).
3) During IVF, most of the embryos are destroyed anyway — screening just allows the selected one to be healthy.
4) Treating disorders costs the Government (and the taxpayers) a lot of money.

Embryonic screening — it's a tricky one...

There's a nice moral argument for you to consider on this page. In the exam you may be asked your opinion — make sure you can back it up with good reasons, and consider other points of view.

Revision Summary for Section Two

And that's another section finished. Award yourself a gold star, relax, get a cup of tea, and take a leisurely glance through these beautiful revision summary questions. Once you've glanced through them, you'll have to answer them. And then you'll have to check your answers and go back and revise any bits you got wrong. And then do the questions again. In fact, it's not really a matter of relaxing at all. More a matter of knuckling down to lots of hard work. Oops. Sorry.

1) Give three ways that the growth of an organism can be measured.
2) Describe two differences in the way plant cells and animal cells grow and develop.
3) Give an example of an animal which can regenerate.
4) Why is it illegal for athletes to use growth factors to enhance their performance?
5) Explain how auxins cause plant shoots to grow towards light.
6) Explain how auxins cause plant roots to grow towards water.
7) Give three ways that plant hormones are used commercially.
8) What is mitosis used for in the human body? Describe the four steps in mitosis.
9) Explain why sexual reproduction produces more variation than asexual reproduction.
10) Give three ways that sperm cells are adapted to their function.
11) What is meant by the 'differentiation' of cells?
12) How are the stem cells in an embryo different from the stem cells in an adult?
13) Give three ways that embryonic stem cells could be used to cure diseases.
14) There are concerns about the ethics of stem cell research. Give one argument in favour of stem cell research and one argument against stem cell research.
15) Why is the legal time limit for terminating a foetus set at 24 weeks?
16) What is selective breeding?
17) Suggest three features that you might selectively breed for in a dairy cow.
18) Give three examples of the use of selective breeding in farming.
19) Describe two disadvantages of selective breeding.
20) What is gene therapy?
21) Give two ways that genetic engineering has been used successfully in plants.
22) Give a balanced account of some of the views that different people have about genetic engineering.
23) Name two ways plants can be cloned.
24) What are the advantages and disadvantages of the cloning technique used in embryo transplants?
25) Describe the process of cloning an animal from an adult cell (e.g. cloning an adult sheep).
26) Describe three risks associated with trying to clone animals.
27) What is an allele?
28) Cystic fibrosis is caused by a recessive allele. If both parents are carriers, what is the probability of their child: a) being a carrier, b) suffering from the disorder?
29) During in vitro fertilisation, it is possible to screen embryos for various genetic disorders before they're implanted into the mother. Only the "good" embryos would be chosen for implantation. Summarise the main arguments for and against embryonic screening.

Respiration and Exercise

Respiration happens in little tiny structures called mitochondria (see page 1).

Respiration is NOT 'Breathing In and Out'

Respiration is really important — it releases the energy that cells need to do just about everything.

1) Respiration is the process of breaking down glucose to release energy, and it goes on in every cell in your body.

2) Respiration happens in plants too. All living things respire. It's how they get energy from their food.

This energy is used to do things like:
• build up larger molecules (like proteins)
• contract muscles
• maintain a steady body temperature

> RESPIRATION is the process of BREAKING DOWN GLUCOSE TO RELEASE ENERGY, which goes on IN EVERY CELL.

Respiration can be Aerobic or Anaerobic

Aerobic respiration is respiration using oxygen ('aerobic' just means 'with air').
It's the most efficient way to release energy from glucose. Learn the word equation:

> Glucose + Oxygen → Carbon Dioxide + Water (+ ENERGY)

Anaerobic respiration happens when there's not enough oxygen available (e.g. when you're exercising hard). Anaerobic just means without air and it's NOT the best way to release energy from glucose — but it's useful in emergencies. The overall word equation is:

> Glucose → Lactic Acid (+ ENERGY)

When You Exercise You Respire More

1) Muscles need energy from respiration to contract. When you exercise some of your muscles contract more frequently than normal so you need more energy. This energy comes from increased respiration.

2) The increase in respiration means you need to get more oxygen into the muscle cells.

3) Your breathing rate increases to get more oxygen into the blood, and your heart rate increases to get this oxygenated blood around the body faster. This removes CO_2 more quickly at the same time.

4) When you do really vigorous exercise (like sprinting) your body can't supply oxygen to your muscles quickly enough, so they start respiring anaerobically.

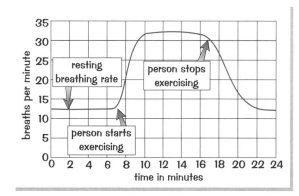

5) Athletes monitor their heart rate and breathing rate to help with their training.

6) The current UK government recommendation is to exercise for at least 30 minutes, five times a week in order to stay fit and healthy. But the official advice changes all the time — not so long ago the recommendation was 20 minutes, three times a week.

Oxygen debt — cheap to pay back...

Advice about exercise (and diet) is based on scientific evidence from many different surveys and studies.

Enzymes and Digestion

The enzymes used in <u>respiration</u> work <u>inside cells</u>. Various different enzymes are used in <u>digestion</u> too, but these enzymes are produced by specialised cells and then <u>released</u> into the <u>gut</u> to mix with the food.

Digestive Enzymes *Break Down* Big Molecules *into* Smaller Ones

1) <u>Starch</u>, <u>proteins</u> and <u>fats</u> are BIG molecules. They're too big to pass through the walls of the digestive system.

2) <u>Sugars</u>, <u>amino acids</u>, <u>glycerol</u> and <u>fatty acids</u> are much smaller molecules. They can pass easily through the walls of the digestive system.

3) The <u>digestive enzymes</u> break down the BIG molecules into the smaller ones.

Amylase *Converts* Starch *into* Simple Sugars

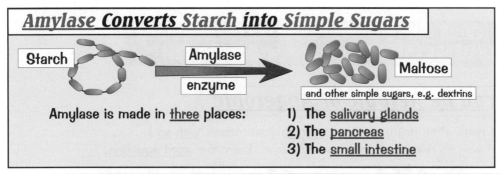

Amylase is made in <u>three</u> places:
1) The <u>salivary glands</u>
2) The <u>pancreas</u>
3) The <u>small intestine</u>

Protease *Converts* Proteins *into* Amino Acids

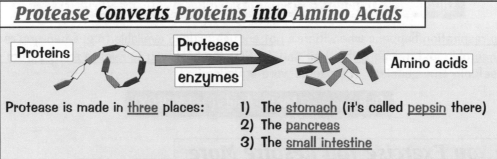

Protease is made in <u>three</u> places:
1) The <u>stomach</u> (it's called <u>pepsin</u> there)
2) The <u>pancreas</u>
3) The <u>small intestine</u>

Lipase *Converts* Fats *into* Glycerol *and* Fatty Acids

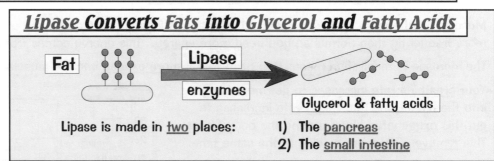

Lipase is made in <u>two</u> places:
1) The <u>pancreas</u>
2) The <u>small intestine</u>

Bile Neutralises the Stomach Acid and Emulsifies Fats

1) Bile is <u>produced</u> in the <u>liver</u>. It's <u>stored</u> in the <u>gall bladder</u> before it's released into the <u>small intestine</u>.

2) The <u>hydrochloric acid</u> in the stomach makes the pH <u>too acidic</u> for enzymes in the small intestine to work properly. Bile is <u>alkaline</u> — it <u>neutralises</u> the acid and makes conditions <u>alkaline</u>. The enzymes in the small intestine <u>work best</u> in these alkaline conditions.

3) Bile also <u>emulsifies</u> fats. In other words it breaks the fat into <u>tiny droplets</u>. This gives a much <u>bigger</u> <u>surface area</u> of fat for the enzyme lipase to work on — which makes its digestion <u>faster</u>.

What do you call an acid that's eaten all the pies...

This all happens inside our digestive system, but there are some microorganisms which secrete their digestive enzymes <u>outside their body</u> onto their food. The food's digested, then the microorganism absorbs the nutrients. Nice. I wouldn't like to empty the contents of my stomach onto my plate before eating it.

The Digestive System

So now you know what the enzymes do, here's a nice <u>big picture</u> of the <u>whole</u> of the digestive system.

The <u>Breakdown</u> of Food is <u>Catalysed by Enzymes</u>

1) Enzymes used in the digestive system are produced by specialised cells in <u>glands</u> and in the <u>gut lining</u>.

2) Different enzymes catalyse the <u>breakdown</u> of different food molecules.

Tongue

<u>Salivary glands</u>

These produce <u>amylase</u> <u>enzyme</u> in the <u>saliva</u>.

<u>Gullet</u>
(Oesophagus)

<u>Liver</u>

Where <u>bile</u> is <u>produced</u>. Bile <u>neutralises stomach</u> <u>acid</u> and <u>emulsifies fats</u>.

<u>Stomach</u>

1) It <u>pummels</u> the food with its muscular walls.

2) It produces the <u>protease</u> enzyme, <u>pepsin</u>.

3) It produces <u>hydrochloric acid</u> for two reasons:
   a) To <u>kill bacteria</u>
   b) To give the <u>right pH</u> for the <u>protease</u> enzyme to work (pH2 — <u>acidic</u>).

<u>Gall bladder</u>

Where <u>bile</u> is <u>stored</u>, before it's released into the <u>small intestine</u>.

<u>Pancreas</u>

Produces <u>protease</u>, <u>amylase</u> and <u>lipase</u> enzymes. It releases these into the <u>small intestine</u>.

<u>Large intestine</u>

Where <u>excess water</u> is <u>absorbed</u> from the food.

<u>Small intestine</u>

1) Produces <u>protease</u>, <u>amylase</u> and <u>lipase</u> enzymes to complete digestion.

2) This is also where the "food" is <u>absorbed</u> out of the digestive system into the body.

<u>Rectum</u>

Where the <u>faeces</u> (made up mainly of indigestible food) are <u>stored</u> before they bid you a fond farewell through the <u>anus</u>.

<u>You don't have to bust a gut to revise this page...</u>

Did you know that the whole of your digestive system is actually a hole that goes right through your body. Think about it. It just gets loads of food, digestive juices and enzymes piled into it.

Functions of the Blood

Blood is very useful stuff. It's a big transport system for moving things around the body. The blood cells do good work too. The red blood cells are responsible for transporting oxygen about, and they carry 100 times more than could be moved just dissolved in the plasma. And as for the white blood cells...

Plasma *is the Liquid Bit of Blood*

It's basically blood minus the blood cells (see below). Plasma is a pale yellow liquid which carries just about everything that needs transporting around your body:

1) Red and white blood cells and platelets (see below).
2) Water.
3) Digested food products like glucose and amino acids from the gut to all the body cells.
4) Carbon dioxide from the body cells to the lungs.
5) Urea from the liver to the kidneys (where it's removed in the urine).
6) Hormones — these acts like chemical messengers.
7) Antibodies and antitoxins produced by the white blood cells (see below).

Red Blood Cells *Have the Job of Carrying* Oxygen

They transport oxygen from the lungs to all the cells in the body. The structure of a red blood cell is adapted to its function:

1) Red blood cells are small and have a biconcave shape (which is a posh way of saying they look a little bit like doughnuts) for maximum absorption of oxygen.
2) They contain haemoglobin, which combines with oxygen — this is the substance that makes them red.
3) Red blood cells don't have a nucleus — this frees up space for more haemoglobin, so they can carry more oxygen.
4) Red blood cells are very flexible. This means they can easily pass through the tiny capillaries.

White Blood Cells *are Used to Fight Disease*

1) Their main role is defence against disease.
2) They produce antibodies to fight microbes.
3) They produce antitoxins to neutralise the toxins produced by microbes.

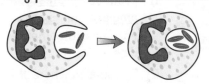

4) They have a flexible shape, which helps them to engulf any microorganisms they come across inside the body. Basically the white blood cell wraps around the microorganism until it's totally surrounded, and then it digests it using enzymes.

Platelets *Help Blood Clot*

1) These are small fragments of cells.
2) They have no nucleus.
3) They help the blood to clot at a wound.
 (So basically they just float about waiting for accidents to happen!)

What do white blood cells and elephants have in common...

The average adult human body contains about five and a half litres of blood altogether, and every single drop contains millions of cells. There are usually about 500 times more red blood cells than white.

The Circulatory System

Blood needs a good system to move it around the body — called the <u>circulatory system</u>.

There are Three Different Types of Blood Vessel

1) <u>ARTERIES</u> — these carry the blood <u>away</u> from the heart at <u>high pressure</u>. They branch into...

2) <u>CAPILLARIES</u> — these are tiny vessels (only one cell thick) involved in the <u>exchange of materials</u> at the tissues.

These join up to form...

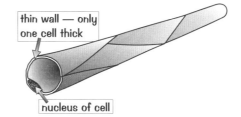

thin wall — only one cell thick

nucleus of cell

3) <u>VEINS</u> — these carry the blood <u>to</u> the heart at low pressure.

Cholesterol can build up in arteries:

<u>Cholesterol</u> is a <u>fatty</u> substance. Eating a diet high in <u>saturated fat</u> has been linked to high levels of cholesterol in the blood.

You need some cholesterol for things like <u>making cell membranes</u>. But if you have <u>too much</u> cholesterol it starts to <u>build up</u> in your <u>arteries</u>. This <u>restricts</u> the flow of blood — <u>bad news</u> for the part of the body the artery is supplying with <u>food</u> and <u>oxygen</u>.

If an artery supplying the <u>heart</u> or <u>brain</u> is affected, it can cause a <u>heart attack</u> or <u>stroke</u>.

Mammals Have a Double Circulatory System

1) The first one connects the <u>heart</u> to the <u>lungs</u>. <u>Deoxygenated</u> blood is pumped to the <u>lungs</u> to take in <u>oxygen</u>. The blood then <u>returns</u> to the heart.

2) The second one connects the <u>heart</u> to the <u>rest of the body</u>. The <u>oxygenated</u> blood in the heart is pumped out to the <u>body</u>. It <u>gives up</u> its oxygen, and then the <u>deoxygenated</u> blood <u>returns</u> to the heart to be pumped out to the <u>lungs</u> again.

3) Not all animals have a double circulatory system — <u>fish</u> don't, for example. So why can't mammals just pump the blood out <u>through the lungs</u> and then on to the rest of the body?

4) Well, returning the blood to the <u>heart</u> after it's picked up oxygen at the <u>lungs</u> means it can be pumped out around the body with <u>much greater force</u>. This is needed so the blood can get to <u>every last tissue</u> in the body and <u>still</u> have enough push left to flow <u>back to the heart</u> through the veins.

Lungs

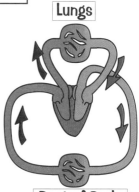

Rest of Body

Learn this page — don't struggle in vein...

Here's an interesting fact for you — your body contains about <u>60 000 miles</u> of blood vessels. That's about <u>six times</u> the distance from <u>London</u> to <u>Sydney</u> in Australia. Of course, capillaries are really tiny, which is how there can be such a big length — they can only be seen with a <u>microscope</u>.

The Heart

Blood doesn't just move around the body <u>on its own</u>, of course. It needs a <u>pump</u> — the <u>heart</u>.

Learn <u>This</u> Diagram <u>of the</u> Heart <u>with All Its</u> Labels

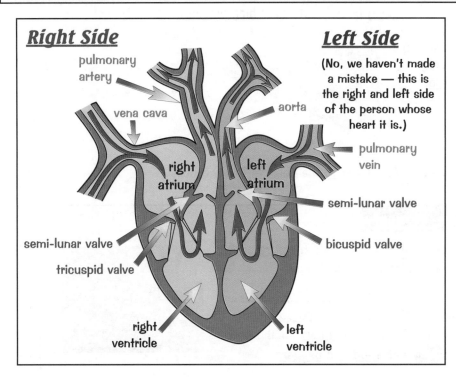

Right Side

pulmonary artery

vena cava

right atrium

semi-lunar valve

tricuspid valve

right ventricle

Left Side

(No, we haven't made a mistake — this is the right and left side of the person whose heart it is.)

aorta

pulmonary vein

left atrium

semi-lunar valve

bicuspid valve

left ventricle

1) The <u>right atrium</u> of the heart receives <u>deoxygenated</u> blood from the <u>body</u> (through the <u>vena cava</u>).
   (The plural of atrium is atria.)

2) The deoxygenated blood moves through to the <u>right ventricle</u>, which pumps it to the <u>lungs</u> (via the <u>pulmonary artery</u>).

3) The <u>left atrium</u> receives <u>oxygenated</u> blood from the <u>lungs</u> (through the <u>pulmonary vein</u>).

4) The oxygenated blood then moves through to the <u>left ventricle</u>, which pumps it out round the <u>whole body</u> (via the <u>aorta</u>).

5) The <u>left</u> ventricle has a much <u>thicker wall</u> than the <u>right</u> ventricle. It needs more <u>muscle</u> because it has to pump blood around the <u>whole body</u>, whereas the right ventricle only has to pump it to the <u>lungs</u>.

6) The <u>semi-lunar</u>, <u>tricuspid</u> and <u>bicuspid valves</u> prevent the <u>backflow</u> of blood.

<u>If the Heart</u> Stops Working <u>Properly — Bits Can be</u> Replaced

The heart has a <u>pacemaker</u> — a group of cells which determine <u>how fast</u> it beats. If this stops working the heartbeat becomes <u>irregular</u>, which can be dangerous. The pacemaker can be <u>replaced</u> with an <u>artificial</u> one.

Defective <u>heart valves</u> can also be replaced — either with <u>animal</u> or <u>mechanical</u> valves.

In extreme cases, the <u>whole heart</u> can be <u>removed</u> and <u>replaced</u> by another one from a <u>human donor</u> — this is called a <u>transplant</u>. It involves <u>major surgery</u> and a lifetime of <u>drugs</u> and <u>medical care</u>. They're only done on patients whose hearts are so damaged that the problems <u>can't</u> be solved in any other way. The new heart must be the <u>right size</u>, <u>relatively young</u> and a <u>close tissue match</u> to prevent rejection:

> TRANSPLANTS CAN BE REJECTED One of the main problems with heart transplants is that the patient's <u>immune system</u> often recognises the new heart as '<u>foreign</u>' and <u>attacks</u> it — this is called <u>rejection</u>. Doctors use <u>drugs</u> that <u>suppress</u> the patient's immune system to help <u>stop</u> the donor heart being rejected, but that leaves the patient more <u>vulnerable</u> to <u>infections</u>.

Okay — let's get to the heart of the matter...

The human heart beats 100 000 times a day on average. You can measure it by feeling a pulse in your wrist or neck — this is the blood being pushed through your arteries by another beat.

Homeostasis

Homeostasis is a fancy word. It covers lots of things, so I guess it has to be. Homeostasis covers all the functions of your body which try to maintain a "constant internal environment". Learn that definition:

HOMEOSTASIS is the maintenance of a constant internal environment.

There are Six Main Things That Need to be Controlled

The first four are all **THINGS YOU NEED**, but at <u>just the right level</u> — not too much and not too little.

1) **Body temperature** You mustn't get <u>too hot</u> or <u>too cold</u> (see below).

2) **Water** The water content of the blood mustn't get <u>too high</u> or <u>low</u>, or too much water could move <u>into</u> or <u>out of cells</u> and <u>damage</u> them. There's more about controlling water on the next page.

3) **Ions** If the <u>ion content</u> of the blood is wrong, you can get similar problems to those you get if the water content's wrong. See page 30.

4) **Sugar** <u>Blood sugar</u> levels need to stay within certain limits (see page 31).

The last two are **WASTE PRODUCTS** — they're produced in the body and you need to get rid of them.

5) **Carbon dioxide** This is a product of <u>respiration</u>. It's toxic in high quantities so it's got to be removed. It leaves the body by the <u>lungs</u> when you breathe out.

6) **Urea** This is a waste product made from the breakdown of <u>excess amino acids</u>. There's more about it on the next page.

Body Temperature Must be Carefully Controlled

All <u>enzymes</u> work best at a certain <u>temperature</u> (see page 4). The enzymes within the <u>human body</u> work best at about <u>37 °C</u>. If the body gets too hot or too cold, the enzymes <u>won't work properly</u> and some really important <u>reactions</u> could be <u>disrupted</u>. In extreme cases, this can even lead to <u>death</u>.

1) There is a <u>thermoregulatory centre</u> in the <u>brain</u> which acts as your own <u>personal thermostat</u>.

2) It contains <u>receptors</u> that are sensitive to the temperature of the <u>blood</u> flowing through the brain.

3) The thermoregulatory centre also receives impulses from the <u>skin</u>, giving information about <u>skin temperature</u>.

4) If you're getting too hot or too cold, your body can <u>respond</u> to try and cool you down (e.g. by sweating) or warm you up (e.g. by shivering).

My sister never goes out — she's a homeostasis...

If you're in really high temperatures for a long time you can get <u>heat stroke</u> — <u>sweating stops</u> because you're so dehydrated and there's a <u>big rise</u> in your body temperature. Your enzymes can't work properly and important reactions get disrupted — if you don't cool down you could collapse and die. Fortunately, good old British drizzle means that heat stroke needn't worry the majority of us. Lucky us.

The Kidneys and Homeostasis

Kidneys are really important in this whole homeostasis thing.

Kidneys Basically Act as Filters to "Clean the Blood"

The <u>kidneys</u> perform **THREE MAIN ROLES**:

1) Removal of Urea

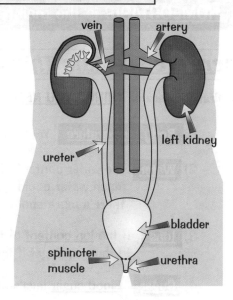

1) Proteins can't be <u>stored</u> by the body — so any excess amino acids are converted into <u>fats</u> and <u>carbohydrates</u>, which can be stored.
2) This happens in the <u>liver</u>. <u>Urea</u> is produced as a <u>waste product</u> from the reactions.
3) Urea is <u>poisonous</u>. It's released into the <u>bloodstream</u> by the liver. The <u>kidneys</u> then filter it out of the blood and it's excreted from the body in <u>urine</u>.
4) The urine is <u>temporarily stored</u> in the <u>bladder</u> before being excreted.

2) Adjustment of Ion Content

1) <u>Ions</u> such as <u>sodium</u> are taken into the body in <u>food</u>, and then absorbed into the blood.
2) If the ion content of the body is <u>wrong</u>, this could mean too much or too little <u>water</u> is drawn into cells by <u>osmosis</u> (see page 7). Having the wrong amount of water can <u>damage</u> cells.
3) Excess ions are <u>removed</u> by the kidneys. For example, a salty meal will contain far too much sodium and so the kidneys will remove the <u>excess</u> sodium ions from the blood.
4) Some ions are also lost in <u>sweat</u> (which tastes salty, you may have noticed).
5) But the important thing to remember is that the <u>balance</u> is always maintained by the <u>kidneys</u>.

3) Adjustment of Water Content

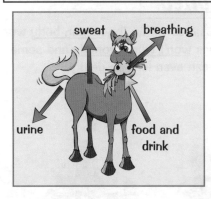

Water is taken into the body as <u>food and drink</u> and is <u>lost</u> from the body in <u>three main ways</u>: 1) In <u>urine</u>
2) In <u>sweat</u>
3) In the air we <u>breathe out</u>.

The body has to <u>constantly balance</u> the water coming in against the water going out. Our bodies can't control how much we lose in our breath, but we do control the other factors. This means the <u>water balance</u> is between: 1) Liquids <u>consumed</u>
2) Amount <u>sweated out</u>
3) Amount <u>excreted by the kidneys</u> in the <u>urine</u>.

On a <u>cold</u> day, if you <u>don't sweat</u>, you'll produce <u>more urine</u> which will be <u>pale</u> and <u>dilute</u>.
On a <u>hot</u> day, you <u>sweat a lot</u>, and you'll produce <u>less urine</u> which will be <u>dark-coloured</u> and <u>concentrated</u>.
The water lost when it is hot has to be <u>replaced</u> with water from food and drink to restore the <u>balance</u>.

Adjusting water content — blood, sweat and, erm, wee...

Scientists have made a machine which can do the kidney's job for us — a <u>kidney dialysis machine</u>. People with kidney failure have to use it for 3-4 hours, 3 times a week. Unfortunately it's not something you can carry around in your back pocket, which makes life difficult for people with kidney failure.

Section Three — Human Biology

Controlling Blood Sugar

Blood sugar is also controlled as part of homeostasis. Insulin is a hormone that controls how much sugar there is in your blood. Learn how it does it:

Insulin Controls Blood Sugar Levels

1) Eating foods containing carbohydrate puts glucose into the blood from the gut.

2) Levels of glucose in the blood must be kept steady. Changes in blood glucose are monitored and controlled by the pancreas, using the hormone insulin.

3) Insulin helps glucose to move from the blood into body cells. This reduces blood glucose and gets the glucose where it needs to be for respiration. Insulin also controls the storage of glucose in the liver:

Blood glucose level TOO HIGH — insulin is ADDED

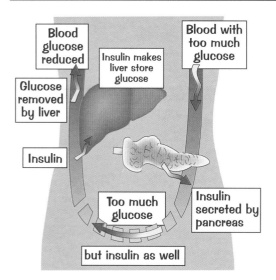

Blood glucose level TOO LOW — insulin is NOT ADDED

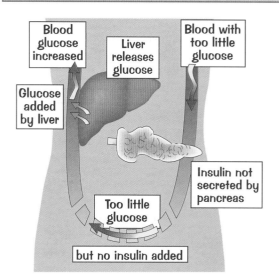

Diabetes (Type 1) — the Pancreas Stops Making Enough Insulin

1) Diabetes (type 1) is a disorder where the pancreas doesn't produce enough insulin.

2) The result is that a person's blood sugar can rise to a level that can kill them.

3) The problem can be controlled in two ways:

   a) Avoiding foods rich in simple carbohydrates, i.e. sugars (which cause glucose levels to rise rapidly). It can also be helpful to take exercise after eating... i.e. trying to use up the extra glucose by doing physical activity — but this isn't usually practical.

   b) Injecting insulin into the blood at mealtimes. This will make the liver remove the glucose as soon as it enters the blood from the gut, when the food is being digested. This stops the level of glucose in the blood from getting too high and is a very effective treatment. However, the person must make sure they eat sensibly after injecting insulin, or their blood sugar could drop dangerously.

4) The amount of insulin that needs to be injected depends on the person's diet and how active they are.

5) Diabetics can check their blood sugar using a glucose-monitoring device. This is a little hand-held machine. They prick their finger to get a drop of blood for the machine to check.

My blood sugar feels low after all that — pass the biscuits...

This stuff can seem a bit confusing at first, but if you concentrate on learning those two diagrams, it'll all start to get a lot easier. Don't forget that only carbohydrate foods put the blood sugar levels up.

Insulin and Diabetes

Scientific discoveries often take a long time, and a lot of trial and error — here's a rather famous example.

Insulin was Discovered by Banting and Best

It has been known for some time that people who suffer from diabetes have a lot of <u>sugar</u> in their <u>urine</u>. In the 19th century, scientists <u>removed pancreases</u> from dogs, and the same sugary urine was observed — the dogs became <u>diabetic</u>. That suggested that the pancreas had to have something to do with the illness. In the 1920s Frederick <u>Banting</u> and his assistant Charles <u>Best</u> managed to successfully <u>isolate insulin</u> — the hormone that controls blood sugar levels.

1) Banting and Best <u>tied string</u> around a dog's pancreas so that a lot of the organ <u>wasted</u> away — but the bits which made the <u>hormones</u> were left <u>intact</u>.

2) They <u>removed</u> the pancreas from the dog, and obtained an <u>extract</u> from it.

3) They then injected this extract into <u>diabetic dogs</u> and observed the effects on their <u>blood sugar levels</u>.

4) After the pancreatic extract was <u>injected</u>, the dog's blood sugar level <u>fell dramatically</u>. This showed that the <u>pancreatic extract</u> caused a <u>temporary decrease</u> in <u>blood sugar level</u>.

5) They went on to <u>isolate</u> the substance in the pancreatic extract — <u>insulin</u>.

Diabetes Can be Controlled by Regular Injections of Insulin

After <u>a lot</u> more experiments, Banting and Best tried <u>injecting insulin</u> into a <u>diabetic human</u>. And it <u>worked</u>. Since then insulin has been <u>mass produced</u> to meet the <u>needs</u> of diabetics. Diabetics have to inject themselves with insulin <u>often</u> — 2-4 times a day. They also need to carefully control their <u>diet</u> and the amount of <u>exercise</u> they do (see page 31).

1) At first, the insulin was extracted from the pancreases of <u>pigs</u> or <u>cows</u>. Diabetics used <u>glass syringes</u> that had to be boiled before use.

2) In the 1980s <u>human</u> insulin made by <u>genetic engineering</u> became available. This didn't cause any <u>adverse reactions</u> in patients, which <u>animal</u> insulin sometimes did.

3) <u>Slow</u>, <u>intermediate</u> and <u>fast</u> acting insulins have been developed to make it easier for diabetics to <u>control</u> their blood sugar levels.

4) Ready sterilised, <u>disposable syringes</u> are now available, as well as <u>needle-free devices</u>.

Improving methods of treatment allow diabetics to <u>control</u> their blood sugar <u>more easily</u>. This helps them avoid some of the damaging side effects of poor control, such as <u>blindness</u> and <u>gangrene</u>.

Diabetics May Have a Pancreas Transplant

Injecting yourself with insulin every day <u>controls</u> the effects of diabetes, but it doesn't help to cure it.

1) Diabetics can have a <u>pancreas transplant</u>. A successful operation means they won't have to inject themselves with insulin again. But as with any organ transplant, your body can <u>reject</u> the tissue. To try to prevent this patients take <u>costly immunosuppressive drugs</u>, which can have <u>serious side-effects</u>.

2) Another method, still in its <u>experimental stage</u>, is to transplant just the <u>cells</u> that produce insulin. There's been <u>varying success</u> with this technique, and there are still problems with <u>rejection</u>.

3) Modern research into <u>artificial pancreases</u> and <u>stem cell research</u> may mean the elimination of organ rejection, but there's a way to go yet (see page 14).

Blimey — all that in the last hundred years...

Insulin can't be taken in a pill or tablet — the <u>enzymes</u> in the stomach completely <u>destroy it</u> before it reaches the bloodstream. That's why diabetics have to <u>inject it</u>. Diabetes is becoming more and more common, partly due to our society becoming increasingly overweight. It's very serious.

Revision Summary for Section Three

And where do you think you're going? It's no use just reading through and thinking you've got it all — this stuff will only stick in your head if you've learnt it properly. And that's what these questions are for. I won't pretend they'll be easy — they're not meant to be, but all the information's in the section somewhere. Have a go at all the questions, then if there are any you can't answer, go back, look stuff up and try again. Enjoy...

1) Write down the word equations for aerobic respiration and anaerobic respiration.

2) Give one advantage and one disadvantage of anaerobic respiration.

3)* Danny measured his heart rate before, during and after exercise. He plotted a graph of the results. Look at the graph and then answer the three questions below.

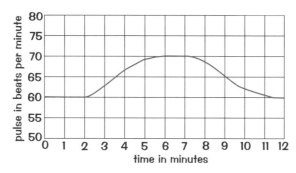

a) What was Danny's heart rate (in beats per minute) when he was at rest?
b) After how many minutes did Danny start exercising?
c) What was Danny's highest heart rate?

4) How much exercise does the UK government recommend you do per week?

5) In which three places in the body is amylase produced?

6) Where in the body is bile: a) produced?   b) stored?   c) used?

7) Explain why the stomach produces hydrochloric acid.

8) Name six things that blood plasma transports around the body.

9) Name the blood vessel that joins to the right ventricle of the heart. Where does it take the blood?

10) Why does the left ventricle have a thicker wall than the right ventricle?

11) Define homeostasis.

12) Write down four conditions that the body needs to keep fairly constant.

13) Which area of the brain is involved in regulating the temperature of the body?

14) What three main jobs do the kidneys do in the body?

15) Where in the body is urea produced?

16) What damage could be done in the body if the ion content is wrong?

17) Explain why your urine is likely to be more concentrated on a hot day.

18) Which organ monitors and controls blood glucose levels?

19) How does insulin lower the blood glucose level if it is too high?

20) Describe the experiments by Banting and Best that led to the isolation of insulin.

* Answers on page 140

Photosynthesis

Plants can make their own food — it's ace. Here's how...

Photosynthesis Produces *Glucose Using Sunlight*

1) Photosynthesis is the process that produces 'food' in plants. The 'food' it produces is glucose.

2) Photosynthesis happens in the leaves of all green plants — this is largely what the leaves are for.

3) Photosynthesis happens inside the chloroplasts, which are found in leaf cells and in other green parts of a plant. Chloroplasts contain a substance called chlorophyll, which absorbs sunlight and uses its energy to convert carbon dioxide and water into glucose. Oxygen is also produced.

$$\text{carbon dioxide} + \text{water} \xrightarrow[\text{chlorophyll}]{\text{SUNLIGHT}} \text{glucose} + \text{oxygen}$$

Four Things are *Needed for Photosynthesis* to Happen:

1) Light

Sunlight beating down on the leaf provides the energy for the process.

2) Chlorophyll

This is the green substance which is found in chloroplasts and which makes leaves look green. Chlorophyll absorbs the energy in sunlight and uses it to combine CO_2 and water to make glucose. Oxygen is just a by-product of this reaction.

3) Carbon dioxide

CO_2 diffuses into the leaf from the air around.

4) Water

Water comes up from the soil, up the roots and stem, and into the leaf via the veins.

Plants Use the Glucose for Different Things

1) **For respiration** — this releases energy. Some of this energy is used to convert the rest of the glucose into various other useful substances which they use to build new cells and grow.

2) **Making fruits** — glucose, along with another sugar called fructose, is turned into sucrose for storing in fruits. Fruits deliberately taste nice so that animals will eat them and spread the seeds all over the place in their poo.

3) **Stored as starch** — glucose is turned into starch and stored in roots, stems and leaves, ready for use when photosynthesis isn't happening, like in winter. Starch is insoluble, which makes it much better for storing because it doesn't bloat the storage cells by osmosis like glucose would.

I'm working on sunshine... woah o...

Plants are pretty crucial in ensuring the flow of energy through nature. They are able to use the Sun's energy to make glucose — the energy source which humans and animals need for respiration (see p.23). Make sure you know the photosynthesis equation inside out — it's important later in the section too.

Rate of Photosynthesis

A plant's rate of photosynthesis is affected by the amount of light, the amount of CO_2, and the temperature of its surroundings. Photosynthesis slows down or stops if the conditions aren't right.

The Limiting Factor Depends on the Conditions

1) A limiting factor is something which stops photosynthesis from happening any faster. The amount of light, amount of CO_2 and the temperature can all be the limiting factor.

2) The limiting factor depends on the environmental conditions. E.g. in winter cold temperatures might be the limiting factor, at night light is likely to be the limiting factor.

There are Three Important Graphs for Rate of Photosynthesis

1) Not Enough LIGHT Slows Down the Rate of Photosynthesis

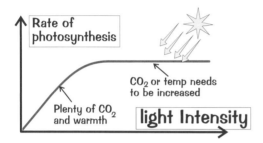

Chlorophyll uses light energy to perform photosynthesis. It can only do it as quickly as the light energy is arriving.

1) If the light level is raised, the rate of photosynthesis will increase steadily, but only up to a certain point.
2) Beyond that, it won't make any difference because then it'll be either the temperature or the CO_2 level which is now the limiting factor.

2) Too Little CARBON DIOXIDE Also Slows It Down

CO_2 is one of the raw materials needed for photosynthesis — only 0.04% of the air is CO_2, so it's pretty scarce as far as plants are concerned.

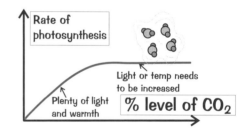

1) As with light intensity, increasing the amount of CO_2 will only increase the rate of photosynthesis up to a point. After this the graph flattens out, showing that CO_2 is no longer the limiting factor.

2) As long as light and CO_2 are in plentiful supply then the factor limiting photosynthesis must be temperature.

3) The TEMPERATURE Has to be Just Right

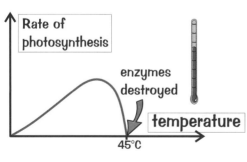

Temperature affects the rate of photosynthesis — because it affects the enzymes involved.

1) As the temperature increases, so does the rate of photosynthesis — up to a point.
2) If the temperature is too high (over about 45 °C), the plant's enzymes will be denatured (destroyed), so the rate of photosynthesis rapidly decreases.
3) Usually though, if the temperature is the limiting factor it's because it's too low, and things need warming up a bit.

No, no... no, no, no, no... no, no, no, no... no, no, there's no limit...

You can create the best conditions for photosynthesis in a greenhouse. Farmers use heaters and artificial lights and they can also increase the level of CO_2 using paraffin burners. By keeping plants in a greenhouse, they're also keeping out pests and diseases. The plants will grow much more quickly.

Leaf Structure

Now's a good time to flick back to pages 5-6 and make sure that you thoroughly know about <u>diffusion</u>.

Leaves are Designed for Making Food by Photosynthesis

The whole structure of leaves is geared towards that.
You need to know all the different parts of a
<u>typical leaf</u> shown on the diagram:

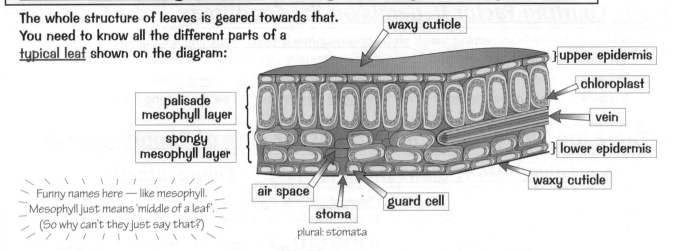

Funny names here — like mesophyll.
Mesophyll just means 'middle of a leaf'.
(So why can't they just say that?)

Leaves are Adapted for Efficient Photosynthesis

<u>Photosynthesis</u> occurs mainly in the <u>leaves</u> of plants.

The leaves are <u>adapted</u> to make it very efficient:

1) Leaves are <u>broad</u>, so there's a large surface area exposed to <u>light</u>.

2) They're also <u>thin</u>, which means <u>carbon dioxide</u>, <u>CO_2</u> and <u>water vapour</u> only have to travel a <u>short distance</u> to reach the photosynthesising cells where they're needed.

3) Leaves contain lots of <u>chloroplasts</u>. These contain <u>chlorophyll</u>, which is the pigment that absorbs light energy for photosynthesis.

4) The lower surface is full of little holes called <u>stomata</u>. They're there to let gases, like <u>CO_2</u> and <u>oxygen</u>, in and out. They also allow <u>water</u> to escape — which is known as <u>transpiration</u> (see page 37).

5) Leaves have a network of <u>veins</u>. These <u>deliver water</u> and other <u>nutrients</u> to every part of the leaf and take away the <u>food</u> produced by the leaf. They also help to <u>support</u> the leaf structure.

Plants Exchange Gases by Diffusion

When plants photosynthesise they <u>use up CO_2</u> from the atmosphere and <u>produce O_2</u> as a product. Plants also <u>respire</u> (see page 23) where they <u>use up O_2</u> and <u>produce CO_2</u> as a product. So there are lots of gases moving to and fro in plants, and this movement happens by <u>diffusion</u>.

1) When the plant is photosynthesising it uses up lots of <u>CO_2</u>, so there's hardly any inside the leaf. Luckily this makes <u>more</u> CO_2 move into the leaf by <u>diffusion</u> (from an area of <u>higher</u> concentration to an area of <u>lower</u> concentration).

2) At the same time lots of <u>O_2</u> is being <u>made</u> as a waste product of photosynthesis. Some is used in <u>respiration</u>, and the rest diffuses <u>out</u> through the stomata (moving from an area of <u>higher</u> concentration to an area of <u>lower</u> concentration).

3) At <u>night</u> it's a different story — there's <u>no photosynthesis</u> going on because there's no <u>light</u>. Lots of carbon dioxide is made in <u>respiration</u> and lots of oxygen is used up. There's a lot of CO_2 in the leaf and not a lot of O_2, so now it's mainly carbon dioxide diffusing <u>out</u> and oxygen diffusing <u>in</u>.

If you don't do much revision, it's time to turn over a new leaf...

Scientists know all this stuff because they've looked and seen the structure of leaves and the cells inside them. Not with the naked eye, of course — they used <u>microscopes</u>. So they're not just making it all up.

Transpiration

If you don't water a house plant for a few days it starts to go all droopy. Then it dies, and the people from the Society for the Protection of Plants come round and have you arrested. Plants need water.

Transpiration *is the Loss of Water from the Plant*

1) Transpiration is caused by the evaporation and diffusion (see p.5) of water from inside the leaves.

2) This creates a slight shortage of water in the leaf, and so more water is drawn up from the rest of the plant through the xylem vessels (see next page) to replace it.

3) This in turn means more water is drawn into the roots, and so there's a constant transpiration stream of water through the plant.

The transpiration stream has some benefits for the plants:

> 1) The constant stream of water from the ground helps to keep the plant cool.
>
> 2) It provides the plant with a constant supply of water for photosynthesis.
>
> 3) The water allows the plant cells to become rigid, which helps support the plant and stops it wilting (see page 38).
>
> 4) Minerals needed by the plant (see page 39) can be brought in from the soil along with the water.

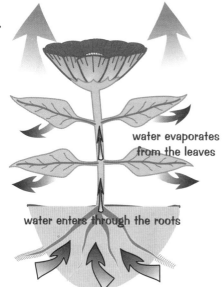

water evaporates from the leaves

water enters through the roots

Transpiration Rate *is Affected by Four Main Things*

To investigate the rate of transpiration, place two identical plants in the same environment, changing only the factor you're investigating (e.g. temperature). To measure the rate, you weigh each plant before and after, using a balance — the plant loses mass as water during transpiration.

The rate of transpiration varies depending on:

1) **LIGHT INTENSITY** — the brighter the light, the greater the transpiration rate.
   To investigate this, you could place one plant in a dark cupboard and the other on a windowsill during the day.

2) **TEMPERATURE** — the warmer it is, the faster transpiration happens.
   To see what effect the temperature has on rate, you could put one plant in a fridge and the other into a similar dark cupboard that's warmer.

3) **AIR MOVEMENT** — if there's lots of air movement (wind) around a leaf, transpiration happens faster.
   In the lab you could place a cool fan beside one of your plants to sweep the water vapour away.

4) **AIR HUMIDITY** — if the air around the leaf is very dry, transpiration happens more quickly.
   If you place a polythene bag around one of the plants, it creates a very humid environment and slows down transpiration.

Transpiration — the plant version of perspiration...

One good way to remember those four factors that affect the rate of transpiration is to think about the best weather for drying washing. Then you'll realise there are far more boring things you could be doing than revision, and you'll try harder. No, only joking — it's the same stuff: sunny, warm, windy and dry.

Water Flow in Plants

Plants Need to Balance Water Loss with Water Uptake

Transpiration can help plants in some ways, but if it hasn't rained for a while and you're <u>short of water</u> it's not a good idea to have it rushing out of your leaves. So plants have <u>adaptations</u> to help <u>reduce water loss</u> from their leaves.

1) Leaves usually have a <u>waxy cuticle</u> covering the <u>upper epidermis</u>. This helps make the upper surface of the leaf <u>waterproof</u>.

2) Most <u>stomata</u> are found on the <u>lower surface</u> of a leaf where it's <u>darker</u> and <u>cooler</u>. This helps slow down <u>diffusion</u> of water out of the leaf (see p.36).

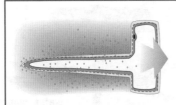

The roots take in water by osmosis

Plant roots have long 'hairs', called <u>root hairs</u> (see next page) which give the roots a really big surface area for taking up water.
There's usually a <u>higher concentration</u> of water in the soil than there is inside the plant, so the water is drawn into the root hair cells by <u>osmosis</u>.

The Cell Wall and Water Support Plant Cells

Plant cell

Water moves in and out of plant cells through the <u>cell wall</u> and the <u>membrane</u>.

1) When a plant is well watered, all its cells will draw water in by <u>osmosis</u>.

2) The contents of the cell <u>push</u> against the cell wall. The cell wall is <u>inelastic</u> so the cell becomes <u>rigid</u>. It provides <u>support</u> to the plant tissues.

3) If there's little water in the soil, a plant starts to <u>wilt</u> (droop). This is because the cells start to lose water and so <u>no longer</u> push against the inelastic cell wall.

Plants Have Xylem and Phloem

Plants have <u>two</u> separate types of vessel — <u>xylem</u> and <u>phloem</u> — for transporting stuff around. <u>Both</u> types of vessel go to <u>every part</u> of the plant, but they are totally <u>separate</u>.

Water and minerals

Xylem tubes take water up:

Xylem carry <u>water</u> and <u>minerals</u> from the <u>roots</u> up the shoot to the leaves in the <u>transpiration stream</u>.

Food (mainly sugars)

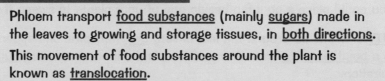
Phloem tubes transport food:

Phloem transport <u>food substances</u> (mainly <u>sugars</u>) made in the leaves to growing and storage tissues, in <u>both directions</u>.
This movement of food substances around the plant is known as <u>translocation</u>.

Don't let revision stress you out — just go with the phloem...

You probably did that really dull experiment at school where you stick a piece of celery in a beaker of water with red food colouring in it. Then you stare at it for half an hour, and once the time is up, hey presto, the red has reached the top of the celery. That's because it travelled there in the xylem.

Minerals Needed for Healthy Growth

Plants Need Three Main Minerals

Plants need certain <u>elements</u> so they can produce important compounds. They get these elements from <u>minerals</u> in the <u>soil</u>. The minerals are usually present in the <u>soil</u> in quite <u>low concentrations</u> — if there aren't enough of them, plants suffer <u>deficiency symptoms</u>.

Gardeners and farmers often add <u>fertilisers</u> to the <u>soil</u> to make their plants and crops <u>grow better</u>.

Fertilisers contain a mixture of compounds containing the <u>main minerals</u>, and often <u>small amounts</u> of any other elements the plants might need, like magnesium.

1) Nitrates

— these are needed for <u>cell growth</u>. If a plant can't get enough nitrates it will be <u>stunted</u> and will have <u>yellow older leaves</u>.

2) Phosphates

— they're needed for <u>respiration</u> and <u>growth</u>. Plants without enough phosphate have <u>poor root growth</u> and <u>purple older leaves</u>.

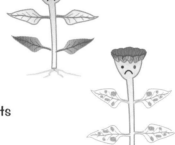

3) Potassium

— to help the <u>enzymes</u>. If there's not enough potassium in the soil, plants have <u>poor flower and fruit growth</u> and <u>discoloured leaves</u>.

Magnesium is Also Needed in Small Amounts

The three main minerals are needed in fairly <u>large amounts</u>, but there are other elements which are needed in much <u>smaller</u> amounts. <u>Magnesium</u> is one of the most significant as it's required for making <u>chlorophyll</u> (needed for <u>photosynthesis</u>). Plants without enough magnesium have <u>yellow leaves</u>.

Root Hairs Take In Minerals As Well As Water

1) The cells on plant roots grow into long '<u>hairs</u>' which stick out into the soil.

2) Each branch of a root will be covered in <u>millions</u> of these microscopic hairs.

3) This gives the plant a <u>big surface area</u> for absorbing <u>minerals</u> and <u>water</u> from the soil.

Minerals are taken in by active transport

1) The <u>concentration</u> of minerals in the <u>soil</u> is usually pretty <u>low</u>. It's normally <u>higher</u> in the <u>root hair cell</u> than in the soil around it.

2) So normal diffusion <u>doesn't</u> explain how minerals are taken up into the root hair cell. They should go <u>the other way</u> if they followed the rules of diffusion.

3) The answer is that a different process called '<u>active transport</u>' is responsible.

4) Active transport uses <u>energy</u> from <u>respiration</u> to help the plant pull minerals into the root hair <u>against the concentration gradient</u>. This is essential for its growth.

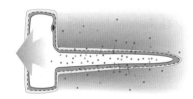

Nitrogen and phosphorus and potassium — oh my...

When a farmer or a gardener buys <u>fertiliser</u>, that's pretty much what he or she is buying — <u>nitrates</u>, <u>phosphates</u> and <u>potassium</u>. A fertiliser's <u>NPK label</u> tells you the relative proportions of nitrogen (N), phosphorus (P) and potassium (K) it contains, so you can choose the right one for your plants and soil.

Pyramids of Number and Biomass

A <u>trophic level</u> is a <u>feeding</u> level. It comes from the Greek word <u>trophe</u> meaning 'nourishment'. The amount of <u>energy</u>, <u>biomass</u> and usually the <u>number of organisms</u> all <u>decrease</u> as you move up a trophic level.

You Need to be Able to Construct Pyramids of Number

Luckily it's pretty easy — they'll give you all the information you need to do it in the exam. Here's an example:

5000 dandelions... feed... 100 rabbits... which feed... 1 fox.

1) Each bar on a pyramid of numbers shows the <u>number of organisms</u> at that stage of the food chain.

2) So the '<u>dandelions</u>' bar on this pyramid would need to be <u>longer</u> than the '<u>rabbits</u>' bar, which in turn should be <u>longer</u> than the '<u>fox</u>' bar.

3) <u>Dandelions</u> go at the <u>bottom</u> because they're at the bottom of the food chain.

This gives a <u>typical pyramid of numbers</u>, where every time you go up a <u>trophic (feeding) level</u>, the number of organisms goes <u>down</u>. This is because it takes a <u>lot</u> of food from the level below to keep one animal alive.

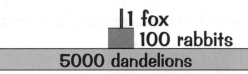

1 fox
100 rabbits
5000 dandelions

There are cases where a number pyramid is <u>not a pyramid at all</u>. For example 1 fox may feed 500 fleas.

You'll Have to Construct Pyramids of Biomass Too

1) Each bar on a <u>pyramid of biomass</u> shows the <u>mass of living material</u> at that stage of the food chain — basically how much all the organisms at each level would '<u>weigh</u>' if you put them <u>all together</u>.

2) So the one fox above would have a <u>big biomass</u> and the <u>hundreds of fleas</u> would have a <u>very small biomass</u>. Biomass pyramids are practically <u>always the right shape</u>:

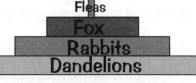

Fleas
Fox
Rabbits
Dandelions

The Species in an Environment are Interdependent

1) In the above food chain, if <u>rabbits</u> were wiped out, then the <u>foxes</u> would soon follow as they have <u>nothing to eat</u>. The foxes are said to be <u>dependent</u> on rabbits for survival.

2) Unfortunately life just isn't as simple as that. There are many different species within an environment, all <u>interdependent</u>. This means if one species changes, it <u>affects all the others</u>. For example, if lots of rabbits died, then:

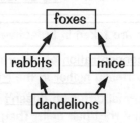

- There would be <u>less food</u> for the <u>foxes</u>, so their numbers might <u>decrease</u>.
- The number of <u>dandelions</u> might <u>increase</u>, because the rabbits wouldn't be eating them.
- The <u>mice</u> wouldn't be <u>competing</u> with the rabbits for food, so their numbers might <u>increase</u>.

Constructing pyramids is a breeze — just ask the Egyptians...

There are actually a couple of exceptions where pyramids of <u>biomass</u> aren't quite pyramid-shaped. It happens when the producer has a very short life but reproduces loads, like with plankton at certain times of year. But it's <u>rare</u>, and you <u>don't</u> need to know about it. Forget I ever mentioned it. Sorry.

Energy Transfer and Energy Flow

All That Energy Just Disappears Somehow...

1) Energy from the Sun is the source of energy for nearly all life on Earth.

2) Plants use a small percentage of the light energy from the Sun to make food during photosynthesis. This energy then works its way through the food web as animals eat the plants and each other.

3) Much of the energy lost at each stage is used for staying alive, i.e. in respiration (see page 23), which powers all life processes.

Material and energy are both lost at each stage of the food chain.

4) Most of this energy is eventually lost to the surroundings as heat. This is especially true for mammals and birds, whose bodies must be kept at a constant temperature which is normally higher than their surroundings.

This explains why you get biomass pyramids. Most of the biomass is lost and so does not become biomass in the next level up.

HEAT LOSS

5) Material and energy are also lost from the food chain in the droppings — you'll need to remember the posh word for producing droppings, which is egestion.

MATERIALS LOST IN ANIMAL'S WASTE

It also explains why you hardly ever get food chains with more than about five trophic levels. So much energy is lost at each stage that there's not enough left to support more organisms after four or five stages.

You Need to be Able to Interpret Data on Energy Flow

rosebush: 80 000 kJ   greenfly: 10 000 kJ   ladybird: 900 kJ   bird: 40 kJ

1) The numbers show the amount of energy available to the next level. So 80 000 kJ is the amount of energy available to the greenfly, and 10 000 kJ is the amount available to the ladybird.

2) You can work out how much energy has been lost at each level by taking away the energy that is available to the next level from the energy that was available from the previous level. Like this:

Energy lost at 1st trophic level as heat and in egestion = 80 000 kJ – 10 000 kJ = 70 000 kJ lost.

So when revising, put the fire on and don't take toilet breaks...

No, I'm being silly — go if you have to. We're talking in general terms about whole food chains here — you won't lose your concentration as a direct result of, erm, egestion.

Biomass and Fermentation

Energy Stored in Biomass Can be Used for Other Things

There are many different ways to release the energy stored in biomass — including eating it, feeding it to livestock, growing the seeds of plants and using it as a fuel.

For a given area of land, you can produce a lot more food for humans by growing crops than by grazing animals — only about 10% of the biomass eaten by beef cattle becomes useful meat for people to eat. It's important to get a balanced diet, though, which is difficult from crops only. It's also worth remembering that some land, like moorland or fellsides, isn't suitable for growing crops. In these places, animals like sheep and deer can be the best way to get food from the land.

As well as using biomass as food, you can use it as fuel. Learn these two examples of biofuels:

1) Fast-growing trees — people tend to think burning trees is a bad thing, but it's not as long as they're fast-growing and planted especially for that purpose. Each time trees are cut down, more can be planted to replace them. There's no overall contribution to CO_2 emissions because the replacement trees are still removing carbon from the atmosphere.

2) Fermenting biomass using bacteria or yeast — fermenting means breaking down by anaerobic respiration. You can use microorganisms to make biogas from plant and animal waste in a simple fermenter called a digester. The biogas can then be burned to release the energy for heating, powering a turbine, etc.

Developing biofuels is a great idea, for these three important reasons:

- Unlike coal, oil and the like, biofuels are renewable — they're not going to run out one day.
- Using biofuels reduces air pollution — no acid rain gases are produced when wood and biogas burn.
- You can be energy self-reliant. Theoretically, you could supply your energy from household waste.

Mycoprotein is Grown in Fermenters

1) Mycoprotein is protein from a fungus, used to make meat substitutes for vegetarian meals, e.g. Quorn.

2) The fungus is grown in huge vessels called fermenters, using glucose syrup as food.

3) Microorganisms can grow very quickly. They can grow miles quicker than plants or animals... which is good if you're using them to make food.

4) They're also easy to look after. All that's needed is something to grow them in, food, oxygen (sometimes) and the right temperature.

5) Another plus is that food can be produced whatever the climate: hot or cold, wet or dry. Many places in the world are pretty unsuitable for growing crops or farming animals, e.g. Siberia, parts of Africa and Outer Mongolia. Microorganisms can be used to produce food anywhere if you have the right equipment.

6) Microorganisms can use waste products from agriculture and industry as food.

7) This often makes using microorganisms cheaper than other methods.

Be energy self-reliant — burn poo...

Microorganisms are really useful — as well as making biogas, and producing mycoprotein, they're used to make antibiotics, AND we can genetically engineer them to make human proteins like insulin (see p.17).

Managing Food Production

There are four main ways to maximise food production:

1) increase the energy transfer,
2) reduce disease,
3) improve feeding/growing conditions,
4) control predators.

- If you reduce the number of stages in the food chain, you reduce the amount of energy lost. For a given area of land, you can produce more food for humans by growing crops than by grazing animals.
- Food production can also be made more efficient by reducing the amount of energy animals use, e.g. if you keep animals warm and still, they won't use as much energy and won't need to eat as much.

Fish Farms and Greenhouses Optimise Food Production

FISH FARMS: The fish are kept in cages in a sea loch, to stop them using energy swimming about looking for food, i.e. they are kept still to maximise the energy transfer. The cage also protects them from predators like birds and seals.

fish farm

GREENHOUSES: They trap the Sun's warmth, making plants grow faster than outside. Carbon dioxide and light levels can be increased to provide optimum conditions for photosynthesis (see p.35) and thereby maximise growth. Pests and diseases can be controlled using pesticides or biological control.

Food Production Involves Compromises and Conflict

Improving the efficiency of food production is useful — it means cheaper food for us, and better standards of living for farmers. But it all comes at a cost.

1) Some people think that forcing animals to live in unnatural and uncomfortable conditions is cruel. There's a growing demand for organic meat, from animals which have not been intensively farmed.

2) The crowded conditions on factory farms create a favourable environment for the spread of diseases, like avian flu and foot-and-mouth disease.

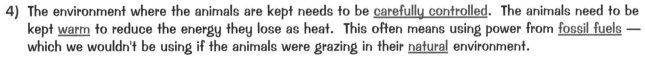

3) To try to prevent disease, animals are given antibiotics. When the animals are eaten these can enter humans. This allows microbes that infect humans to develop immunity to those antibiotics — so the antibiotics become less effective as human medicines.

4) The environment where the animals are kept needs to be carefully controlled. The animals need to be kept warm to reduce the energy they lose as heat. This often means using power from fossil fuels — which we wouldn't be using if the animals were grazing in their natural environment.

5) Our fish stocks are getting low. Yet a lot of fish goes on feeding animals that are intensively farmed — these animals wouldn't usually eat this source of food.

In an exam, you may be asked to give an account of the positive and negative aspects of food management. You will need to put both sides, whatever your personal opinion is. If you get given some information on a particular case, make sure you use it — they want to see that you've read it carefully.

Locked in a little cage with no sunlight — who'd work in a bank...

The world produces enough food to feed the Earth's population, but there are millions of undernourished people worldwide. The food is not equally distributed. Many people think that countries with food surpluses should give food to countries with food shortages (or sell them cheaply).

Intensive Farming

Intensive Farming is Used to Produce More Food

Intensive farming means trying to produce as much food as possible from your land, animals and plants. Farmers can do this in different ways, but they all involve increasing the productivity (getting bigger and better yields). Here's some examples of how they do it:

1) Fish farming

2) Glasshouses (greenhouses)

See previous page for details.

3) Battery farming

4) Hydroponics — this is where food such as tomatoes and cucumbers are commercially grown in nutrient solutions (water and fertilisers) instead of in soil.

Intensive farming allows us to produce a lot of food from less and less land, which means a huge variety of top quality foods, all year round, at cheap prices.

Intensive Farming Uses Pesticides and Herbicides

Intensive farming methods use chemicals to increase the amount of food they can produce.

1) Pesticides kill pests. More specifically, insecticides kill insects and fungicides kill fungi. This increases the productivity as it stops the destruction of the crop from these types of organism.

2) Herbicides kill weeds. If you remove plants that compete for the same resources (e.g. nutrients from the soil), it means the crop gets more of them.

Pesticides Disturb Food Chains

1) Pesticides are sprayed onto crops to kill the creatures that damage them, but unfortunately they also kill lots of harmless animals such as bees and beetles.

2) This can cause a shortage of food for animals further up the food chain.

3) Pesticides also tend to be toxic to creatures that aren't pests and there's a danger of the poison passing on through the food chain to other animals. There's even a risk that they could harm humans.

This is well illustrated by the case of otters which were almost wiped out over much of crop-dominated southern England by a pesticide called DDT in the early 1960s. The diagram shows the food chain which ends with the otter. DDT can't be excreted, so it accumulates along the food chain and the otter ends up with a lot of the DDT collected by the other animals.

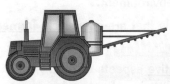

③ Each little tiny animal eats lots of small plants

⑤ Each eel eats lots of small fish

① Insecticide seeps into the river

② Small water plants take up a little insecticide

④ Each small fish eats lots of tiny animals

⑥ Each otter eats lots of eels

Plants without soil? It's not like when I was a lad...

One of the saddest things about intensive farming methods is that it reduces the wildlife in the countryside. If there are no plants (except crops) and few insects, there's not much around to eat...

Alternatives to Intensive Farming

Intensive farming methods are still used, a lot. But people are also using other methods more and more.

You Can Use Biological Control Instead of Pesticides

Biological control means using living things instead of chemicals to control a pest.
You could use a predator, a parasite or a disease to kill the pest. For example:

1) Aphids are a pest because they eat roses and vegetables. Ladybirds are aphid predators, so people release them into their fields and gardens to keep aphid numbers down.

2) Certain types of wasps and flies produce larvae which develop on (or in, yuck) a host insect. This eventually kills the insect host. Lots of insect pests have parasites like this.

3) Myxomatosis is a disease which kills rabbits. The myxoma virus was released in Australia as a biological control when the rabbit population there grew out of control and ruined crops.

> You need to be able to explain the advantages and disadvantages of biological control:
>
> ADVANTAGES:
>
> * The predator, parasite or disease usually only affects the pest animal. You don't kill all the harmless and helpful creatures as well like you often do with a pesticide.
> * No chemicals are used, so there's less pollution, disruption of food chains and risk to people eating the food that's been sprayed.
>
> DISADVANTAGES:
>
> * It's slower than pesticides — you have to wait for your control organism to build up its numbers.
> * Biological control won't kill all the pests, and it usually only kills one type of pest.
> * It takes more management and planning, and workers might need training or educating.
> * Control organisms can drive out native species, or become pests in their own right.

Remember that removing an organism from a food web, whether you use biological control or pesticides, can affect all the other organisms too. For example, if you remove a pest insect, you're removing a source of food from all the organisms that normally eat it. These might die out, and another insect that they normally feed on could breed out of control and become a pest instead. You have to be very careful.

Organic Farming is Still Perfectly Viable

Modern intensive farming produces lots of food and we all appreciate it on the supermarket shelves. But traditional organic farming methods do still work (amazingly!), and they don't use artificial fertilisers, herbicides or pesticides. You need to know about these organic farming techniques:

1) Use of organic fertilisers (e.g. animal manure and compost). This recycles the nutrients left in plant and animal waste. It doesn't work as well as artificial fertilisers, but it is better for the environment.

2) Crop rotation — growing a cycle of different crops in a field each year. This stops the pests and diseases of one crop building up, and stops nutrients running out (as each crop has different needs).

3) Weeding — this means physically removing the weeds, rather than just spraying them with a herbicide. Obviously it's a lot more labour-intensive, but there are no nasty chemicals involved.

4) Varying seed planting times — sowing seeds later or earlier in the season will avoid the major pests for that crop. This means the farmer won't need to use pesticides.

5) Biological control — see above.

Don't get bugged by biological pest control...

You can't just learn about the methods used in different types of farming — you have to think about their impact too. That means weighing up the advantages and disadvantages and being able to discuss them.

<u>Decay</u>

Microorganisms are great because they <u>break down</u> plant and animal remains which are lying around and looking unsightly. But they also break down plant and animal remains that we just bought at the shops.

<u>Things Decay **Because of** Microorganisms</u>

1) <u>Living things</u> are made of materials they take from the world around them.
2) When they <u>die and decompose</u>, or release material as <u>waste</u>, the elements they contain are returned to the <u>soil</u> or <u>air</u> where they originally came from.
3) These elements are then <u>used</u> by plants to <u>grow</u> and the whole cycle <u>repeats</u> over and over again.
4) Nearly all the <u>decomposition</u> is done by <u>microorganisms</u>, in particular <u>soil bacteria</u> and <u>fungi</u>.
5) All the important <u>elements</u> are thus <u>recycled</u>, including <u>carbon</u>, <u>oxygen</u>, <u>hydrogen</u> and <u>nitrogen</u>.
6) The rate of decay depends on three main things:
    a) <u>Temperature</u> — a <u>warm</u> temperature makes things decay <u>faster</u>.
    b) <u>Moisture</u> — things decay <u>faster</u> when they're moist.
    c) <u>Oxygen</u> (air) — decay is <u>faster</u> when there's oxygen <u>available</u>.
7) Microorganisms are also used in <u>compost heaps</u> to break down plant material, and in <u>sewage works</u> to break down human waste.

An energetic decomposer

<u>Detritivores **Feed on** Decaying Material</u>

1) <u>Detritivores</u> are a type of organism important in <u>decay</u>. They feed on dead and decaying material (<u>detritus</u>). Examples of detritivores include <u>earthworms</u>, <u>maggots</u> and <u>woodlice</u>.
2) As these detritivores feed on the decaying material, they break it up into <u>smaller bits</u>. This gives a <u>bigger surface area</u> for smaller decomposers to work on and so <u>speeds up</u> decay.

<u>Food Preservation **Methods** Reduce **the** Rate of Decay</u>

Decomposers are good for <u>returning nutrients</u> to the soil, but they're <u>not so good</u> when they start decomposing your lunch. So people have come up with ways to <u>stop them</u>:

1) <u>Canning</u> — the food is put in an <u>airtight can</u> to keep decomposers <u>out</u>. After canning, the tin and its contents are <u>heated</u> to a high temperature to <u>kill</u> any microorganisms that were in there <u>already</u>.
2) <u>Cooling</u> — the easiest way to keep food cool is put it in a <u>fridge</u>. Cooling <u>slows down decay</u> because it slows down <u>respiration</u> in the microorganisms. They can't <u>reproduce</u> as fast either.
3) <u>Freezing</u> — food lasts longer in the <u>freezer</u> than in the fridge because the microorganisms can't respire or reproduce <u>at all</u> at such low temperatures. Some (but not all) are <u>killed</u> when the water inside them <u>expands</u> as it freezes.
4) <u>Drying</u> — dried food lasts longer because microorganisms need <u>water</u>. Lots of <u>fruits</u> are preserved by drying them out, and sometimes <u>meat</u> is too.
5) <u>Adding salt</u> — if there's a high concentration of salt around decomposers, they'll lose <u>water</u> by <u>osmosis</u>. This damages them so they can't work properly. Things like <u>tuna</u> and <u>olives</u> are often stored in <u>brine</u> (salt water).
6) <u>Adding vinegar</u> — mmm, pickled onions. Vinegar is <u>acidic</u>, and the <u>low pH</u> inhibits the <u>enzymes</u> inside the microorganisms. This stops them decomposing the delicious onions.

<u>Decomposers — they're just misunderstood...</u>

Without decomposers we'd be up to our eyes in <u>dead things</u>, and there'd be <u>no nutrients</u> in the soil.

Recycling Nutrients

Carbon and nitrogen are constantly being <u>recycled</u>. Round and round and round...

The Carbon Cycle Shows How Carbon is Recycled

<u>Carbon</u> is an important element in the materials that living things are made from. It's constantly <u>recycled</u>:

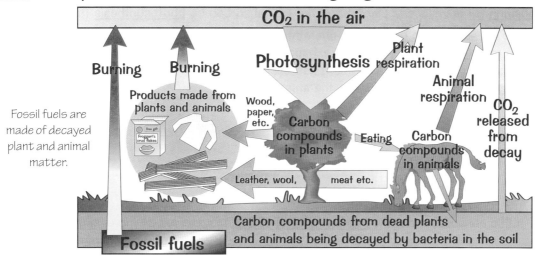

This diagram isn't half as bad as it looks. Learn these important points:

1) There's only <u>one arrow</u> going <u>down</u>. The whole thing is 'powered' by <u>photosynthesis</u>.

2) In photosynthesis <u>plants</u> convert the carbon from CO_2 in the air into <u>sugars</u>. Plants can then incorporate this carbon into <u>fats</u>, <u>proteins</u> and other <u>carbohydrates</u>.

3) <u>Eating</u> passes the carbon compounds in plants to <u>animals</u> in a food chain or web.

4) Both plants and animals <u>respire</u> when they're alive, <u>releasing CO_2</u> back into the <u>air</u>.

5) Plants and animals eventually <u>die</u> and <u>decay</u>, or are killed and turned into <u>useful products</u>.

6) When plants and animals <u>decay</u> they're broken down by <u>bacteria</u> and <u>fungi</u>. These decomposers <u>release CO_2</u> back into the air as they break down the material.

7) Some useful plant and animal <u>products</u>, e.g. wood and fossil fuels, are <u>burned</u> (<u>combustion</u>). This also <u>releases CO_2</u> back into the air.

Nitrogen is Also Recycled in the Nitrogen Cycle

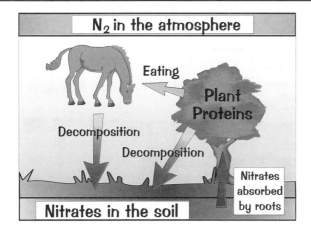

1) The <u>atmosphere</u> contains <u>78% nitrogen gas</u>, N_2. This is <u>very unreactive</u> and so it can't be used <u>directly</u> by plants or animals.

2) <u>Nitrogen</u> is <u>needed</u> for making <u>proteins</u> for growth, so living organisms have to get it somehow.

3) Plants get their nitrogen from <u>nitrates</u> in the <u>soil</u>. <u>Animals</u> can only get <u>proteins</u> by eating plants (or each other).

4) <u>Decomposers</u> break down <u>nitrogen compounds</u> in rotting plants and animals back into <u>nitrates</u>. So the nitrogen in these organisms is <u>recycled</u>.

It's the cyyyycle of liiiiife...

Carbon is a very <u>important element</u> for living things — it's the basis for all the organic molecules. Nitrogen is also <u>vital</u>, because it's found in <u>proteins</u>, which are needed for things like enzymes.

Air Pollution

High levels of gases released through human activity can cause havoc in the air.

The Level of CO_2 in the Atmosphere is Increasing

1) The level of CO_2 in the atmosphere used to be nicely balanced between the CO_2 released by respiration and decomposition (of animals and plants) and the CO_2 absorbed by photosynthesis (see p.34).

2) However, people release carbon dioxide into the atmosphere all the time as part of everyday life — from car exhausts, industrial processes, burning fossil fuels etc. As society has become more industrialised over the last 300 years, the amount of CO_2 released has increased.

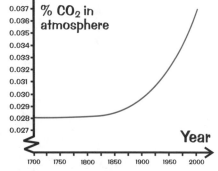

3) We have also been cutting down trees all over the world to make space for living and farming. This is called deforestation.

4) The level of CO_2 in the atmosphere has gone up by about 20%, and will continue to rise as long as we keep burning fossil fuels — just look at that graph — eek!

5) There's a scientific consensus that the increasing level of CO_2 has caused an increase in global temperature ('global warming') and this is causing other types of climate change.

Carbon Monoxide is Poisonous

1) When fossil fuels are burnt without enough air supply they produce the gas carbon monoxide (CO).

2) It's a poisonous gas. If it combines with red blood cells, it prevents them from carrying oxygen.

3) Carbon monoxide's mostly released in car emissions. Most modern cars are fitted with catalytic converters that oxidise the carbon monoxide (to make carbon dioxide), decreasing the amount that's released into the atmosphere.

Acid Rain is Caused by Sulfur Dioxide

1) As well as releasing CO_2, burning fossil fuels releases other harmful gases, including sulfur dioxide.

2) The sulfur dioxide (SO_2) comes from sulfur impurities in the fossil fuels.

3) When SO_2 mixes with rain clouds it forms dilute sulfuric acid.

4) This then falls as acid rain.

5) Cars and power stations are the main causes of acid rain.

6) Acid rain can cause a lake to become more acidic. This has a severe effect on the lake's ecosystem. Many organisms are sensitive to changes in pH and can't survive in more acidic conditions. Many plants and animals die.

7) Acid rain can kill trees.

8) Acid rain damages limestone buildings and statues.

It's raining, it's pouring — quick, cover the rhododendron...

Exam questions on this topic may give you a graph or table to interpret. If they ask you to describe the data, just say what you see (e.g. the number of species in a lake decreases with increased acidity of the water). But if they ask you to explain the data, you're going to need some scientific knowledge to suggest why the data shows that trend (e.g. some species can't survive in acidic conditions).

Water Pollution

All living things <u>need water</u>. You need water to <u>survive</u>. So it's important it doesn't become polluted...

Many Different Substances Can Pollute Water

1) Fertilisers and Sewage

<u>Fertilisers</u> and <u>sewage</u> are high in nutrients like <u>nitrates</u> and <u>phosphates</u>. Fertilisers used in agriculture sometimes run off into rivers and streams. Treated sewage is released into rivers or the sea (sewage is <u>treated</u> to <u>reduce</u> the amount of nutrients it contains — but it still contains more than clean water). Pollution of water by fertilisers and sewage causes EUTROPHICATION.

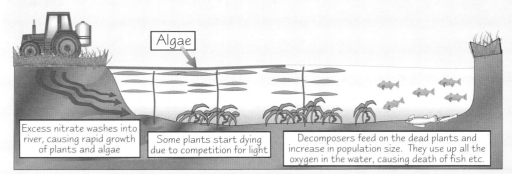

Algae

Excess nitrate washes into river, causing rapid growth of plants and algae

Some plants start dying due to competition for light

Decomposers feed on the dead plants and increase in population size. They use up all the oxygen in the water, causing death of fish etc.

As the picture shows, <u>too many nitrates</u> in the water cause a sequence of '<u>mega-growth</u>', '<u>mega-death</u>' and '<u>mega-decay</u>' involving most of the <u>plant and animal life</u> in the water.

2) Industrial Chemicals and Pesticides

Chemicals which can cause water pollution include <u>pesticides</u> like <u>DDT</u> (which is now banned in the UK) and <u>industrial chemicals</u> like <u>PCBs</u>. If <u>water</u> is <u>polluted</u> by these, they are <u>taken up</u> by <u>organisms</u> at the bottom of the food chain. Many of these chemicals <u>aren't broken down</u> by the organisms, so when they're eaten the chemical is <u>passed on</u> (see page 44).

3) Oil

Spills from <u>oil tanker accidents</u> and also oil from <u>boat engines</u> harm water life.

4) Metals

Some <u>metals</u> (e.g. lead and mercury) are <u>poisonous</u>. They can get into the water supply from old <u>lead pipes</u> or <u>careless waste disposal</u>.

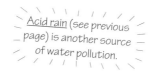

<u>Acid rain</u> (see previous page) is another source of water pollution.

Water Pollution Can be Measured Directly and Indirectly

1) A <u>direct measurement</u> of water pollution is made by taking a <u>sample of water</u> and doing a <u>chemical test</u> to find the concentration of pollutants in it. E.g.
   - The concentration of <u>nitrates</u>, <u>phosphates</u> and <u>pesticides</u>.
   - <u>Oxygen (O_2) concentration</u> (<u>eutrophication</u> would make the O_2 concentration lower).
   - The <u>pH</u> of the water (acid rain reduces the pH).

2) An <u>indirect measurement</u> of water pollution is made by <u>observing</u> the <u>organisms</u> which live in the habitat.
   - <u>Some species</u> (like mayfly larvae) only live in <u>clean water</u> — their presence means pollution is low.
   - <u>Some species</u> (like the rat-tailed maggot) are more common in <u>polluted water</u>.
   - In general, <u>polluted water</u> will contain <u>fewer organisms</u>, and fewer different species.

Polluted water is bad news...

Oil spills are really awful. They coat animals living in the sea, like seals and penguins, and many die. A major oil spill happened in February 1996, when the 'Sea Empress' crashed off the Welsh coast. 71 800 tonnes of oil were spilt, covering an estimated 17 000 seabirds with oil.

Pollution Indicators

Getting an accurate picture of the human impact on the environment is hard.
But there are some <u>useful indicators</u> of how polluted an area is.

Lichen Distribution Indicates the Amount of Air Pollution

1) Some organisms are <u>very sensitive</u> to changes in their environment. These organisms can be used by scientists as an <u>indicator</u> of human impact on the environment (e.g. pollution).

> For example, <u>air pollution</u> can be monitored by looking at the number and type of <u>lichen</u>, which are very sensitive to levels of <u>sulfur dioxide</u> (and other pollutants) in the atmosphere. This means they can give a good idea about the level of pollution from <u>car exhausts</u>, power stations, etc. The number and type of lichen at a particular location will indicate <u>how clean</u> the air is (e.g. the air is clean if there's <u>lots of lichen</u>).

2) Organisms like lichen are called '<u>indicator species</u>' or '<u>living indicators</u>'.

3) You can do a similar sort of thing to monitor <u>water pollution</u> (see previous page). Freshwater clams can be used as a measure of the acidity of a lake — some species are <u>very sensitive to pH</u>.

Skin Cancer is an Indicator of Ozone Layer Depletion

Another <u>indicator of pollution</u> (and one which affects humans directly) is the number of <u>cases of skin cancer</u>.

This has increased dramatically in the UK in recent years — there are about <u>5 times as many</u> cases per year now as there were 30 years ago.

1) It's thought that <u>one reason</u> for the <u>increase in skin cancer</u> is the <u>depletion</u> (thinning) of the <u>ozone layer</u> in the Earth's atmosphere.

2) The ozone layer has got <u>thinner</u> because of <u>air pollution</u> by <u>CFCs</u> (gases which can be used in aerosols and refrigerator coolants). CFCs react with ozone molecules in the atmosphere and destroy them.

3) Ozone <u>absorbs</u> harmful <u>ultraviolet (UV) radiation</u> from the Sun. The damage to the ozone layer means it <u>absorbs less UV radiation</u> from the Sun. UV radiation can <u>trigger skin cancer</u> in humans.

4) Now that the <u>dangers</u> of <u>CFCs</u> are known, they have been <u>banned in many countries</u>. The ozone layer is <u>starting to recover</u>, but this will take time. At the moment, the incidence of skin cancer is high.

5) By the way, the incidence of skin cancer isn't the only way that scientists can monitor the state of the ozone layer — they can <u>measure it directly</u> with <u>satellites</u> and <u>ground stations</u> too.

Non-Living Indicators can be Direct or Indirect

1) You can also monitor the environment by looking at <u>non-living indicators</u>.

2) These could be <u>direct</u> or <u>indirect</u> indicators of pollution.

3) A direct indicator could be a <u>chemical test</u> or <u>satellite picture</u>.

4) Indirect indicators include the amount and type of <u>weathering on rocks and buildings</u> (acid rain), <u>visibility</u> (smog) and <u>melting ice</u> (global warming).

My indicators were faulty — I had to keep going left...

Some species, like the rat-tailed maggot, have evolved to live in places where there's lots of pollution. These are great living indicators. It's amazing where some creatures can live — like in hot deserts, in volcanic vents, or even in the deep sea where there's practically no light at all.

Conservation and Recycling

Conservation and recycling are all about what humans can do to reduce our impact on the environment.

Conservation is Important for Protecting Food, Nature and Culture

1) Conservation measures protect species by maintaining their habitats and protecting them from poachers and over-hunting / over-harvesting.

2) There are several reasons why it's important to conserve species and natural habitats:

- Protecting endangered species — Many species are becoming endangered, often due to hunting and the destruction of their habitats. They need to be protected to stop them becoming extinct.

- Protecting the human food supply — Overfishing has greatly reduced fish stocks in the sea. Conservation measures (e.g. quotas on how many fish can be caught) encourage the survival and growth of fish stocks. This protects the food supply for future generations.

- Maintaining biodiversity — Biodiversity is the variety of different species in a habitat — the more species there are, the greater the biodiversity. If one species in a habitat is destroyed it affects the other species living there — the food web will be affected. It's important to protect biodiversity.

Example: Woodland Conservation

Conservation measures in a woodland habitat may include:

1) Coppicing — This is an ancient form of woodland management. It involves cutting trees down to just above ground level. The stumps sprout straight, new stems which can be regularly harvested.

2) Reforestation — Where forests have been cut down in the past, they can be replanted, to try to recreate the habitat that has been lost.

3) Replacement planting — This is when new trees are planted at the same rate that others are cut down. So the total number of trees stays the same.

Recycling Conserves Our Natural Resources

If materials aren't recycled they get thrown away as waste. This means that:

1) There is more waste, so more land has to be used for landfill sites (waste dumps). Some waste is toxic (poisonous), so this also means more polluted land.

2) More materials have to be manufactured or extracted to make new products (rather than recycling existing ones) — using up more of the Earth's resources and more energy.

Recycling processes usually use less energy and create less pollution than manufacturing or extracting materials from scratch. Recyclable materials include metals, paper, plastics and glass.

There are Some Problems with Recycling

1) Recycling still uses energy, e.g. for collecting, sorting, cleaning and processing waste.

2) Some waste materials can be difficult and time-consuming to sort out, e.g. different types of plastic have to be separated from each other before they can be recycled.

3) The equipment needed for recycling can be expensive, e.g. equipment for sorting plastics automatically.

4) In some cases, the quality of recycled materials isn't as good as new materials, e.g. recycled paper.

5) Some materials can only be recycled a limited number of times (e.g. plastics, paper). Others can be recycled indefinitely though (e.g. aluminium).

Recycling — doing the Tour de France twice...

The organisms in a habitat are dependent on each other, e.g. for food. You need to protect all species — animals, trees, fungi, bacteria... because if one of them dies out it affects the others (see p.40).

Revision Summary for Section Four

Here goes, folks — another beautiful page of revision questions to keep you at your desk studying hard until your parents have gone out and you can finally nip downstairs to watch TV. Think twice though before you reach for that remote control. These questions are actually pretty good — certainly more entertaining than 'Train Your Husband Like He's a Dog' or 'Celebrities Dance Around'. Question 14 is almost as good as an episode of 'Supernanny'. Question 4 is the corker though — like a reunion episode of 'Friends' but a lot funnier. Give the questions a go. Oh go on.

1) Write down the equation for photosynthesis.

2) Write down three ways that plants can use the glucose produced by photosynthesis.

3)* The graph shows how the rate of a plant's growth is affected by increasing the level of carbon dioxide. Look at the graph and answer the two questions below.

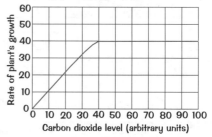

a) At what level of carbon dioxide is the plant's growth limited by another factor?

b) Suggest two possible limiting factors on the plant's growth above this level.

4) How does being broad and thin help a leaf to photosynthesise?

5) Why does carbon dioxide tend to move into leaves when they're photosynthesising?

6) Give three ways that the transpiration stream benefits a plant.

7) How is the transpiration rate affected by: a) increased temperature, b) increased air humidity?

8) Stomata close automatically when a plant is short of water. How does this benefit the plant?

9) Name the three main minerals plants need for healthy growth.

10) How can you tell by looking at a plant that it isn't getting enough phosphates?

11) What is active transport? Why is it used in the roots of a plant?

12) Explain why number pyramids are not always pyramid-shaped.

13) What is the source of all the energy in a typical food chain?

14) Why is it unusual to find a food chain with more than five trophic levels?

15) Give three reasons for developing biofuels.

16) What is mycoprotein used for?

17) Give the four main ways in which it is possible to maximise food production.

18) What is meant by the term hydroponics?

19) Give two advantages and two disadvantages of biological pest control.

20) Give an example of a detritivore. How do detritivores increase the rate of decay?

21) How does carbon enter the carbon cycle from the air?

22) Which gas can cause acid rain? How is it produced?

23) Describe the damage which can be caused by acid rain.

24) How do fertilisers and sewage cause water pollution?

25) What type of pollution are lichen very sensitive to?

26) What can be used as a living indicator of ozone layer depletion?

27) Describe three reasons why conservation of habitats and species is important.

28) Give two advantages and two disadvantages of recycling.

* Answers on page 140

Section Four — Plants and the Environment

Atoms

There are quite a few different (and equally useful) models of the atom — but chemists tend to like this nuclear model best. You can use it to explain pretty much the whole of Chemistry... which is nice.

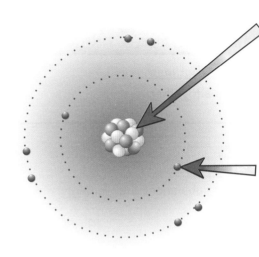

Atoms are really tiny, don't forget. They're too small to see, even with a microscope.

The Nucleus

1) It's in the middle of the atom.
2) It contains protons and neutrons.
3) It has a positive charge because of the protons.
4) Almost the whole mass of the atom is concentrated in the nucleus.
5) But size-wise it's tiny compared to the rest of the atom.

The Electrons

1) Move around the nucleus.
2) They're negatively charged.
3) They're tiny, but they cover a lot of space.
4) The volume of their orbits determines how big the atom is.
5) They have virtually no mass.
6) They occupy shells around the nucleus.
7) These shells explain the whole of Chemistry.

PARTICLE	RELATIVE MASS	RELATIVE CHARGE
Proton	1	+1
Neutron	1	0
Electron	0.0005	−1

Protons are heavy and positively charged.
Neutrons are heavy and neutral.
Electrons are tiny and negatively charged. (Electron mass is often taken as zero.)

Atoms are Neutral

1) Neutral atoms have no charge overall.
2) If some electrons are added or removed, the atom becomes charged and is then an ion.

Atomic Number and Mass Number Describe an Atom

These two numbers tell you how many of each kind of particle an atom has.

1) The atomic (proton) number tells you how many protons there are.
2) Atoms of the same element all have the same number of protons — so atoms of different elements will have different numbers of protons.
3) The mass (nucleon) number is always the biggest number.
4) The mass number tends to be roughly double the proton number.
5) Which means there's about the same number of protons as neutrons in any nucleus.

You might see "Relative Atomic Mass" instead of "Mass Number" but you don't need to worry about it too much.

The Mass Number ➡ **23**
— Total of protons and neutrons

The Atomic Number ➡ **11**   **Na**
— Number of protons

Number of protons = number of electrons...

This stuff might seem a bit useless at first, but it should be permanently engraved into your mind.
If you don't know these basic facts, you've got no chance of understanding the rest of Chemistry.
So learn it now, and watch as the Universe unfolds and reveals its timeless mysteries to you...

Isotopes, Elements and Compounds

And the question on everybody's lips is — what are isotopes...

Isotopes are the Same Except for an Extra Neutron or Two

Isotopes are: different atomic forms of the same element, which have the SAME number of PROTONS but a DIFFERENT number of NEUTRONS.

1) The upshot is: isotopes must have the same atomic number but different mass numbers.
2) If they had different atomic numbers, they'd be different elements altogether.

Elements Consist of One Type of Atom Only

Elements cannot be broken down chemically. Quite a lot of everyday substances are elements:

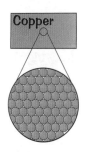 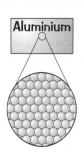 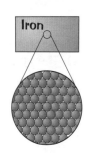 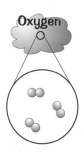 

Compounds are Chemically Bonded

1) Carbon dioxide is a compound formed from a chemical reaction between carbon and oxygen.
2) It's very difficult to separate the two original elements again. There's a chemical bond holding them together.

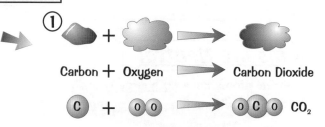

Carbon + Oxygen ⟶ Carbon Dioxide

3) The properties of a compound are totally different from the properties of the original elements.
4) If iron and sulfur react to form iron sulfide, the compound formed is a grey solid lump, and doesn't behave anything like either iron or sulfur.

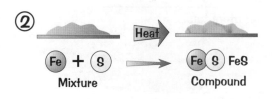

Mixture   Compound

There are two types of chemical bonding:

1) Ionic Bonding — the attraction between positive and negative particles called ions.
2) Covalent Bonding — sharing a pair of electrons.
   You'll find out more about these types of bond later in this section.
   Until then, you'll just have to hold your breath...

Don't mix these up — it'll only compound your problems...

There are loads of natural isotopes out there, and some of them are radioactive. Carbon dating uses different isotopes of carbon to date old materials... wonder if it'd work on my Dad...
And make sure you know exactly what the difference between an element and a compound is.

Section Five — Classifying Materials

The Periodic Table

The periodic table is a chemist's bestest friend — start getting to know it now... seriously...

The Periodic Table is a Table of All Known Elements

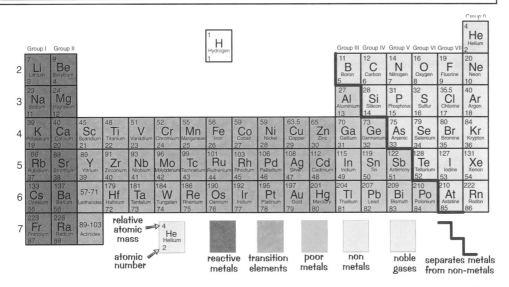

1) There are 100ish elements, which all materials are made of. More are still being 'discovered'.

2) The modern periodic table shows the elements in order of ascending atomic number.

3) The periodic table is laid out so that elements with similar properties form columns.

4) These vertical columns are called groups and Roman numerals are sometimes used for them.

5) The group to which the element belongs corresponds to the number of electrons it has in its outer shell. E.g. Group 1 elements have 1 outer shell electron, Group 7 elements have 7 outer shell electrons and so on.

6) Some of the groups have special names. Group 1 elements are called alkali metals. Group 7 elements are called halogens, and Group 0 are called the noble gases.

Elements in a Group Have the Same Number of Outer Electrons

1) The elements in each group all have the same number of electrons in their outer shell.

2) That's why they have similar properties. And that's why we arrange them in this way.

3) When only 50 or so elements were known, the periodic table was made by looking at the properties of the elements and arranging them in groups — the same groups that they are in today.

4) This idea is extremely important to chemistry — so make sure you understand it.

> The properties of the elements are decided entirely by how many electrons they have.
> Atomic number is therefore very significant because it is equal to the number of electrons each atom has.
> But it's the number of electrons in the outer shell which is the really important thing.

Electron Shells are Just Totally Brill

> The fact that electrons form shells around atoms is the basis for the whole of chemistry.
> If they just whizzed round the nucleus any old how and didn't care about shells or any of that stuff there'd be no chemical reactions. No, nothing in fact — because nothing would happen.
> The atoms would just slob about, all day long. Just like teenagers.
> But amazingly, they do form shells (if they didn't, we wouldn't even be here to wonder about it), and the electron arrangement of each atom determines the whole of its chemical behaviour.
> Phew. I mean electron arrangements explain practically the whole Universe. They're just totally brill.

I've got a periodic table — Queen Anne legs and everything...

Physicists can produce new elements in particle accelerators, but they're all radioactive. Most only last a fraction of a second before they decay. They haven't even got round to giving most of them proper names yet, but then even "element 114" sounds pretty cool when you say it in Latin — ununquadium...

Electron Shells

I said it on the last page, but as it's got such a huge wow factor, I'll say it again — the fact that electrons occupy "shells" around the nucleus is what causes the whole of chemistry. Remember that, it's ace.

Electron Shell Rules:

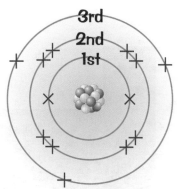

3rd
2nd
1st

3rd shell still filling

1) Electrons always occupy <u>shells</u> (also called <u>energy levels</u>).

2) The <u>lowest</u> energy levels are <u>always filled first</u> — these are the ones closest to the nucleus.

3) Only <u>a certain number</u> of electrons are allowed in each shell:
   <u>1st shell:</u> 2   <u>2nd Shell:</u> 8   <u>3rd Shell:</u> 8

4) Atoms are much <u>happier</u> when they have <u>full electron shells</u> — like the <u>noble gases</u> in <u>Group 0</u> (see p.60).

5) In most atoms the <u>outer shell</u> is <u>not full</u> and this makes the atom want to <u>react</u>.

Follow the Rules to Work Out Electron Configurations

You need to know the <u>electron configurations</u> for the first <u>20</u> elements (things get a bit more complicated after that). But they're not hard to work out. For a quick example, take nitrogen. <u>Follow the steps...</u>

1) The periodic table tells us nitrogen has <u>seven</u> protons... so it must have <u>seven</u> electrons.

2) Follow the 'Electron Shell Rules' above. The <u>first</u> shell can only take 2 electrons and the <u>second</u> shell can take a <u>maximum</u> of 8 electrons.

3) So the electron configuration for nitrogen <u>must</u> be <u>2, 5</u>. Easy peasy.

4) Now <u>you</u> try it for argon.

The periodic table has a big gap here where the transition metals fit in on row four.

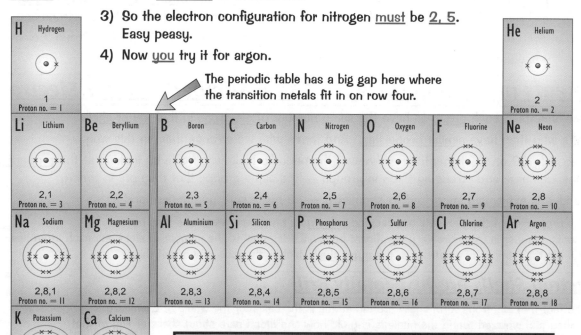

Answer... To calculate the electron configuration of argon, <u>follow the rules</u>. It's got 18 protons, so it <u>must</u> have 18 electrons. The first shell must have <u>2</u> electrons, the second shell must have <u>8</u>, and so the third shell must have <u>8</u> as well. It's as easy as <u>2, 8, 8</u>.

One little duck and two fat ladies — 2, 8, 8...

You need to know enough about electron shells to draw out that <u>whole diagram</u> at the bottom of the page without looking at it. Obviously, you don't have to learn each element separately, just <u>learn the pattern</u>. Cover the page and, using a periodic table, find the atom with the electron configuration 2, 8, 6.

Ionic Bonding

Ionic Bonding — Transferring Electrons

In ionic bonding, atoms lose or gain electrons to form charged particles (called ions) which are then strongly attracted to one another (because of the attraction of opposite charges, + and –).

A Shell with Just One Electron is Well Keen to Get Rid...

1) All the atoms over at the left-hand side of the periodic table, e.g. sodium, potassium, calcium, etc., have just one or two electrons in their outer shell.

2) And they're pretty keen to get shot of them, because then they'll only have full shells left, which is how they like it.

3) So given half a chance they do get rid, and that leaves the atom as an ion instead.

4) Now ions aren't the kind of things that sit around quietly watching the world go by. They tend to leap at the first passing ion with an opposite charge and stick to it like glue.

A Nearly Full Shell is Well Keen to Get That Extra Electron...

1) On the other side of the periodic table, the elements in Group 6 and Group 7, such as oxygen and chlorine, have outer shells which are nearly full.

2) They're obviously pretty keen to gain that extra one or two electrons to fill the shell up.

3) When they do of course they become ions (you know, not the kind of things to sit around) and before you know it, pop, they've latched onto the atom (ion) that gave up the electron a moment earlier.

Sodium Chloride — a Classic Example:

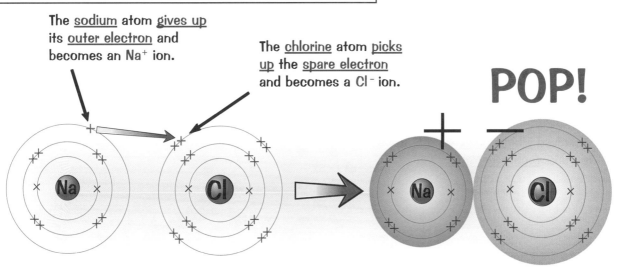

The sodium atom gives up its outer electron and becomes an Na+ ion.

The chlorine atom picks up the spare electron and becomes a Cl– ion.

POP!

The + and – charges we talk about, e.g. Na+ for sodium, just tell you what type of ion the atom WILL FORM in a chemical reaction. In sodium metal there are only neutral sodium atoms, Na. The Na+ ions will only appear if the sodium metal reacts with something like water or chlorine.

Full Shells — it's the name of the game...

There are quite a lot of words on this page and all to hammer home two really basic points: 1) atoms can react by swapping electrons, 2) some atoms lose electrons and some gain them to get full shells.

Ionic Compounds

Ionic compounds are all kinda similar...

Giant Ionic Structures Don't Melt Easily, but When They Do...

1) Ionic bonds always produce giant ionic structures.

2) The ions form a closely packed regular lattice arrangement.

3) There are very strong chemical bonds between all the ions.

4) A single crystal of salt is one giant ionic lattice, which is why salt crystals tend to be cuboid in shape.

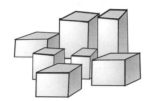

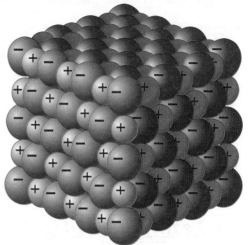

1) They Have High Melting Points and Boiling Points

Ionic bonds are very strong.

All the ions in the giant structure are joined together with these strong bonds, so they're hard to melt or boil.

For example:

NaCl — melting point: 801 °C, boiling point: 1465 °C

MgO — melting point: 2830 °C, boiling point: 3600 °C

2) They Dissolve to Form Solutions That Conduct Electricity

When dissolved the ions separate and are all free to move in the solution.

Free charges can carry electric current, so dissolved salts are good electrical conductors.

Dissolved lithium salts are used to make rechargeable batteries.

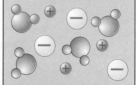

Dissolved in Water

Melted

3) They Conduct Electricity When Molten

When an ionic compound melts, the ions are free to move and they'll carry electric current.

Giant ionic lattices — all over your chips...

Because they conduct electricity when they're dissolved in water, ionic compounds are used to make some types of battery. In the olden days, most batteries had actual liquid in, so they tended to leak all over the place. Now they've come up with a sort of paste that doesn't leak but still conducts. Clever.

Electron Shells and Ions

Groups 1 & 2 and 6 & 7 are the Most Likely to Form Ions

1) Remember, atoms that have <u>lost</u> or <u>gained</u> an electron (or electrons) are <u>ions</u>.
2) The elements that most readily form ions are those in Groups 1, 2, 6 and 7.
3) <u>Group 1 and 2 elements</u> are <u>metals</u> and they <u>lose</u> electrons to form <u>+ve ions</u> or <u>cations</u>.
4) <u>Group 6 and 7 elements</u> are <u>non-metals</u>. They <u>gain</u> electrons to form <u>–ve ions</u> or <u>anions</u>.
5) Make sure you know these easy ones:

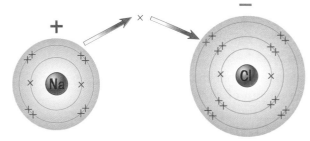

Cations		Anions	
Gr 1	Gr 2	Gr 6	Gr 7
Li^+	Be^{2+}	O^{2-}	F^-
Na^+	Mg^{2+}		Cl^-
K^+	Ca^{2+}		Br^-

6) When any of the above cations <u>react</u> with the anions, they form <u>ionic bonds</u>.
7) Only elements at <u>opposite sides</u> of the periodic table will form ionic bonds, e.g. Na and Cl, where one of them becomes a <u>cation</u> (+ve) and one becomes an <u>anion</u> (–ve).

Remember, the + and – charges we talk about, e.g. Na^+ for sodium, just tell you <u>what type of ion the atom WILL FORM</u> in a chemical reaction. In sodium <u>metal</u> there are <u>only neutral sodium atoms, Na</u>. The Na^+ ions <u>will only appear</u> if the sodium metal <u>reacts</u> with something like water or chlorine.

Show the Electronic Structure of Simple Ions with Brackets [ ]

A useful way of representing ions is by specifying the <u>ion's name</u>, followed by its <u>electron configuration</u> and the <u>charge</u> on the ion. For example, the electronic structure of the sodium ion Na^+ can be represented by Na [2, 8]$^+$. That's the electron configuration followed by the charge on the ion. Simple enough. A few <u>ions</u> and the <u>ionic compounds</u> they form are shown below.

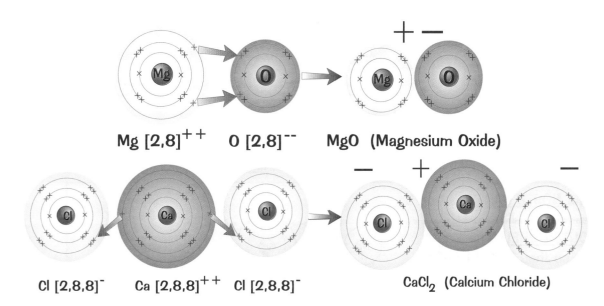

Mg [2,8]$^{++}$ O [2,8]$^{--}$ MgO (Magnesium Oxide)

Cl [2,8,8]$^-$ Ca [2,8,8]$^{++}$ Cl [2,8,8]$^-$ CaCl$_2$ (Calcium Chloride)

Any old ion, any old ion — any, any, any old ion...

Learn which atoms will form 1$^+$, 1$^-$, 2$^+$ and 2$^-$ ions, and <u>why</u>. Then have a go at these:
1) What ions will each of these elements form? Write out their electron configurations:
   a) potassium, b) aluminium, c) beryllium, d) sulfur, e) fluorine (using a periodic table) Answers on page 140.

Reactivity Trends

The reactivity of the elements in Groups 1 and 7 changes as you go down each group. It's all to do with how keen the atoms are to lose or gain electrons to form ions — which is all down to <u>electron configurations</u>...

Reactivity *Changes Down a Group Due to Shielding*

1) As atoms get <u>bigger</u>, they have <u>more full shells</u> of electrons.

2) As you go down any group, each <u>new row</u> has <u>one more</u> full shell.

3) The number of <u>outer</u> electrons is the <u>same</u> for each element in a group.

4) However, going down the group, the outer shell of electrons becomes <u>increasingly far</u> from the nucleus.

5) You have to learn to say that the inner shells provide '<u>SHIELDING</u>'.

6) This means that the <u>outer shell electrons</u> get <u>shielded</u> from the <u>attraction</u> of the <u>+ve nucleus</u>. The <u>upshot</u> of all this is:

For *Group 1 — the Alkali Metals*

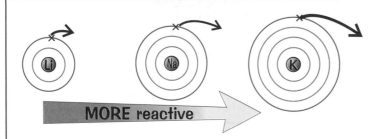

As Group 1 atoms get **BIGGER**, the outer electron is <u>MORE EASILY LOST</u>.

This makes the alkali metals <u>MORE REACTIVE</u> as you go <u>DOWN</u> the group.

For *Group 7 — the Halogens*

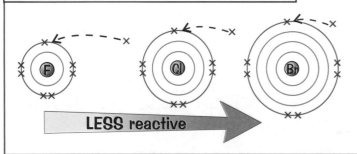

As Group 7 atoms get **BIGGER**, the extra electron is <u>HARDER TO GAIN</u>.

This makes the halogens <u>LESS REACTIVE</u> as you go <u>DOWN</u> the group.

(See p63 for more on the halogens.)

The Noble Gases aren't Reactive At All

When atoms <u>react</u> with each other, they're trying to form <u>full outer shells</u>.

The <u>NOBLE GASES</u>, Group 0 elements, all have <u>FULL OUTER SHELLS</u> already — so they <u>DON'T REACT</u>.

Learn about electron shielding — keep up with the trends...

The <u>physical properties</u> of the alkali metals and the halogens also change as you go down the groups. As you go down the <u>halogens</u>, their boiling points increase and they get darker in colour. Going down the <u>alkali metals</u>, they get softer, denser and easier to melt. <u>Learn</u> the trends.

Covalent Bonding

Covalent Bonds — Sharing Electrons

1) Sometimes atoms prefer to make <u>covalent bonds</u> by <u>sharing</u> electrons with other atoms.
2) This way <u>both</u> atoms feel that they have a <u>full outer shell</u>, and that makes them happy.
3) Each <u>covalent bond</u> provides one <u>extra</u> shared electron for each atom.
4) Each atom involved has to make <u>enough</u> covalent bonds to <u>fill up</u> its outer shell.
5) <u>Learn</u> these <u>seven important examples</u>:

You only have to draw the outer shell of electrons.

1) Hydrogen, H_2

Hydrogen atoms have just one electron. They <u>only need one more</u> to complete the first shell...

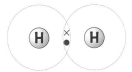

Or H—H

...so they often form <u>single covalent bonds</u> to achieve this.

2) Chlorine, Cl_2

...chlorine atoms also need <u>only one more</u> electron...

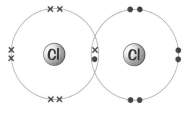

Or Cl—Cl

3) Hydrogen Chloride, HCl

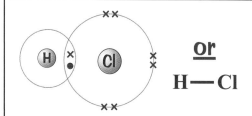

or H—Cl

This is very similar to H_2 and Cl_2. Again, both atoms <u>only need one more electron</u> to complete their outer shells.

4) Ammonia, NH_3

Nitrogen has <u>five</u> outer electrons...

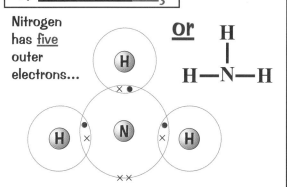

Or
$$H—N—H$$ with H above

...so it needs to form <u>three covalent bonds</u> to make up the extra <u>three</u> electrons needed.

5) Methane, CH_4

Carbon has <u>four outer electrons</u>, which is <u>half a full</u> shell.

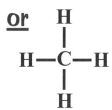
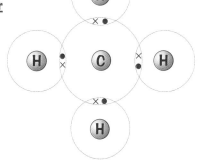

or H—C—H

To become a 4+ or a 4– ion is hard work so it forms <u>four covalent bonds</u> to make up its outer shell.

6) Water, H_2O
7) Oxygen, O_2

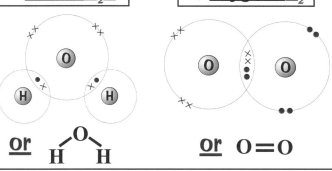

or O=O

<u>Oxygen</u> atoms have <u>six</u> outer electrons. They sometimes form <u>ionic</u> bonds by <u>taking</u> two electrons to complete their outer shell.

However they'll also cheerfully form <u>covalent bonds</u> and <u>share</u> two electrons instead. In <u>water molecules</u>, the oxygen <u>shares</u> electrons with the H atoms and in oxygen gas it shares with another oxygen atom.

Covalent bonding — it's good to share...

Make sure you learn these seven really basic examples and <u>why they work</u>. Every atom wants a full outer shell, and they can get that either by becoming an <u>ion</u> (p.57) or by <u>sharing electrons</u>. Once you understand that, you should be able to apply it to any example they give you in the exam.

Covalent Substances: Two Kinds

Substances formed from <u>covalent bonds</u> can either be <u>simple molecules</u> or <u>giant structures</u>.

Simple Molecular Substances

1) The small number of atoms within a molecule are held together by <u>very strong</u> covalent bonds.

2) By contrast, the forces of attraction <u>between</u> the molecules are <u>very weak</u>.

3) These feeble <u>intermolecular forces</u> mean that the <u>melting</u> and <u>boiling points</u> are <u>very low</u>, because the molecules are <u>easily parted</u> from each other.

4) Most molecular substances are <u>gases or liquids</u> at room temperature.

5) Molecular substances <u>don't conduct electricity</u>, simply because there are <u>no ions</u>.

6) You can usually tell a molecular substance just from its <u>physical state</u>, which is always kinda '<u>mushy</u>' — i.e. <u>liquid</u> or <u>gas</u> or an <u>easily melted solid</u>.

Very weak intermolecular forces

The rest of the halogens form two-atom (diatomic) molecules too — see the next page.

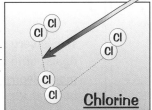
Chlorine

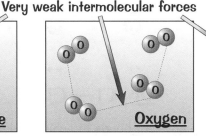
Oxygen

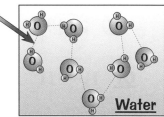
Water

Giant Covalent Structures

1) These are similar to giant ionic structures except that there are <u>no charged ions</u>.

2) <u>All</u> the atoms are <u>bonded</u> to <u>each other</u> by <u>strong</u> covalent bonds.

3) They have <u>very high</u> melting and boiling points.

4) They <u>don't conduct electricity</u> — not even when <u>molten</u> (except for graphite that is — see below).

5) They're usually <u>insoluble</u> in water.

6) Important examples are <u>diamond</u> and <u>graphite</u>, which are both made only from <u>carbon atoms</u>, and silicon dioxide (silica).

Diamond

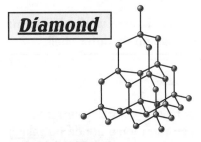

Each carbon atom forms <u>four covalent bonds</u> in a <u>very rigid</u> giant covalent structure. This structure makes diamond the <u>hardest</u> natural substance, so it's used for drill tips.

(And it's all <u>pretty</u> and <u>sparkly</u> too.)

Graphite

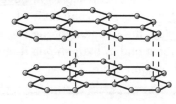

The carbon atoms in graphite are bonded together in <u>layers</u>. The layers are held together so <u>loosely</u> that they can <u>slide over each other</u>, which makes it soft and slippery. These layers can be <u>rubbed off</u> onto paper — that's how a <u>pencil</u> works.

This structure also leaves <u>free electrons</u>, so graphite is the only <u>non-metal</u> which is a <u>good conductor of electricity</u>.

Carbon is a girl's best friend...

The <u>two different types</u> of covalent substance are very different — make sure you know about them both.

Molecular Substances: the Halogens

The halogens are all <u>simple molecular</u> substances made up of <u>pairs</u> of atoms <u>covalently</u> bonded together. That's why you'll usually see the symbols for halogen elements with a <u>little 2</u> next to them — e.g. Cl_2, F_2.

The 'Halogens' are Fluorine, Chlorine, etc.

The Halogens are the Group 7 elements: <u>fluorine</u>, <u>chlorine</u>, <u>bromine</u> and <u>iodine</u>. *(plus astatine, but you don't need to know that one)*

<u>Chlorine</u> is a fairly reactive, poisonous, <u>dense green gas</u>.
<u>Bromine</u> is a dense, poisonous, <u>orange liquid</u>.
<u>Iodine</u> is a <u>dark grey crystalline solid</u>.

All Group 7 elements have <u>7 electrons in their outer shell</u> — so they've all got similar properties.

| As you go <u>DOWN</u> Group 7, the halogens become <u>less reactive</u>.
| So chlorine's more reactive than bromine, and bromine's more reactive than iodine.

	Group 5	Group 6	Group 7		He
		O	19 F Fluorine 9	Ne
		S	35.5 Cl Chlorine 17	Ar
		Se	80 Br Bromine 35	Kr
		Te	127 I Iodine 53	Xe
		Po	210 At Astatine 85	Rn

The Halogens React with Alkali Metals to Form Salts

They react vigorously with alkali metals to form <u>salts</u> called '<u>metal halides</u>'.

> Sodium + Chlorine → Sodium Chloride
>
> Potassium + Bromine → Potassium Bromide

Chlorine makes chlorides, bromine makes bromides, iodine makes iodides... etc.

More Reactive Halogens Will Displace Less Reactive Ones

A halogen closer to the <u>top</u> of the group is <u>more reactive</u>, and can kick <u>less reactive</u> halogens out of compounds. This kind of reaction is called a <u>displacement</u> reaction.

So <u>chlorine</u> can displace <u>bromine</u> and <u>iodine</u> from a solution of <u>bromide</u> or <u>iodide</u>.

And <u>bromine</u> will also displace <u>iodine</u> because of the <u>trend</u> in <u>reactivity</u>.

You need to know the reactions:

> Chlorine + Potassium Iodide → Iodine + Potassium Chloride
>
> Chlorine + Potassium Bromide → Bromine + Potassium Chloride

Halogens and Halides Have Various Uses

CHLORINE IS USED IN BLEACH AND FOR STERILISING WATER...

1) Chlorine's used in <u>bleach</u>, for <u>sterilising water</u>, and for making <u>pesticides</u>.
2) It's also used to make <u>plastics</u> (e.g. PVC, which is polyvinyl chloride).

...IODINE IS USED AS AN ANTISEPTIC...

...but it stings like nobody's business and stains the skin brown. Nice.

...AND SODIUM CHLORIDE'S USED IN THE FOOD INDUSTRY

1) <u>Sodium chloride</u> (<u>salt</u>) is added to most <u>processed foods</u> to enhance the <u>flavour</u>, and to act as a <u>preservative</u>. (But it's now reckoned to be unhealthy to eat too much salt.)
2) Sodium chloride's also used for making <u>chlorine</u>. They do this by <u>electrolysis</u> (see page 85).

Halogens — one electron short of a full shell...

You've got to learn trends and equations. You know the routine.

Metallic Structures

Most Metals are Good Conductors and are Strong and Bendy

...and it's all to do with their 'sea of free electrons'.

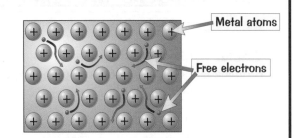

Metal atoms

Free electrons

1) Metals also consist of a giant structure.
2) Metallic bonds involve the all-important 'free electrons', which produce all the properties of metals. These free electrons come from the outer shell of every metal atom in the structure.
3) These electrons are free to move and so metals are good conductors of heat and electricity.

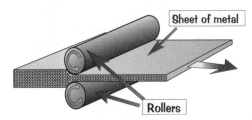

Sheet of metal

Rollers

4) These electrons also hold the atoms together in a regular structure, which gives metals a high tensile strength (in other words they're strong and hard to break).
5) The electrons also allow the atoms to slide over each other, causing metals to be bendy and malleable (you can hammer them into a different shape).

Metals in the Middle of the Periodic Table are Transition Metals

A lot of everyday metals are transition metals (e.g. copper, iron, zinc, gold, silver) — but there are loads of others as well.

1) Transition metals have typical 'metallic' properties (see above).
2) Compounds of transition elements often have pretty colours:
   copper compounds are blue
   iron(II) compounds are light green
   iron(III) compounds are orange/brown

These are the transition metals

Sc	Ti	V	Cr	Mn	Fe	Co	Ni	Cu	Zn

3) Transition metals and their compounds make good catalysts:
   Iron is the catalyst used in the Haber process for making ammonia.
   Nickel is useful for the hydrogenation of alkenes (e.g. to make margarine).

At Very Low Temperatures, Some Metals are Superconductors

1) Normally, all metals have some electrical resistance — even really good conductors like copper.
2) That resistance means that whenever electricity flows through them, they heat up, and some of the electrical energy is wasted as heat.
3) If you make some metals cold enough, though, their resistance disappears completely. The metal becomes a superconductor.
4) Without any resistance, no energy is turned into heat, so none of it's wasted.
5) With superconducting wires you could potentially make:
   a) Power cables that transmit electricity without any loss of power.
   b) Really strong electromagnets that don't need a constant power source.
   c) Electronic circuits that work really fast, because there's no resistance to slow them down.

Metal fatigue — yeah, we've all had enough of this page...

Metals all share a similar structure and conduct well, but they still behave in radically different ways. Take the alkali metals of Group I — they react vigorously with water, producing alkalis and hydrogen gas. Transition metals don't do this. Lucky really, or the Statue of Liberty would disappear in the rain.

New Materials

New materials are continually being developed, with new properties. The two groups of materials you really need to know about are <u>smart materials</u> and <u>nanomaterials</u>.

Smart Materials Have Some Really Weird Properties

1) <u>Smart</u> materials <u>behave differently</u> depending on the <u>conditions</u>, e.g. temperature.

2) A good example is <u>nitinol</u> — a "<u>shape memory alloy</u>" made from about half <u>nickel</u>, half <u>titanium</u>. It's a metal, but you can <u>bend it</u> and <u>twist it</u> like rubber. Bend it too far, though, and it stays bent. But here's the really clever bit — if you heat it above a certain temperature, it goes back to its "<u>remembered</u>" shape (hence the name). It's really handy for glasses frames — if you accidentally sit on them, you can just pop them into a bowl of hot water and they'll <u>jump</u> back <u>into shape</u>.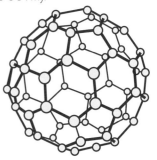

3) Other examples of smart materials include <u>dyes</u> that change <u>colour</u> depending on the <u>temperature</u> or <u>light intensity</u>, <u>liquids</u> that turn <u>solid</u> when you put them in a <u>magnetic field</u>, and materials that <u>expand</u> or <u>contract</u> when you put an <u>electric current</u> through them.

Fullerenes are Nanoparticles

Nanoparticles are only a few nanometres (nm) across (1 nm = 0.000 000 001 m).

1) <u>Fullerenes</u> are molecules of <u>carbon</u>, shaped like <u>hollow balls</u> or <u>closed tubes</u>.

2) The smallest fullerene is <u>buckminsterfullerene</u>, which has <u>60</u> carbon atoms joined in a <u>ball</u> — its molecular formula is C_{60}.

3) Buckminsterfullerene is a <u>black solid</u> that dissolves in <u>petrol</u> to give a <u>deep red</u> solution.

4) Fullerenes can be joined together to form <u>nanotubes</u> — teeny tiny hollow carbon tubes:

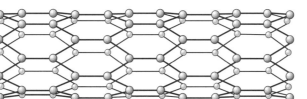

Buckminsterfullerene
(or a 'bucky ball', as it's affectionately known ☺)

a) Carbon nanotubes are <u>very strong</u>. They can be used to reinforce graphite in tennis rackets and to make stronger, lighter building materials.

b) Nanotubes <u>conduct</u> electricity, so they can be used in tiny <u>electric circuits</u> for computer chips.

c) They have a <u>huge surface area</u>, so they could help make great industrial <u>catalysts</u> (the bigger the surface area of a catalyst the better).

d) With nanoparticles, you can build surfaces with very <u>specific properties</u>. That means you can use them to make <u>sensors</u> to detect one type of molecule and nothing else. These <u>highly specific</u> sensors are already being used to test water purity.

While ordinary chemistry works with materials on a large scale, <u>nanochemistry</u> is all on an <u>atomic</u> level. Nanoparticles have <u>very different properties</u> from the 'bulk' chemical. Nanoparticles of normally unreactive silver can kill bacteria. The colour of gold nanoparticles actually varies from red to purple.

Bendy specs, tennis rackets and computer chips — cool...

Like a lot of scientific discoveries, C_{60} was discovered by <u>chance</u>. In the 1980s some scientists investigating how carbon chains form in stars fired laser beams at graphite discs. When they analysed the soot formed they found clusters of 60 carbon atoms — the first 'sightings' of buckminsterfullerene.

Revision Summary for Section Five

Now, my spies tell me that some naughty people skip these pages without so much as reading through the list of questions. Well, you shouldn't, because what's the point in reading that great big section if you're not going to check if you really know it or not? Look, just read the first 10 questions, and I guarantee there'll be an answer you'll have to look up. And when it comes up in the exam, you'll be so glad you did. Plus, if you don't do as you're told my spies will tell me, and then you won't get any toys. Or something.

1) Sketch the nuclear model of an atom.
   Give five details about the nucleus and five details about the electrons.
2) Draw a table showing the relative masses and charges of the three types of particle in an atom.
3) What do the mass number and atomic number represent?
4) Define the term isotope.
5) Describe the difference between an element and a compound. Give an example of each.
6) What feature of atoms determines the order of the modern periodic table?
7) What are groups in the periodic table? Explain their significance in terms of electrons.
8) Describe how you would work out the electron configuration of an atom given its atomic number.
   Find the electron configuration of potassium (using the periodic table at the front of the book).
9) Describe the process of ionic bonding.
10) Draw a diagram to show the ionic bonding in sodium chloride.
11) List the main properties of ionic compounds.
12) Show the electronic structure of a magnesium ion using brackets.
13) State the trends in reactivity as you go down Groups 1 and 7 of the periodic table.
    Explain these trends using the idea of shielding.
14) Explain in terms of electrons why the noble gases are unreactive.
15) What is covalent bonding?
16) Sketch a dot and cross diagram showing the bonding in molecules of:
    a) hydrogen, b) hydrogen chloride, c) water, d)* carbon dioxide.
17) What are the two types of covalent substance? Give three examples of each.
18) Industrial diamonds are used in drill tips and precision cutting tools. What property of diamond makes it suitable for this use? Explain how the bonding in diamond causes its physical properties.
19) Which is more reactive: chlorine or fluorine?
    * What products would you get if you reacted sodium chloride with fluorine?
20) Write down one use of chlorine and one use of iodine.
21) List three properties of metals and explain how metallic bonding causes these properties.
22) Whereabouts in the periodic table will you find the transition metals?
    Name one important use of a transition metal.
23) How can you make some metals become superconductors?
    List two possible uses of superconducting wires.
24) Give an example of a "smart" material and describe how it behaves.
25) What are nanoparticles? Describe two different applications of nanoparticles.
26) Describe briefly how buckminsterfullerene was discovered.

* Answers on page 140.

Balancing Equations

Equations need practice if you're going to get them right, and you'll need them all through Chemistry. Every time you do an equation you need to practise getting it right rather than skating over it.

The Symbol Equation Shows the Atoms on Both Sides:

A chemical reaction can be described by the process REACTANTS → PRODUCTS.

E.g. magnesium reacts with oxygen to produce magnesium oxide.

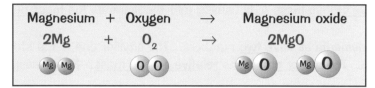

Magnesium + Oxygen → Magnesium oxide

$2Mg$ + O_2 → $2MgO$

Balancing the Equation — Match Them Up One by One

1) There must always be the same number of atoms on both sides — they can't just disappear.
2) You balance the equation by putting numbers in front of the formulas where needed.

Take this equation for burning propane in oxygen to make carbon dioxide and water:

$$C_3H_8 \ + \ O_2 \ \rightarrow \ CO_2 \ + \ H_2O$$

The formulas are all correct but the numbers of some atoms don't match up on both sides. You can't change formulas like C_3H_8 to C_4H_8. You can only put numbers in front of them:

Method: Balance just ONE type of atom at a time

The more you practise, the quicker you'll get, but all you do is this:

> 1) Find an element that doesn't balance and pencil in a number to try and sort it out.
> 2) See where it gets you. It may create another imbalance, but pencil in another number and see where that gets you.
> 3) Carry on chasing unbalanced elements and it'll sort itself out pretty quickly.

I'll show you. In the equation above you soon notice we're short of H atoms on the RHS (right-hand side).
1) The only thing you can do about that is make it $4H_2O$ instead of just H_2O:
$$C_3H_8 \ + \ O_2 \ \rightarrow \ CO_2 \ + \ 4H_2O$$

2) We're also short of C atoms on the RHS, so to balance that up change CO_2 to $3CO_2$:
$$C_3H_8 \ + \ O_2 \ \rightarrow \ 3CO_2 \ + \ 4H_2O$$

3) Now the O atoms are out of balance. You can sort that out by making it $5O_2$ on the left-hand side:
$$C_3H_8 \ + \ 5O_2 \ \rightarrow \ 3CO_2 \ + \ 4H_2O$$

4) And suddenly there it is. Everything balances.

State Symbols Tell You What Physical State It's In

These are easy enough, so make sure you know them — especially aq (aqueous).

(s) — Solid	(l) — Liquid	(g) — Gas	(aq) — Dissolved in water

E.g. $2Mg(s)$ + $O_2(g)$ → $2MgO(s)$

Balanced diet — a biscuit in one hand, an apple in the other...

Write balanced symbol equations for these, and put the state symbols in too:
1) Iron(III) oxide + hydrogen → iron + water
2) Dilute hydrochloric acid + aluminium → aluminium chloride solution + hydrogen

iron(III) oxide = Fe_2O_3
aluminium chloride = $AlCl_3$

Relative Formula Mass

The biggest trouble with <u>relative atomic mass</u> and <u>relative formula mass</u> is that they <u>sound</u> so blood-curdling. Take a few deep breaths, and just enjoy, as the mists slowly clear...

Relative Atomic Mass, A_r — Easy Peasy

1) This is just a way of saying how <u>heavy</u> different atoms are <u>compared</u> with the mass of an atom of carbon-12. So carbon-12 has A_r of <u>exactly 12</u>.

2) It turns out that the <u>relative atomic mass</u> A_r is usually just the same as the <u>mass number</u> of the element.

3) In the periodic table, the elements all have <u>two</u> numbers. The smaller one is the atomic number (how many protons it has). The <u>bigger one</u> is the <u>relative atomic mass</u>. Easy peasy, I'd say.

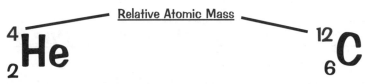

Relative Atomic Mass

$${}^{4}_{2}\text{He} \qquad\qquad {}^{12}_{6}\text{C}$$

Helium has A_r = 4. Carbon has A_r = 12.

Relative Formula Mass, M_r — Also Easy Peasy

If you have a compound like $MgCl_2$ then it has a <u>relative formula mass</u>, M_r, which is just all the relative atomic masses <u>added together</u>.

For $MgCl_2$ it would be:

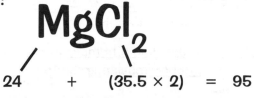

$$\text{MgCl}_2$$

$$24 \quad + \quad (35.5 \times 2) \quad = \quad 95$$

The formula mass of a substance, in grams, is known as a "<u>mole</u>" of that substance. Chemists, eh.

So M_r for $MgCl_2$ is simply <u>95</u>.

You can easily get A_r for any element from the periodic table (see inside front cover), but in a lot of questions they give you them anyway. I'll tell you what, since it's nearly Christmas I'll run through another example for you:

Question: Find the relative formula mass for calcium carbonate, $CaCO_3$, using the given data:
A_r for Ca = 40 A_r for C = 12 A_r for O = 16

<u>ANSWER:</u>

$$\text{CaCO}_3$$

$$40 \quad + \quad 12 \quad + \quad (16 \times 3) = 100$$

So the relative formula mass for $CaCO_3$ is <u>100</u>.

And that's all it is. A big fancy name like <u>relative formula mass</u> and all it means is "<u>add up all the mass numbers</u>". What a swizz, eh? You'd have thought it'd be something a bit juicier than that, wouldn't you. Still, that's life — it's all a big disappointment in the end. Sigh.

Numbers? — and you thought you were doing chemistry...

Learn the definitions of relative atomic mass and relative formula mass, then have a go at these:
1) Use the periodic table to find the relative atomic mass of these elements: Cu, K, Kr, Cl
2) Find the relative formula mass of: NaOH, Fe_2O_3, C_6H_{14}, $Mg(NO_3)_2$ Answers on page 140.

0

Two Formula Mass Calculations

Although relative atomic mass and relative formula mass are easy enough, it can get a tad trickier when you get into other calculations that use them. It's all to do with ratios and percentages, basically.

Calculating % Mass of an Element in a Compound

This is actually dead easy — so long as you've learnt this formula:

$$\text{Percentage mass OF AN ELEMENT IN A COMPOUND} = \frac{A_r \times \text{No. of atoms (of that element)}}{M_r \text{ (of whole compound)}} \times 100$$

If you don't learn the formula then you'd better be pretty smart — or you'll struggle.

EXAMPLE: Find the percentage mass of sodium in sodium carbonate, Na_2CO_3.
ANSWER:
A_r of sodium = 23, A_r of carbon = 12, A_r of oxygen = 16
M_r of Na_2CO_3 = $(2 \times 23) + 12 + (3 \times 16)$ = 106

Now use the formula:

$$\text{Percentage mass} = \frac{A_r \times n}{M_r} \times 100 = \frac{23 \times 2}{106} \times 100 = 43.4\%$$

And there you have it. Sodium makes up 43.4% of the mass of sodium carbonate.

Finding the Formula from Masses or Percentages

This also sounds a lot worse than it really is. Try this for an easy peasy stepwise method:

1) List all the elements in the compound (there's usually only two or three).
2) Underneath them, write their experimental masses or percentages.
3) Divide each mass or percentage by the A_r for that particular element.
4) Turn the numbers you get into a nice simple ratio by multiplying and/or dividing them by well-chosen numbers.
5) Get the ratio in its simplest form, and that tells you the empirical formula of the compound.

Example: Find the empirical formula of the iron oxide produced when 44.8 g of iron react with 19.2 g of oxygen. (A_r for iron = 56, A_r for oxygen =16)
Method:

	Fe	O
1) List the two elements:	Fe	O
2) Write in the experimental masses:	44.8	19.2
3) Divide by the A_r for each element:	$44.8/56 = 0.8$	$19.2/16 = 1.2$
4) Multiply by 10...	8	12
...then divide by 4:	2	3

5) So the simplest formula is 2 atoms of Fe to 3 atoms of O, i.e. Fe_2O_3. And that's it done.

You need to realise (for the exam) that this method is empirical (i.e. based on experiment) and that it's the only way of finding out the formula of a compound. Rust is iron oxide, sure, but is it FeO, or Fe_2O_3? Only an experiment to determine the empirical formula will tell you for certain.

With this empirical formula I can rule the world! — mwa ha ha ha...

Make sure you learn the formula in the red box and the method above. Then try these: Answers on page 140.
1) Find the percentage mass of oxygen in each of these: a) Fe_2O_3 b) H_2O c) $CaCO_3$ d) H_2SO_4.
2) Find the empirical formula of the compound formed from 2.4 g of carbon and 0.8 g of hydrogen.

Calculating Masses in Reactions

These can be kinda scary too, but chill out, little trembling one — just relax and enjoy.

Calculating Masses — No Problem If You Learn This Method

These questions are all about calculating the mass of a reactant or product in a reaction. To answer them you need to write down the ratio of masses they give you in the question, then apply this rule:

> ### Divide to get one, then multiply to get all
> (But you have to apply this first to the substance they give information about, and then the other one.)

Don't worry — this rule should make sense when you look at the example below.

Example: 48 g of magnesium, Mg, burns in air to give 80 g of magnesium oxide, MgO. What mass of magnesium oxide is produced when 60 g of magnesium is burned in air?

Answer: Write down the ratio of masses you're given: 48 g of Mg reacts to give 80 g of MgO

Now apply the rule: Divide to get one, then multiply to get all

This is the tricky bit. You've got to be able to write this down:

> 48 g of Mg ......reacts to give.....80 g of MgO
>
> 1 g of Mg ......reacts to give.....
>
> 60 g of Mg .....reacts to give......

The big clue is that in the question they've said we want to burn '60 g of magnesium', i.e. they've told us how much magnesium to have, and that's how you know to write down the left-hand side of it first, because:

We'll first need to divide by 48 to get 1 g of Mg

and then we'll need to multiply by 60 to get 60 g of Mg.

Then you can work out the numbers on the other side (shown in orange below) by realising that you must divide both sides by 48 and then multiply both sides by 60. It's tricky.

$$\div48 \left\{ \begin{array}{l} 48 \text{ g of Mg} \ldots\ldots\ldots\ldots\ 80 \text{ g of MgO} \\ 1 \text{ g of Mg} \ldots\ldots\ldots\ldots\ 1.67 \text{ g of MgO} \\ 60 \text{ g of Mg} \ldots\ldots\ldots\ldots\ 100 \text{ g of MgO} \end{array} \right\} \div48$$
$$\times60 \qquad\qquad\qquad\qquad\qquad\qquad\qquad\qquad \times60$$

This finally tells us that 60 g of magnesium will produce 100 g of magnesium oxide. If the question had said, 'Find how much magnesium gives 500 g of magnesium oxide', you'd fill in the MgO side first, because that's the one you'd have the information about. Got it? Good-O!

An Important Principle...

> **THE TOTAL MASS OF REACTANTS AT THE START OF A REACTION IS EQUAL TO THE TOTAL MASS OF PRODUCTS MADE.**

In theory anyway... in real life it's not that simple — see p72.

So going back to the example, we can use this principle to calculate the mass of oxygen that reacted with the 60 g of magnesium. Let's call the mass of oxygen 'x'. Then, by the above principle we can say that:

$60 + x = 100$, which gives $x = 100 - 60 = 40$. So the mass of oxygen is 40 g.

Reaction mass calculations? — no worries, matey...

The only way to get good at these is to practise. So have a go at this question:
40 g of calcium reacts with oxygen to produce 56 g of calcium oxide.
Find the mass of calcium needed to produce 30 g of calcium oxide. Answer on page 140.

Atom Economy

It's important in industrial reactions that as much of the reactants as possible get turned into useful products. This depends on the atom economy of the reaction.

"Atom Economy" — "Efficiency" of a Reaction

1) A lot of reactions make more than one product. Some of these products will be useful, but others will just be waste, e.g. when you make quicklime from limestone, you also get CO_2 as a waste product.

2) The atom economy of a reaction tells you how much of the mass of the reactants ends up as useful products, compared with the amount of waste.

> Example: Hydrogen gas is made on a large scale by reacting natural gas (methane) with steam:
>
> $$CH_4(g) + H_2O(g) \rightarrow CO(g) + 3H_2(g)$$

1) In this reaction, only 17.6% of the mass of the reactants is converted into the useful product — hydrogen.
2) The other 82.4% of the starting materials are wasted as carbon monoxide, which has to be disposed of somehow.
3) In industry, the waste carbon monoxide is reacted with more steam to make carbon dioxide (and a bit more hydrogen). That brings the overall "atom economy" down to only 15% — but the final waste product is much less nasty that way.

High Atom Economy is Better for Profits and the Environment

1) Pretty obviously, if you're making lots of waste, that's a problem.

2) Reactions with low atom economy use up resources very quickly. At the same time, they make lots of waste materials that have to be disposed of somehow. That tends to make these reactions unsustainable — the raw materials will run out and the waste has to go somewhere.

3) For the same reasons, low atom economy reactions aren't usually profitable. Raw materials are expensive to buy, and waste products can be expensive to remove and dispose of responsibly.

4) One way around the problem is to find a use for the waste products rather than just throwing them away. There's often more than one way to make the product you want, so the trick is to come up with a reaction that gives useful 'by-products' rather than useless ones.

5) That doesn't get round all the problems, though. It can be really hard to separate out the different things made in the reaction to get pure products.

6) The reactions with the highest atom economy are the ones that only have one product — like the Haber process (see page 79). Those reactions have an atom economy of 100%.

Atom economy — important, but not the whole story...

You could get asked about any industrial reaction in the exam. Don't panic — whatever example they give you, the same stuff applies. In the real world, high atom economy isn't enough, though. You need to think about other factors like the energy cost as well.

Percentage Yield

Of course, things are never as simple in practice as they are in theory. The mass of product is called the <u>yield</u> of a reaction. In theory this is equal to the total mass of the reactants (see p70), but the <u>actual yield</u> will be <u>slightly less</u> — not even the most efficient reaction will have a 100% yield.

Percentage Yield Compares Actual and Predicted Yield

The more reactants you start with, the higher the <u>actual yield</u> will be — that's pretty obvious. But the <u>percentage yield doesn't</u> depend on the amount of reactants you started with — it's a <u>percentage</u>.

1) The <u>predicted yield</u> of a reaction is the mass of product you <u>expect</u> to get. You can calculate it using the method on page 70. In the example, the predicted yield was 100 g.

2) Percentage yield is given by the formula:

$$\text{percentage yield} = \frac{\text{actual yield (grams)}}{\text{predicted yield (grams)}} \times 100$$

3) Percentage yield is <u>always</u> somewhere between 0 and 100%.

4) 100% yield means that you got <u>all</u> the product you expected to get.

5) 0% yield means that <u>no</u> reactants were converted into product, i.e. no product at all was <u>made</u>.

Yields are Always Less Than 100%

In real life, you <u>never</u> get a 100% yield. Some product or reactant <u>always</u> gets lost along the way — and that goes for big <u>industrial processes</u> as well as school lab experiments.
How this happens depends on <u>what sort of reaction</u> it is and what <u>apparatus</u> is being used.

Lots of things can go wrong, but the four you need to <u>know about</u> are:

1) Evaporation

Liquids evaporate <u>all the time</u> — not just while they're being heated.

Liquid evaporating...

2) Heating

Losses while heating can be due to <u>evaporation</u>, or for more complicated reasons.

In <u>reversible reactions</u> (see P.79), increasing the temperature can change the amount of product that's produced. So heating the reaction to speed it up might mean a <u>lower yield</u>.

3) Filtration

When you <u>filter a liquid</u> to remove <u>solid particles</u>, you nearly always lose a bit of liquid or solid.

1) If you want to <u>keep the liquid</u>, you lose the bit that remains with the solid and filter paper (they always stay a bit wet).

2) If you want to <u>keep the solid</u>, some of it usually gets left behind when you scrape it off the filter paper — even if you're really careful.

4) Transferring Liquids

You always lose a bit of liquid when you <u>transfer</u> it from one container to another — even if you manage not to spill it.

Some of it always gets left behind on the <u>inside surface</u> of the old container. Think about it — it's always wet when you finish.

You can't always get what you want...

Unfortunately, no matter how careful you are, you're not going to get a 100% yield in any reaction. So you'll <u>always</u> get a little loss of product. In industry, people work very hard to keep wastage as <u>low</u> as possible — so <u>reactants</u> that don't react first time are <u>collected</u> and <u>recycled</u> whenever possible.

Revision Summary for Section Six

Some more tricky questions to stress you out. The thing is though, why bother doing easy questions? These meaty monsters find out what you really know, and worse, what you really don't. Yeah, I know, it's kinda scary, but if you want to get anywhere in life you've got to face up to a bit of hardship. That's just the way it is. Take a few deep breaths and then try these.

1)* Write down the chemical formulas for the following substances:
   a) zinc carbonate

   b) sodium hydroxide

   c) lithium oxide

   d) Iron(III) chloride

2)* Give three rules for balancing equations, then try balancing these equations:

   a) $CaCO_3 + HCl \rightarrow CaCl_2 + H_2O + CO_2$

   b) $Ca + H_2O \rightarrow Ca(OH)_2 + H_2$

   c) $H_2SO_4 + KOH \rightarrow K_2SO_4 + H_2O$

   d) $Mg + HNO_3 \rightarrow Mg(NO_3)_2 + H_2$

3) Use the correct state symbols to show the physical state of the following substances:
   a) oxygen (O_2) gas   b) $CuSO_4$ dissolved in water   c) liquid water (H_2O)   d) ice (H_2O)

4) Define the relative atomic mass of an element.

5)* Find A_r or M_r for each of these (use the periodic table inside the front cover):
   a) Ca   b) Ag   c) CO_2 d) $MgCO_3$ e) $Al(OH)_3$
   f) ZnO   g) Na_2CO_3 h) sodium chloride

6)* Find the percentage mass of carbon in the following:
   a) CH_4 b) K_2CO_3 c) CO_2

7)* Find the percentage mass of oxygen in the following:
   a) CO   b) K_2CO_3 c) CO_2

8)* Find the formula of the compound formed when 21.9 g of magnesium, 29.3 g of sulfur and 58.4 g of oxygen react.

9)* Write down the method for calculating reacting masses.

   a) What mass of magnesium oxide is produced when 112.1 g of magnesium burns in air?

   b) What mass of sodium is needed to produce 108.2 g of sodium oxide?

   c) What mass of carbon will react with hydrogen to produce 24.6 g of propane (C_3H_8)?

10) What is meant by the term "atom economy"?

11) Is it better to have a high atom economy or a low atom economy? Explain why.

12) What is the formula for percentage yield?

13) How does predicted yield differ from actual yield?

14) Name four factors that prevent the percentage yield being 100%.

* Answers on page 140.

Rates of Reaction

Reactions Can Go at All Sorts of *Different Rates*

1) One of the <u>slowest</u> is the <u>rusting</u> of iron (it's not slow enough though — what about my little MGB).

2) A <u>moderate speed</u> reaction is a <u>metal</u> (like magnesium) reacting with <u>acid</u> to produce a gentle stream of <u>bubbles</u>.

3) A <u>really fast</u> reaction is an <u>explosion</u>, where it's all over in a <u>fraction</u> of a second.

The Rate of a Reaction Depends on Four Things:

1) <u>Temperature</u>
2) <u>Concentration</u>   — (or <u>pressure</u> for gases)
3) <u>Catalyst</u>
4) <u>Size of particles</u>   — (or <u>surface area</u>)

LEARN THEM!

Typical Graphs for Rate of Reaction

The plot below shows how the speed of a particular reaction varies under <u>different conditions</u>. The quickest reaction is shown by the line that becomes <u>flat</u> in the <u>least</u> time. The line that flattens out first must have the <u>steepest slope</u> compared to all the others, making it possible to spot the slowest and fastest reactions.

1) <u>Graph 1</u> represents the original <u>fairly slow</u> reaction. The graph is not too steep.

2) <u>Graphs 2 and 3</u> represent the reaction taking place <u>quicker</u> but with the <u>same initial amounts</u>. The slope of the graphs gets steeper.

3) The <u>increased rate</u> could be due to <u>any</u> of these:

> a) increase in <u>temperature</u>
> b) increase in <u>concentration</u> (or pressure)
> c) <u>catalyst</u> added
> d) solid reactant crushed up into <u>smaller bits</u>

Graph (Amount of product evolved vs Time):
- ④ faster, and more reactants
- **End of Reaction**
- ③ much faster reaction
- ② faster reaction
- ① original reaction

4) <u>Graph 4</u> produces <u>more product</u> as well as going <u>faster</u>. This can <u>only</u> happen if <u>more reactant(s)</u> are added at the start. <u>Graphs 1, 2 and 3</u> all converge at the same level, showing that they all produce the same amount of product, although they take <u>different</u> times to get there.

How to get a fast, furious reaction — crack a wee joke...

<u>Industrial</u> reactions generally use a <u>catalyst</u> and are done at <u>high temperature and pressure</u>. Time is money, so the faster an industrial reaction goes the better... but only <u>up to a point</u>. Chemical plants are quite expensive to rebuild if they get blown into lots and lots of teeny tiny pieces.

Measuring Rates of Reaction

Three Ways to Measure the Speed of a Reaction

The speed of a reaction can be observed either by how quickly the reactants are used up or how quickly the products are formed. It's usually a lot easier to measure products forming.

The rate of reaction can be calculated using the following equation:

$$\text{Rate of Reaction} = \frac{\text{Amount of reactant used or amount of product formed}}{\text{Time}}$$

There are different ways that the speed of a reaction can be measured. Learn these three:

1) Precipitation

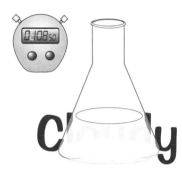

1) This is when the product of the reaction is a precipitate which clouds the solution.
2) Observe a marker through the solution and measure how long it takes for it to disappear.
3) The quicker the marker disappears, the quicker the reaction.
4) This only works for reactions where the initial solution is rather see-through.
5) The result is very subjective — different people might not agree over the exact point when the mark 'disappears'.

2) Change in Mass (Usually Gas Given Off)

1) Measuring the speed of a reaction that produces a gas can be carried out on a mass balance.
2) As the gas is released the mass disappearing is easily measured on the balance.
3) The quicker the reading on the balance drops, the faster the reaction.
4) This is the most accurate of the three methods described on this page because the mass balance is very accurate. But it has the disadvantage of releasing the gas straight into the room.

3) The Volume of Gas Given Off

1) This involves the use of a gas syringe to measure the volume of gas given off.
2) The more gas given off during a given time interval, the faster the reaction.
3) A graph of gas volume against time elapsed could be plotted to give a rate of reaction graph.
4) Gas syringes usually give volumes accurate to the nearest millilitre, so they're quite accurate. You have to be quite careful though — if the reaction is too vigorous, you can easily blow the plunger out of the end of the syringe!

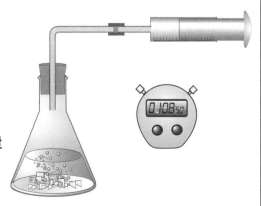

OK have you got your stopwatch ready *BANG!* — oh...

Each method has its pros and cons. The mass balance method is only accurate as long as the flask isn't too hot, otherwise you lose mass by evaporation as well as by the reaction. The first method isn't very accurate, but if you're not producing a gas you can't use either of the other two. Ah well.

Collision Theory

The four ways to <u>speed up reactions</u> are <u>increasing temperature</u>, <u>increasing pressure or concentration</u>, chopping it into <u>smaller bits</u> and <u>adding a catalyst</u>. But WHY, I hear you cry...

It's All to Do with Colliding Particles

1) <u>Reaction rates</u> are explained perfectly by <u>colliding particles</u>. It's really simple.

2) <u>Collision theory</u> says that <u>the rate of a reaction</u> simply depends on <u>how often</u> and <u>how hard</u> the reacting particles <u>collide</u> with each other.

3) The basic idea is that particles have to <u>collide</u> in order to <u>react</u>, and they have to collide <u>hard enough</u> (with enough energy). This minimum energy is called the <u>activation energy</u>.

4) Each of the four methods of increasing the <u>rate of a reaction</u> can be <u>explained</u> in terms of increasing the <u>number of successful collisions</u> between the reacting particles.

5) The <u>GOOD NEWS</u> is — you only need to know how <u>two</u> of them work:

1) HIGHER TEMPERATURE Increases Collisions

When the <u>temperature is increased</u> the particles all <u>move quicker</u>. If they're moving quicker, they're going to have <u>more collisions</u>, and collide with <u>more energy</u>.

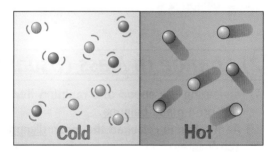

Cold   Hot

2) HIGHER CONCENTRATION (or PRESSURE) Increases Collisions

If a solution is made more <u>concentrated</u> it means there are more particles of <u>reactant</u> knocking about <u>between the water molecules</u> (or other solvent molecules, see p92). This makes collisions between the <u>important</u> particles <u>more likely</u>.

In a <u>gas</u>, increasing the <u>pressure</u> means the particles are <u>more squashed up</u> together so there are going to be <u>more collisions</u>.

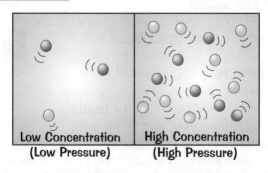

Low Concentration   High Concentration
(Low Pressure)   (High Pressure)

Collision theory — the lamppost ran into me...

Once you've learnt everything off this page, the rates of reaction stuff should make <u>a lot more sense</u>. The concept's fairly simple — the <u>more often</u> particles bump into each other, and the <u>harder</u> they hit when they do, the <u>faster</u> the reaction happens.

Catalysts

Many reactions can be speeded up by adding a catalyst.

> A catalyst is a substance which changes the speed of a reaction, without being changed or used up in the reaction.

1) Catalysts Lower the Activation Energy

1) The activation energy is the minimum amount of energy needed for a reaction to happen.
2) Catalysts lower the activation energy of reactions, making it easier for them to happen.
3) This means a lower temperature can be used.

2) Solid Catalysts Work Best When They Have a Big Surface Area

1) Catalysts are usually used as a powder or pellets or a fine gauze.
2) This gives them a large surface area to help the reacting particles meet up and do the business.

Catalyst Powder

Catalyst Pellets

Catalyst Gauzes

3) Transition metals are common catalysts in many industrial reactions, e.g. nickel is used for cracking hydrocarbons and iron catalyses the Haber process (see p.79).

3) Catalysts Help Reduce Costs in Industrial Reactions

1) Catalysts are very important for commercial reasons — most industrial reactions use them.
2) Catalysts increase the rate of the reaction, which saves money because the plant doesn't need to operate for as long to produce the same amount of stuff.
3) Alternatively, a catalyst will let the reaction work at a much lower temperature. That reduces the energy used up in the reaction (the energy cost), which is good for sustainable development and can save a lot of money too.
4) There are disadvantages to using catalysts, though.
5) Catalysts can be very expensive to buy, and often need to be removed and cleaned. But they never get used up in the reaction, so once you've got them you can use them over and over again.
6) Different reactions use different catalysts, so if you make more than one product at your plant, you'll probably need to buy different catalysts for them.
7) Catalysts can be 'poisoned' by impurities, so they stop working. That means you have to keep your reaction mixture very clean.

Catalysts are like great jokes — they can be used over and over...

And they're not only used in industry... every useful chemical reaction in the human body is catalysed by a biological catalyst (an enzyme). If the reactions in the body were just left to their own devices, they'd take so long to happen, we couldn't exist. Quite handy then, these catalysts.

Section Seven — Industrial Chemistry

Energy Transfer in Reactions

Whenever chemical reactions occur <u>energy</u> is usually <u>transferred</u> to or from the <u>surroundings</u>.

In an Exothermic Reaction, Heat is Given Out

An <u>EXOTHERMIC reaction</u> is one which <u>gives out energy</u> to the surroundings, usually in the form of <u>heat</u> and usually shown by a <u>rise in temperature.</u>

1) Burning Fuels

The best example of an <u>exothermic</u> reaction is <u>burning fuels</u> — also called <u>COMBUSTION</u>. This gives out a lot of heat — it's very exothermic.

2) Neutralisation Reactions

<u>Neutralisation reactions</u> (acid + alkali) are also exothermic — see page 81.

3) Oxidation Reactions

Many oxidation reactions are exothermic...
Addition of water to anhydrous <u>copper(II) sulfate</u> to turn it into blue hydrated copper sulfate crystals <u>produces heat</u>, so it must be <u>exothermic</u>.
("Anhydrous" just means "without water", and "hydrated" means "with water".)

ACID
Don't do it like this!!
ALKALI
Steam

In an Endothermic Reaction, Heat is Taken In

An <u>ENDOTHERMIC reaction</u> is one which <u>takes in energy</u> from the surroundings, usually in the form of <u>heat</u> and usually shown by a <u>fall in temperature.</u>

Endothermic reactions are much <u>less common</u>. <u>Thermal decompositions</u> are a good example:

<u>THERMAL DECOMPOSITION OF CALCIUM CARBONATE</u>:

Heat must be supplied to make the compound <u>decompose</u> to make quicklime.

$$CaCO_3 \rightarrow CaO + CO_2$$

<u>A lot of heat energy</u> is needed to make this happen. In fact the calcium carbonate has to be <u>heated in a kiln</u> and kept at about <u>800 °C</u>. It takes almost <u>18 000 kJ</u> of heat to make <u>10 kg</u> of calcium carbonate decompose. That's pretty endothermic I'd say.

The Thermal Decomposition of Hydrated Copper Sulfate

<u>Copper(II) sulfate</u> crystals can be used as a <u>test</u> for <u>water</u>.

1) If you <u>heat blue hydrated</u> copper(II) sulfate crystals it drives the water off and leaves <u>white anhydrous</u> copper(II) sulfate powder. This is endothermic.

Water vapour

2) If you then <u>add</u> a couple of drops of <u>water</u> to the <u>white powder</u> you get the <u>blue crystals</u> back again. This is exothermic.

This is a <u>reversible reaction</u> (see p.79). In reversible reactions, if the reaction is <u>endothermic</u> in <u>one direction</u>, it will be <u>exothermic</u> in the <u>other direction</u>. The energy absorbed by the endothermic reaction is <u>equal</u> to the energy released during the exothermic reaction.

Right, so burning gives out heat — really...

This whole energy transfer thing is a fairly simple idea — don't be put off by the long words.
Remember, "<u>exo-</u>" = <u>exit</u>, "<u>-thermic</u>" = <u>heat</u>, so an exothermic reaction is one that <u>gives out</u> heat.
And "<u>endo-</u>" = erm... the other one. Okay, so there's no easy way to remember that one. Tough.

Reversible Reactions and Ammonia

A <u>reversible reaction</u> is one where the <u>products</u> of the reaction can react with each other and <u>convert back</u> to the original reactants. In other words, <u>it can go both ways</u>. Eventually it'll usually reach equilibrium — a kind of <u>balance</u> point between the forwards and backwards reactions.

> A <u>reversible reaction</u> is one where the <u>products</u> of the reaction can <u>themselves react</u> to produce the <u>original reactants</u>
> A + B ⇌ C + D

The Haber Process to Make Ammonia is Reversible

$$N_{2(g)} + 3H_{2(g)} \rightleftharpoons 2NH_{3(g)} \quad (+ \text{ heat})$$

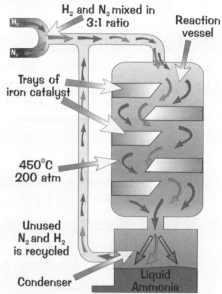

1) The <u>nitrogen</u> is obtained easily from the <u>air</u>, which is <u>78% nitrogen</u> (and 21% oxygen).

2) The <u>hydrogen</u> comes from <u>natural gas</u> or from <u>other sources</u> like crude oil.

3) The reaction is <u>reversible</u> — it occurs in both directions — so not all of the nitrogen and hydrogen will <u>convert</u> to ammonia. The reaction eventually reaches an <u>equilibrium</u>.

4) But remember, the unused hydrogen, H_2, and nitrogen, N_2, are <u>recycled</u> so <u>nothing is wasted</u>.

5) The <u>ammonia</u> is formed as a <u>gas</u> but as it cools in the condenser it <u>liquefies</u> and is <u>removed</u>.

6) This is an <u>important industrial process</u> — ammonia is used to make <u>fertilisers</u> (see below), to make <u>nitric acid</u>, and in <u>cleaning fluids</u>.

INDUSTRIAL CONDITIONS:
<u>Pressure</u>: 200 atmospheres
<u>Temperature</u>: 450 °C <u>Catalyst</u>: Iron

Ammonia is Used to Make Ammonium Nitrate Fertiliser

1) If you react <u>ammonia</u> with <u>nitric acid</u>, you get <u>ammonium nitrate</u>.

2) Ammonium nitrate is an especially good fertiliser because it has <u>nitrogen</u> from <u>two sources</u>, the ammonia and the nitric acid. Kind of a <u>double dose</u>. Plants need nitrogen to make <u>proteins</u>.

3) Ammonium nitrate is a much more <u>effective</u> fertiliser than <u>organic alternatives</u> (e.g. pig poo), so it helps farmers produce crops from land that otherwise wouldn't have been <u>fertile</u> enough. As you can imagine, this can be very important in countries hit by famine.

4) But there are some <u>serious problems</u> with artificial fertilisers:

   a) If they get into <u>streams</u>, they can cause <u>plants and algae</u> to <u>grow out of control</u>. This can completely <u>change the ecosystem</u> and can lead to all the <u>fish dying</u>. Not nice.

   b) If too many <u>nitrates</u> get into <u>drinking water</u> it can cause <u>health problems</u>, especially for <u>babies</u>.

You need to learn this stuff — go on, Haber go at it...

So remember: the Haber process is a reversible reaction — so you don't get 100% yield (see p72). But it doesn't matter, because the hydrogen and nitrogen are recycled. It's all clever stuff.

Minimising the Cost of Production

Things like <u>fast reaction rates</u> are nice in industry — but in the end, the important thing is <u>keeping costs down</u>. It all comes down to <u>maximum efficiency</u>...

Production Cost <u>Depends</u> on <u>Several Different</u> Factors

There are <u>five</u> main things that affect the <u>cost</u> of making a new substance. It's these five factors that companies have to consider when deciding <u>if</u>, and then <u>how</u>, to produce a chemical.

1) Price of Energy

a) Industry needs to keep its <u>energy bills</u> as low as possible.

b) If a reaction needs a <u>high temperature</u>, the <u>running costs</u> will be higher.

2) Cost of Raw Materials

a) This is kept to a minimum by <u>recycling</u> any <u>materials</u> that haven't reacted.

b) A good example of this is the <u>Haber process</u> (see p79). The % yield of the reaction is quite <u>low</u> (about 10%), but the unreacted N_2 and H_2 can be <u>recycled</u> to keep waste to a minimum.

3) Labour Costs (Wages)

a) Everyone who works for a company has got to be <u>paid</u>.

b) <u>Labour-intensive</u> processes (i.e. those that involve many people) can be very expensive.

c) <u>Automation</u> cuts <u>running costs</u> by reducing the number of people involved.

d) But companies have always got to weigh any <u>savings</u> they make on their <u>wage bill</u> against the <u>initial cost</u> and <u>running costs</u> of the machinery.

4) Plant Costs (Equipment)

a) The cost of equipment depends on the <u>conditions</u> it has to cope with.

b) For example, it costs far more to make something to withstand <u>very high pressures</u> than something which only needs to work at atmospheric pressure.

5) Rate of Production

a) Generally speaking, the <u>faster</u> the reaction goes, the better it is in terms of reducing the time and costs of production.

b) So rates of reaction are often increased by using <u>catalysts</u>.

c) But the increase in production rate has to <u>balance the cost</u> of buying the catalyst in the first place and replacing any that gets lost.

This will make it as cheap as chips...

In industry, <u>compromises</u> must be made, just like in life, and the Haber process is a prime example of this. You need to learn those <u>five</u> different factors affecting cost, along with the details about each factor. Cover the page and scribble it all down — and keep doing it until you get it all right.

Acids and Bases

You'll find acids and bases <u>at home</u>, in <u>industry</u> and in <u>the lab</u> — they're an important set of chemicals.

The pH Scale and Universal Indicator

pH 0 1 2 3 4 5 6 7 8 9 10 11 12 13 14

ACIDS | ALKALIS

NEUTRAL

car battery acid, stomach acid | vinegar, lemon juice | acid rain | normal rain | pure water | washing-up liquid | pancreatic juice | soap powder | caustic soda (drain cleaner)

An Indicator is Just a Dye That Changes Colour

The dye in the indicator <u>changes colour</u> depending on whether it's <u>above</u> or <u>below</u> a certain pH. <u>Universal indicator</u> is a very useful <u>combination of dyes</u> which gives the colours shown above.

It's very useful for <u>estimating</u> the pH of a solution.

The pH Scale Goes from 0 to 14

1) A <u>very strong acid</u> has <u>pH 0</u>. A <u>very strong alkali</u> has <u>pH 14</u>.
2) A <u>neutral</u> substance has <u>pH 7</u> (e.g. pure water).

Acids and Bases Neutralise Each Other

An <u>ACID</u> is a substance with a pH of less than 7. Acids form H^+ ions in <u>water</u>.
A <u>BASE</u> is a substance with a pH of greater than 7.
An <u>ALKALI</u> is a base that <u>DISSOLVES IN WATER</u>. Alkalis form OH^- ions in <u>water</u>.

The reaction between acids and bases is called <u>neutralisation</u>. Make sure you learn it:

$$acid + base \rightarrow salt + water$$

Neutralisation can also be seen in terms of <u>H</u>$^+$ and <u>OH</u>$^-$ <u>ions</u> like this, so learn it too:

$$H^+ + OH^- \rightarrow H_2O$$

When an acid neutralises a base (or vice versa), the <u>products</u> are <u>neutral</u>, i.e. they have a <u>pH of 7</u>.

Modern Industry Uses Tonnes of Sulfuric Acid

1) Sulfuric acid is used in <u>car batteries</u>, where it's concentrated enough to cause severe <u>burns</u>.
2) It's also used in many <u>manufacturing</u> processes, such as making <u>fertilisers</u> and <u>detergents</u>.
3) You can also use it to <u>clean</u> and <u>prepare metal surfaces</u>, e.g. before painting or welding. A metal surface is usually covered with a layer of <u>insoluble metal oxide</u>. Sulfuric acid reacts with this layer, forming a <u>soluble metal salt</u> which washes away nice and easily.

This'll give you a firm base for Chemistry...

There's no getting away from acids and bases in Chemistry, or even in real life. They are everywhere — acids are found in loads of <u>foods</u>, like vinegar and fruit, and as <u>food flavourings</u> and <u>preservatives</u>, whilst alkalis (particularly sodium hydroxide) are used to help make all sorts of things, from <u>soaps</u> to <u>ceramics</u>.

Acids Reacting with Metals

Acid + Metal → Salt + Hydrogen

That's written big 'cos it's kinda worth remembering. Here's the <u>typical experiment</u>:

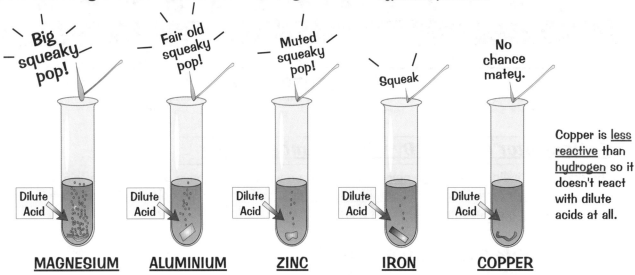

Big squeaky pop!   Fair old squeaky pop!   Muted squeaky pop!   Squeak   No chance matey.

Dilute Acid   Dilute Acid   Dilute Acid   Dilute Acid   Dilute Acid

MAGNESIUM   **ALUMINIUM**   **ZINC**   **IRON**   **COPPER**

Copper is <u>less reactive</u> than <u>hydrogen</u> so it doesn't react with dilute acids at all.

1) The more <u>reactive</u> the metal, the <u>faster</u> the reaction will go — very reactive metals (e.g. sodium) react <u>explosively</u>.

2) <u>Copper</u> does <u>not</u> react with dilute acids <u>at all</u> — because it's <u>less</u> reactive than <u>hydrogen</u>.

3) The <u>speed</u> of reaction is indicated by the <u>rate</u> at which the <u>bubbles</u> of hydrogen are given off.

4) The <u>hydrogen</u> is confirmed by the <u>burning splint test</u> giving the notorious 'squeaky pop'.

5) The <u>name</u> of the <u>salt</u> produced depends on which <u>metal</u> is used, and which <u>acid</u> is used:

Hydrochloric Acid Will Always Produce Chloride Salts:

$$2HCl + Mg \rightarrow MgCl_2 + H_2 \qquad \text{(Magnesium chloride)}$$
$$6HCl + 2Al \rightarrow 2AlCl_3 + 3H_2 \qquad \text{(Aluminium chloride)}$$
$$2HCl + Zn \rightarrow ZnCl_2 + H_2 \qquad \text{(Zinc chloride)}$$

Sulfuric Acid Will Always Produce Sulfate Salts:

$$H_2SO_4 + Mg \rightarrow MgSO_4 + H_2 \qquad \text{(Magnesium sulfate)}$$
$$3H_2SO_4 + 2Al \rightarrow Al_2(SO_4)_3 + 3H_2 \qquad \text{(Aluminium sulfate)}$$
$$H_2SO_4 + Zn \rightarrow ZnSO_4 + H_2 \qquad \text{(Zinc sulfate)}$$

Chloride and sulfate salts are generally <u>soluble in water</u>
(the main exceptions are lead chloride, lead sulfate and silver chloride, which are insoluble).

Nitric Acid Produces Nitrate Salts When NEUTRALISED, But...

Nitric acid reacts fine with alkalis, to produce nitrates, but it can play silly devils with metals and produce nitrogen oxides instead, so we'll ignore it here. Chemistry's a real messy subject sometimes, innit.

Nitric acid, tut — there's always one...

Okay, so this stuff isn't exactly a laugh a minute, but at least it's fairly straightforward learning. Metals that are <u>less</u> reactive than <u>hydrogen</u> don't react with acid, and some metals like sodium and potassium are <u>too</u> reactive to mix with acid — your beaker would <u>explode</u>.

Neutralisation Reactions

Metal Oxides and Metal Hydroxides are Bases

1) Some metal oxides and metal hydroxides dissolve in water. These soluble compounds are alkalis.
2) Even bases that won't dissolve in water will still react with acids.
3) So, all metal oxides and metal hydroxides react with acids to form a salt and water.

Acid + Metal Oxide → Salt + Water

Acid + Metal Hydroxide → Salt + Water

(These are neutralisation reactions, of course.)

| Hydrochloric acid | + | Copper oxide | → | Copper chloride | + | water |
| $2HCl$ | + | CuO | → | $CuCl_2$ | + | H_2O |

| Sulfuric acid | + | Potassium hydroxide | → | Potassium sulfate | + | water |
| H_2SO_4 | + | $2KOH$ | → | K_2SO_4 | + | $2H_2O$ |

| Nitric acid | + | Sodium hydroxide | → | Sodium nitrate | + | water |
| HNO_3 | + | $NaOH$ | → | $NaNO_3$ | + | H_2O |

Acids and Carbonates Produce Carbon Dioxide

These are very like the ones above — they just produce carbon dioxide as well.

Acid + Carbonate → Salt + Water + Carbon Dioxide

| Hydrochloric acid | + | Sodium carbonate | → | Sodium chloride | + | water | + | carbon dioxide |
| $2HCl$ | + | Na_2CO_3 | → | $2NaCl$ | + | H_2O | + | CO_2 |

| Hydrochloric acid | + | Calcium carbonate | → | Calcium chloride | + | water | + | carbon dioxide |
| $2HCl$ | + | $CaCO_3$ | → | $CaCl_2$ | + | H_2O | + | CO_2 |

Acids and Ammonia Produce Ammonium Salts

And lastly... **Acid + Ammonia → Ammonium Salt**

| Hydrochloric acid | + | Ammonia | → | Ammonium chloride |
| HCl | + | NH_3 | → | NH_4Cl |

| Sulfuric acid | + | Ammonia | → | Ammonium sulfate |
| H_2SO_4 | + | $2NH_3$ | → | $(NH_4)_2SO_4$ |

| Nitric acid | + | Ammonia | → | Ammonium nitrate |
| HNO_3 | + | NH_3 | → | NH_4NO_3 |

This last reaction with nitric acid produces the famous ammonium nitrate fertiliser, much appreciated for its double dose of essential nitrogen. (See P. 79.)

Acid + Revision → Insomnia Cure...

Some of these reactions are really useful, and some are just for fun (who said Chemistry was dull).
Try doing different combinations of acids and alkalis, acids and carbonates, acids and ammonia. Balance them. Cover the page and scribble all the equations down. If you make any mistakes, try again...

Making Salts

Most <u>chlorides</u>, <u>sulfates</u> and <u>nitrates</u> are <u>soluble</u> in water (the main exceptions are lead chloride, lead sulfate and silver chloride). Most <u>oxides</u>, <u>hydroxides</u> and <u>carbonates</u> are <u>insoluble</u> in water.

Making Soluble Salts from Insoluble Bases

1) You need to pick the right <u>acid</u>, plus a <u>metal carbonate</u> or <u>metal hydroxide</u>, as long as it's <u>insoluble</u>. You can't use <u>sodium</u>, <u>potassium</u> or <u>ammonium</u> carbonates or hydroxides, as they're soluble (so you can't tell whether the reaction has finished — see below).

2) You add the <u>carbonate</u> or <u>hydroxide</u> to the <u>acid</u> until <u>all</u> the acid is neutralised. (The excess carbonate or hydroxide will just <u>sink</u> to the bottom of the flask when all the acid has reacted.)

3) Then <u>filter</u> out the excess carbonate, and <u>evaporate</u> off the water — and you should be left with a <u>pure</u>, <u>dry</u> salt.

<u>Filtering</u> — to get rid of the excess carbonate or hydroxide.

E.g. you can use <u>copper carbonate</u> and <u>nitric acid</u> to make <u>copper nitrate</u>:

$$CuCO_{3\,(s)} + 2HNO_{3\,(aq)} \longrightarrow Cu(NO_3)_{2\,(aq)} + CO_{2\,(g)} + H_2O_{(l)}$$

Ammonia itself is a base, but it's <u>SOLUBLE</u>, as are all other ammonium bases. This means making soluble ammonium salts, such as <u>ammonium nitrate</u>, is a bit tricky. You can't just add an <u>excess</u> of base and filter out what's left — you have to add <u>exactly</u> the right amount of base to just neutralise the acid. You need to use an <u>indicator</u> to show when the reaction's finished. Then <u>repeat</u> using exactly the same volumes of base and acid so the salt isn't contaminated with indicator. All this is quite <u>fiddly</u>. But ammonium nitrate is a great <u>fertiliser</u>, so it's all worthwhile in the end (if you want nice big crops to grow that is).

Making Insoluble Salts — Precipitation Reactions

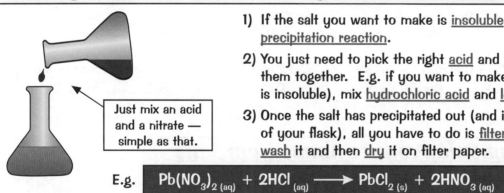

Just mix an acid and a nitrate — simple as that.

1) If the salt you want to make is <u>insoluble</u>, you can use a <u>precipitation reaction</u>.

2) You just need to pick the right <u>acid</u> and <u>nitrate</u>, then mix them together. E.g. if you want to make <u>lead chloride</u> (which is insoluble), mix <u>hydrochloric acid</u> and <u>lead nitrate</u>.

3) Once the salt has precipitated out (and is lying at the bottom of your flask), all you have to do is <u>filter</u> it from the solution, <u>wash</u> it and then <u>dry</u> it on filter paper.

E.g. $$Pb(NO_3)_{2\,(aq)} + 2HCl_{(aq)} \longrightarrow PbCl_{2\,(s)} + 2HNO_{3\,(aq)}$$

4) <u>Precipitation reactions</u> can be used to remove <u>poisonous ions</u> (e.g. lead) from <u>drinking water</u>. <u>Calcium</u> and <u>magnesium</u> ions can also be removed from water this way — they make water "<u>hard</u>", which stops soap lathering properly.

Making Salts by Displacement

1) If you put a <u>more reactive metal</u> like magnesium into a <u>salt solution</u> of a less reactive metal, like copper sulfate, then the magnesium will <u>take the place</u> of the copper — and make magnesium sulfate.

2) The "kicked-out" (or <u>displaced</u>) metal then <u>coats itself</u> onto the more reactive metal.

3) But once the magnesium has been <u>completely coated</u> with copper, the reaction <u>stops</u> — so this isn't a very practical way to make a salt.

Get two beakers, mix 'em together — job's a good 'un...

It's hard to find the precise <u>neutral point</u> using universal indicator. There's quite a wide range of "green"s between blue and yellow. There are more accurate indicators, but you don't need to know about them.

Electrolysis

Electrolysis Means "Splitting Up with Electricity"

1) Electrolysis is the breaking down of a substance using electricity.
2) It requires a liquid to conduct the electricity, called the electrolyte.
3) Electrolytes are usually free ions dissolved in water
   e.g. dissolved salts, or molten ionic substances.
4) In either case it's the free ions which conduct the electricity and allow the whole thing to work.
5) For an electrical circuit to be complete, there's got to be a flow of electrons. Electrons are taken away from ions at the positive anode and given to other ions at the negative cathode. As ions gain or lose electrons they become atoms or molecules and are released.

 NaCl dissolved
 Molten NaCl

The Electrolysis of a Salt Solution

When common salt (sodium chloride) is electrolysed, it produces three very useful products.

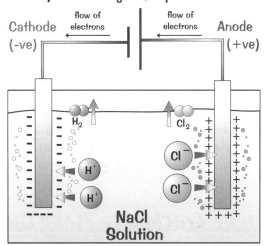

+ve ions are called CATIONS because they're attracted to the -ve cathode.

Hydrogen is produced at the -ve cathode.

-ve ions are called ANIONS because they're attracted to the +ve anode.

Chlorine is produced at the +ve anode.

1) At the cathode, two hydrogen ions accept two electrons to become one hydrogen molecule.
2) At the anode, two chloride (Cl^-) ions lose their electrons and become one chlorine molecule.
3) NaOH is left in the solution.

Electrolysis is Used to Purify Copper

1) The purer copper is, the better it conducts, so electrolysis is used to obtain very pure copper.
2) Electrons are pulled off copper atoms at the anode, causing them to go into solution as Cu^{2+} ions.
3) Cu^{2+} ions near the cathode gain electrons and turn back into copper atoms.
4) The impurities are dropped at the anode as a sludge, whilst pure copper atoms bond to the cathode.

The CATHODE is a thin piece of pure copper — more pure copper adds to it.

The ANODE is impure copper, which will dissolve.

Copper(II) sulfate solution containing $Cu^{2+}_{(aq)}$ ions.

Faster shopping at Tesco — use Electrolleys...

Electrolysis is also used for extracting aluminium from its ore (aluminium oxide). You have to melt the ore first so the ions can move. The positive Al^{3+} ions are attracted to the cathode where they pick up electrons and "zup", they turn into aluminium atoms. These conveniently then sink to the bottom.

Crude Oil

Nothing as amazingly useful as crude oil would be without its problems. No, that'd be too good to be true.

Crude Oil Provides an Important Fuel for Modern Life

1) Crude oil fractions (e.g. petrol, diesel, kerosene) burn cleanly, so they make good <u>fuels</u>. Most modern transport is fuelled by a crude oil fraction. Gas and oil are also burnt in <u>central heating</u> in homes, and in <u>power stations</u> to <u>generate electricity</u>.
2) Often there are <u>alternatives</u>, e.g. electricity can be generated by <u>nuclear</u> or <u>wind</u> power, <u>ethanol</u> can fuel cars, and <u>solar</u> panels can heat water.
3) But things tend to be <u>set up</u> for using oil fractions. For example, cars are designed for <u>petrol or diesel</u> and they're <u>readily available</u>. There are filling stations all over the country, with specially designed storage facilities and pumps. So crude oil fractions are often the <u>easiest and cheapest</u> things to use.
4) They're often <u>more reliable</u> too — e.g. solar and wind power need the right weather conditions. Nuclear energy is reliable, but there are lots of concerns about its <u>safety</u>.

It Also Provides Raw Materials for Plastics and Chemicals

1) As well as fuels, crude oil provides the raw materials for making various <u>chemicals</u>, including <u>plastics</u>, <u>paints</u>, <u>solvents</u>, <u>detergents</u> and lots of <u>medicines</u>.
2) Crude oil is so useful because it's mainly <u>carbon</u>.
3) Each carbon atom forms <u>four covalent bonds</u>, which can join atoms together in lots of <u>different ways</u>. Carbons can be arranged in <u>chains</u> or <u>rings</u>, they can be linked together with <u>single</u>, <u>double</u> or even <u>triple</u> covalent bonds and can have many <u>other elements</u> bonded onto them.
4) Unlike most other elements, carbon can form <u>huge molecules</u> containing hundreds of atoms joined together, e.g. <u>plastics</u> (see page 89).

Heavy Fractions can be Cracked to Make them More Useful

1) Heavy crude oil fractions contain <u>long-chain</u> hydrocarbons. They form <u>thick</u> gloopy liquids like <u>tar</u> which aren't all that useful.
2) A process called <u>cracking</u> turns them into <u>shorter</u> molecules which are <u>much</u> more useful.
3) <u>Cracking</u> is a form of <u>thermal decomposition</u>, which just means <u>breaking</u> molecules down into <u>simpler</u> molecules by <u>heating</u> them.
4) A lot of the longer molecules produced from fractional distillation are <u>cracked</u> into smaller ones because there's <u>more demand</u> for products like <u>petrol</u> than for diesel or lubricating oil.

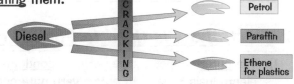

5) Just as importantly, cracking produces <u>alkenes</u> (see next page) which are needed for making <u>plastics</u>.

<u>MOST SCIENTISTS THINK THAT OIL WILL RUN OUT.</u> But no one knows exactly when.

In the <u>worst-case scenario</u>, oil may be gone in about 25 years — and that's not far off.

Some people think we should <u>immediately stop</u> using oil for things like transport, for which there are alternatives, and keep it for things that it's absolutely <u>essential</u> for, like some chemicals and medicines.

It will take time to <u>develop</u> alternative fuels to satisfy all our energy needs, so however long oil does last for, it's probably a good idea to start <u>conserving</u> it and finding <u>alternatives</u> now.

If oil alternatives aren't developed, we might get caught short...

In industry, cracking is done at a scorching 400-700 °C using a catalyst such as aluminium oxide. But believe it or not, you can also do cracking in the <u>lab</u> (well, with a bit of help from Teach). You just pass some <u>vaporised paraffin</u> over some <u>heated porcelain chips</u>. And Bob's your builder — the porcelain acts as a catalyst and you end up with a bunch of shorter molecules. Great stuff, eh?

Alkanes and Alkenes

When you crack crude oil (previous page) you get <u>alkanes</u> and <u>alkenes</u>. Know the differences between them.

ALKANES Have All C–C SINGLE Bonds

1) They're made up of <u>chains</u> of carbon atoms with <u>single</u> covalent bonds between them.
2) They're called <u>saturated</u> hydrocarbons because they have <u>no</u> spare bonds.
3) This is also why they <u>don't</u> decolourise <u>bromine water</u> — <u>no</u> spare bonds.
4) They <u>won't</u> form polymers — same reason again, <u>no</u> spare bonds.
5) The first four alkanes are <u>methane</u> (natural gas), <u>ethane</u>, <u>propane</u> and <u>butane</u>.

Bromine water
+ alkane
—still brown.

1) Methane
Formula: CH_4

H
|
H–C–H (natural
| gas)
H

2) Ethane
Formula: C_2H_6

H H
| |
H–C–C–H
| |
H H

3) Propane
Formula: C_3H_8

H H H
| | |
H–C–C–C–H
| | |
H H H

4) Butane
Formula: C_4H_{10}

H H H H
| | | |
H–C–C–C–C–H
| | | |
H H H H

ALKENES Have a C=C DOUBLE Bond

1) They're <u>chains</u> of carbon atoms with some <u>double</u> bonds.
2) They are called <u>unsaturated</u> hydrocarbons because they have some 'spare' bonds left.
3) This is why they will decolourise <u>bromine water</u>. They form <u>bonds</u> with bromine atoms.
4) They form <u>polymers</u> by <u>opening up</u> their double bonds to 'hold hands' in a long chain.
5) The first two alkenes are <u>ethene</u> and <u>propene</u>.

Bromine water
+ alkene —
decolourised

1) Ethene
Formula: C_2H_4

H   H
 \   /
  C = C
 /   \
H   H

2) Propene
Formula: C_3H_6

H H
| | H
H–C–C=C
| \
H   H

Notice the names: "<u>meth-</u>" means "<u>one</u> carbon atom", "<u>eth-</u>" means "<u>two</u> C atoms",
"<u>prop-</u>" means "<u>three</u> C atoms", "<u>but-</u>" means "<u>four</u> C atoms", etc. The only difference
then between the names of <u>alkanes</u> and <u>alkenes</u> is just the "<u>-ane</u>" or "<u>-ene</u>" on the end.

Alkane anybody who doesn't learn this lot properly...

Hydrating alkenes is a good way to produce industrial alcohol because it needs to be very <u>pure</u>. You can
also make alcohol by fermenting sugar then distilling the product, but you can't get it as pure that way.

Vegetable Oils

Oils can be saturated (no C-C double bonds — see p.87), monounsaturated or polyunsaturated.

Vegetable Oils are Usually Unsaturated

Unsaturated compounds are ones that contain carbon-carbon double bonds (like alkenes, see p.87).

> MONO means one. An oil molecule with only one carbon-carbon double bond is monounsaturated.
> POLY means many. If an oil molecule has more than one double bond, it's polyunsaturated.

1) The sort of oils that you eat in your food can be important for your health.
2) Polyunsaturated oils are thought to be the healthiest and saturated oils the least healthy, because of what they do to the amount of cholesterol in your blood.
3) Cholesterol is a fatty substance that's made in the liver. High levels of cholesterol in the blood are linked to an increased risk of heart disease.
4) You can reduce the level of cholesterol in your blood and so reduce your risk of heart disease by eating polyunsaturated oils in place of saturated oils.

Unsaturated Oils are Runnier than Saturated Ones

1) Double bonds change the shape of molecules by making an inflexible 'kink' in the carbon chain.

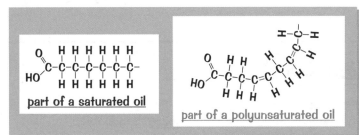

part of a saturated oil

part of a polyunsaturated oil

2) Kinked and less flexible chains can't pack together as tightly as straighter, flexible ones, so the forces between the molecules aren't as strong.
3) Weaker forces make oils less viscous (less thick). So unsaturated oils are runnier than saturated oils.

Vegetable Oils are Hydrogenated for the Food Industry

1) Unsaturated oils (ones with double bonds) can be changed to saturated oils by breaking a double bond and adding hydrogen — a process called hydrogenation.
2) A nickel catalyst is used to help the reaction along:

part of an unsaturated oil + H-H → (High temperature, High pressure, Ni catalyst) → part of a saturated oil

3) The nickel catalyst is a solid and can be filtered out and used again.
4) As the filtered oil cools down to room temperature it turns into a solid fat (a fat is just an oil that is solid at room temperature).
5) Polyunsaturated vegetable oils can be hydrogenated to make margarine. Not all the double bonds in the oil are hydrogenated, so some of the margarine is still unsaturated — it's called a partially hydrogenated oil. It's firm enough to spread on your toast, but still low in saturates compared with butter.

What do you call a parrot in a raincoat? Polyunsaturated...

Some of the double bonds that are left in partially hydrogenated vegetable oils get a bit 'mangled' and you end up with things called trans fats. Most trans fats are completely artificial (you don't get them in nature), and studies have linked them to an increased risk of heart disease.

Plastics

Plastics are made up of lots of small molecules joined together.

Plastics are Long-Chain Molecules Called Polymers

1) Plastics are formed when lots of small molecules called monomers join together to give a polymer.
2) There are two basic types of polymer — addition and condensation. Addition polymerisation only makes one product (see below). Condensation polymerisation makes two — the polymer and a simple compound like water or HCl. You don't need to know any details about condensation polymers, though.

Addition Polymers are Made Under High Pressure

The monomers that make up addition polymers have a carbon double bond — they're unsaturated.

Under high pressure and with a catalyst to help them along, many unsaturated small molecules will open up those double bonds and 'join hands' (polymerise) to form very long saturated chains — polymers.

Ethene becoming polyethene or "polythene", is the easiest example:

Many single ethenes

Polyethene

The 'n' just means there can be any number of monomers.

You'll need to be able to construct the displayed formula of an addition polymer given the displayed formula of its monomer. Dead easy — the carbons just all join together in a row with no double bonds between them.

The name of the plastic comes from the type of monomer it's made from — you just stick the word 'poly' in front of it:

Propene can form polypropene:

Propene

Polypropene

A molecule called styrene will polymerise into polystyrene:

Styrene

Polystyrene

$\bigcirc = C_6H_5$

Most Plastics Don't Rot, so They're Hard to Get Rid Of

1) UK households produce over 2 million tonnes of plastic waste every year — so it's a big problem.
2) Toxic gases are given off if you burn plastic, so that's not a good idea.
3) It's best to recycle them as this helps to conserve resources. But recycling is expensive and difficult — lots of types of plastic have to be separated before recycling.
4) Most plastics are 'non-biodegradable' — they're not broken down by microorganisms, so they don't rot. If you bury them in a landfill site, they'll still be there years later.
5) Some polythene bags are now made with starch granules in them. If the plastic is buried, the starch is broken down by microorganisms in the soil, and the bag breaks up into tiny pieces of polythene.
6) There are currently some fully biodegradable plastics, but they're about 10 times more expensive than ordinary ones. Scientists are working on genetically modifying plants to produce the raw materials for more biodegradable plastics. With any new product like this tests have to be done to find out exactly what happens when the plastic breaks down to make sure that nothing harmful is produced.
7) You can also get plastics that break down in sunlight — they tend to be used in agriculture.

You're not done yet — more plasticky goodness over the page...

Getting rid of plastic is a big problem, but recycling can help. There are recycling points all around the country for plastic bottles, and many supermarkets collect old polythene bags for recycling.

Plastics

Forces Between Molecules Determine the Properties of Plastics

Strong covalent bonds hold the atoms together in long chains. But it's the bonds between the different molecule chains that determine the properties of the plastic.

Weak Forces:
Long chains held together by weak forces are free to slide over each other.

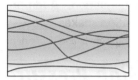

THERMOPLASTIC POLYMERS, like polythene, don't have cross-linking between chains. The forces between the chains are easy to overcome, so it's easy to melt the plastic. When it cools, it hardens into a new shape. You can melt these plastics and remould them as many times as you like.

Strong Forces:
Some plastics have stronger bonds between the polymer chains, called crosslinks, that hold the chains firmly together.

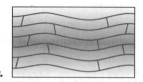

THERMOSETTING POLYMERS, like Bakelite, have crosslinks. These hold the chains together in a solid structure. The polymer doesn't soften when it's heated — but too much heat makes it burn. Thermosetting polymers are the tough guys of the plastic world. They're strong, hard and rigid.

You Can Add Plasticisers and Preservatives to Polymers

1) The starting materials, reaction conditions and additives will all affect the properties of a polymer.

2) Using styrene as a starting material produces polystyrene, which is a brittle polymer. Whereas using ethene as a starting material will make polythene, which is more flexible (see p.89).

3) Polythene can be made by heating ethene to about 200 °C under high pressure. This makes the light, flexible polythene used for bags and bottles. Polythene made at a lower temperature and pressure (with a catalyst) is denser and more rigid. It's used for water tanks and drainpipes.

4) Additives can also change the properties of plastics. Pure PVC is rigid and brittle at room temperature. To make PVC cloth, plasticisers are added. These are small molecules that get between the polymer chains and allow them to move past each other more easily — making the plastic more flexible.

5) Many plastics will become brittle and change colour if left in the Sun. Preservatives can be added to plastics such as uPVC in window frames to help prolong their useful life and appearance.

The Use of a Plastic Depends on Its Properties

You've got to be able to answer a question like this one in the exam.

Choose from the table the plastic that would be best suited for making:

a) a disposable cup for hot drinks,

b) clothing,

c) a measuring cylinder.

Give reasons for each choice.

Plastic	Cost	Resistance to chemicals	Melting point	Transparency	Rigidity	Can be made into fibres
W	High	High	High	Low	High	No
X	Low	Low	Low	Low	Low	Yes
Y	High	High	High	High	High	No
Z	Low	Low	High	High	High	No

Answers

a) Z — low cost (disposable) and high melting point (for hot drinks),

b) X — flexible (essential for clothing) and able to be made into fibres (clothing is usually woven),

c) Y — transparent and resistant to chemicals (you need to be able to see the liquid inside and the liquid and measuring cylinder mustn't react with each other).

Platinum cards — my favourite sort of plastic...

You don't have to learn the properties of different plastics — you'll be given those in the exam — you just need to think about which properties are good for which uses. It's just common sense.

Chemical Production

The Type of Manufacturing Process Depends on the Product

Continuous production: large-scale industrial manufacture of popular chemicals,
e.g. the Haber process for making ammonia (see p.79).

1) Production <u>never stops</u>, so you don't waste time emptying the reactor and setting it up again.
2) It runs <u>automatically</u> — you only need to interfere if something goes wrong.
3) The <u>quality</u> of the product is <u>very consistent</u>.
4) Usually the manufacturing plant only makes <u>one</u> product, so there's little risk of <u>contamination</u>.
5) <u>Start-up costs</u> to build the plant are <u>huge</u>, and it isn't cost-effective to run at less than <u>full</u> capacity.

Batch production: <u>small quantities</u> of <u>specialist chemicals</u>, e.g. pharmaceutical drugs, often on demand.

1) It's <u>flexible</u> — <u>several different products</u> can be made using the <u>same</u> equipment.
2) <u>Start-up costs</u> are relatively low — small-scale, multi-purpose equipment can be bought off the shelf.
3) It's <u>labour-intensive</u> — the equipment needs to be set up and manually controlled for each batch and then cleaned out at the end.
4) '<u>Downtime</u>' between batches means there are times when you're <u>not producing anything</u>.
5) It's trickier to keep the <u>same quality</u> from batch to batch. Also, there's more chance of <u>contamination</u> because the same equipment is used to make more than one thing.
   On the other hand, any problems can be traced to a <u>specific batch</u>, which can be recalled.

<u>Pharmaceutical drugs</u> are <u>complicated</u> to make and there's low demand for them. So batch production's often the most <u>cost-effective</u> way for a company to produce small quantities of different drugs to order.

Several Factors Affect the Cost of Pharmaceutical Drugs

1) <u>Market Research</u> — identifying a possible new drug. Is there any <u>competition</u> already out there? Is there enough <u>demand</u> for it to make it worthwhile developing?

2) <u>Research and Development</u> — finding a <u>suitable compound</u>, testing it, modifying it, testing again, until it's ready. This involves the work of lots of highly paid scientists.

3) <u>Trialling</u> — no drug can be sold until it's gone through loads of time-consuming tests including <u>animal trials</u> and <u>human trials</u> to prove that it <u>works</u> and it's <u>safe</u>.

4) <u>Marketing</u> — advertising in medical magazines and buttering up doctors.

5) <u>Manufacture</u> — multi-step batch production is <u>labour-intensive</u> and <u>can't be automated</u>. Other costs include <u>energy</u> and <u>raw materials</u>. The raw materials for pharmaceuticals are often rare and sometimes need to be <u>extracted from plants</u> (an expensive process).

> It takes about <u>12 years</u> and <u>£900 million</u> to develop a new drug and get it onto the market. Ouch.

To extract a substance from a plant, it has to be <u>crushed</u> and <u>dissolved</u> in a suitable solvent. Then, you can extract the substance you want by <u>chromatography</u>.

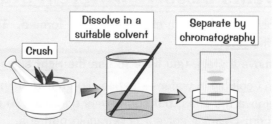

Crush | Dissolve in a suitable solvent | Separate by chromatography

> Once the active ingredient has been isolated, it can be analysed, and its chemical structure worked out.
>
> It's often possible to make a synthetic version of the chemical.

6) The actual <u>price per dose</u> depends on the demand and how long the company is willing to wait to get back its <u>initial investment</u>. A company only holds a drug patent for 20 years — after that anyone can make it. Some drugs can cost <u>thousands of pounds</u> for just <u>one dose</u>.

I wish they'd find a drug to cure exams...

£900 million. You could buy yourself an island. And one for your mum. And a couple for your mates...

Washing-Up Liquids and Detergents

Cleanliness is next to godliness... or so they say.

Washing-Up Liquids Have Five Main Ingredients

1) <u>ACTIVE DETERGENT</u>: This is the bit that actually does the <u>cleaning</u>.
2) <u>WATER SOFTENER</u>: To help the <u>soap lather</u> properly.
3) <u>WATER</u>: Washing-up liquids are <u>thinned</u> with water to make them easier to pour out.
4) <u>COLOUR AND FRAGRANCE</u>: To make it <u>look</u> and <u>smell</u> nice. ☺
5) <u>RINSE AGENT</u>: This helps the water <u>drain off</u> your dishes quickly and evenly.

Clothes Powders Also Have Five Main Ingredients

1) <u>ACTIVE DETERGENT</u> (see above)　　2) <u>WATER SOFTENER</u> (see above)
3) <u>BLEACHES</u>: Some contain bleaches to remove <u>coloured stains</u> from pale-coloured clothes.
4) <u>OPTICAL BRIGHTENERS</u>: These are special dyes that give your clothes the "<u>whiter than white</u>" look.
5) <u>ENZYMES</u>: <u>Biological powders</u> contain enzymes to break down <u>protein-based</u>, <u>carbohydrate-based</u> and <u>fat-based</u> stains. They only work at low temperatures, since the enzymes are destroyed above 40 °C.

Low Temperature Washes Save Energy (and Your Clothes)

1) When you're washing clothes, <u>high temperatures</u> usually work best for getting things clean. They <u>melt</u> greasy dirt deposits, so your <u>detergent</u> can break up and remove the stain more easily.

2) But if the <u>temperature is too high</u>, it can make some <u>clothes shrink</u> or <u>lose shape</u>. It can also make some <u>dyes run</u>, so your clothes look dull.

3) Clothes have <u>care labels</u> that use a standard range of <u>symbols</u> that tell you what conditions you should use to wash them. Learn these ones:

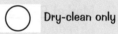

40° Machine wash at 40 °C		Hand wash only
40° Gentle machine wash at 40 °C		Do not wash in water
60° Machine wash at 60 °C		Dry-clean only

4) The <u>enzymes</u> in biological detergents can digest <u>food</u> stains without the need for high temperatures, which protects your clothes.

5) <u>Low-temperature washes</u> also <u>save energy</u>, which is great for the environment and your energy bill.

Most Detergents are Salts

Modern <u>synthetic detergents</u> are mostly made using substances that come from <u>crude oil</u>, which are turned into organic acids. An organic acid would then be <u>neutralised</u> with a strong <u>alkali</u>, to form a <u>salt</u>:　organic acid + strong alkali → salt (detergent) + water

Different Solvents Dissolve Different Stains

1) When a solid dissolves in a liquid, a clear <u>solution</u> is formed. The liquid is called the <u>solvent</u>, and the solid is called the <u>solute</u>.

2) To successfully remove a <u>stain</u>, you have to use the <u>right solvent</u> to dissolve it off the fabric.

3) A lot of stains aren't <u>soluble</u> in water — especially greasy stains, paints and varnishes. Sometimes a detergent can remove the stain, but sometimes you need to use a different, <u>dry-cleaning</u> solvent. The most common dry-cleaning solvent is <u>tetrachloroethene</u>.

4) Dry-cleaning is usually used for clothes that would get <u>damaged</u> if you washed them in water, or if you have a stain that <u>won't dissolve</u> in water or detergent, such as <u>paints</u> and <u>varnishes</u>.

Would your whites pass the Exam challenge...

Yes, I'm afraid you are going to have to do some washing at some point — you will run out of clothes eventually. And when you do, you'll have the pleasure of knowing <u>how it all works</u>. Isn't that nice. ☺

Water Purity

Water, water, everywhere... well, there is if you live in Cumbria.

There are a Variety of Limited Water Resources in the UK

1) As well as for drinking, we need water for loads of <u>domestic</u> uses (mainly washing things).

2) <u>Industrially</u>, water is important as a <u>cheap raw material</u>, a <u>coolant</u> (especially in power stations) and a <u>solvent</u>. Between half and two thirds of all the fresh water used in the UK goes into industry.

> In the UK, we get our water from:
> 1) <u>SURFACE WATER</u>: <u>lakes</u>, <u>rivers</u> and <u>reservoirs</u> (artificial lakes). In much of England and Wales, these sources start to run dry during the summer months.
> 2) <u>GROUNDWATER</u>: <u>aquifers</u> (rocks that trap water underground). In parts of the south-east where surface water is very limited, as much as 70% of the domestic water supply comes from groundwater.

All these resources are <u>limited</u>, depending on <u>annual rainfall</u>, and demand for water increases every year. Experts worry that, unless we limit our water use, by 2025 we might not have enough water to supply everybody's needs. Ways to <u>conserve water</u> include:

1) <u>Stopping leaks</u> in pipes. About 20% of all the water that enters the mains is lost through leaks.

2) <u>Not wasting water at home</u>, e.g. not leaving taps running, using a bucket instead of a hose to wash the car, avoiding sprinklers in the garden (they use up to 1000 litres per hour), washing up by hand rather than using a dishwasher, using a water-efficient washing machine (fully loaded each time).

3) <u>Recycling</u> water, e.g. collecting rainwater to use in the garden.

4) Installing a <u>water meter</u> — you tend to waste less water if you're paying for it by the bath-full.

Water is Purified in Water Treatment Plants

How much purification the water needs depends on the source. <u>Groundwater</u> from aquifers is usually quite pure, but <u>surface water</u> needs a lot of treatment.

The processes include:

1) <u>Filtration</u> — a wire mesh screens out large twigs etc., and then gravel and sand beds filter out any other solid bits.

2) <u>Sedimentation</u> — iron sulfate or aluminium sulfate is added to the water, which makes fine particles clump together and settle at the bottom.

3) <u>Chlorination</u> — chlorine gas is bubbled through to kill <u>harmful bacteria</u> and <u>microbes</u>.

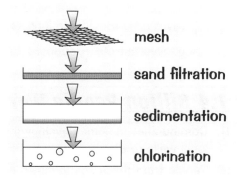

mesh

sand filtration

sedimentation

chlorination

Tap Water Can Still Contain Impurities

The water that comes out of our taps has to meet <u>strict safety standards</u>, but low levels of pollutants are still found. These pollutants come from various sources:

1) <u>Nitrate residues</u> from excess fertiliser 'run-off' into rivers and lakes. If too many nitrates get into drinking water it can cause serious health problems, especially for young babies. Nitrates prevent the blood from carrying oxygen properly.

2) <u>Lead compounds</u> from old lead pipes. Lead is very poisonous, particularly in children.

3) <u>Pesticide residues</u> from spraying too near to rivers and lakes.

Water Purity

You Can Test Water for Various Dissolved Ions

Water companies have to test their water regularly to make sure that pollutant levels don't exceed strict limits. You can test for some <u>dissolved ions</u> very easily using precipitation reactions (where two dissolved compounds react to form an insoluble solid — the <u>precipitate</u>).

1) <u>TEST FOR SULFATE IONS</u>: add some dilute hydrochloric acid, then 10 drops of <u>barium chloride solution</u> to the test sample. If you see a <u>white precipitate</u>, there are sulfate ions in the sample.

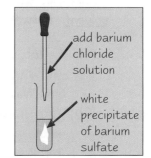

add barium chloride solution

white precipitate of barium sulfate

> barium chloride + sulfate ions → barium sulfate + chloride ions

e.g. barium chloride + copper sulfate → barium sulfate + copper chloride

2) <u>TEST FOR HALIDE IONS</u>: add some dilute nitric acid, then 10 drops of <u>silver nitrate solution</u> to the sample.
<u>Chloride ions</u> will produce a <u>white precipitate</u>.
<u>Bromide ions</u> will produce a <u>cream precipitate</u>.
<u>Iodide ions</u> will produce a <u>pale yellow precipitate</u>.

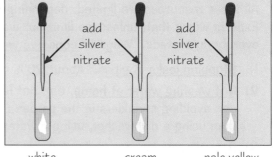

add silver nitrate   add silver nitrate   add silver nitrate

white precipitate of silver chloride   cream precipitate of silver bromide   pale yellow precipitate of silver iodide

> silver nitrate + chloride ions
>   → silver chloride + nitrate ions

e.g. silver nitrate + copper chloride
    → silver chloride + copper nitrate

> silver nitrate + bromide ions → silver bromide + nitrate ions

e.g. silver nitrate + copper bromide → silver bromide + copper nitrate

> silver nitrate + iodide ions → silver iodide + nitrate ions

e.g. silver nitrate + copper iodide → silver iodide + copper nitrate

1.4 Billion People Worldwide Can't Get Clean Water to Drink

1) Communities in some <u>developing countries</u> often don't have access to sources of <u>clean water</u>, such as local wells or distribution networks.

2) People from these communities often have to <u>walk for miles</u> every day to fetch water from sources which may be <u>contaminated</u>.

3) <u>Dirty water</u> can carry dangerous microbes which cause outbreaks of <u>serious diseases</u> such as cholera and dysentery. About 3.4 million people (mainly children) <u>die</u> from water-borne diseases each year.

4) Giving a community a <u>clean water source</u> and teaching them the <u>skills</u> to maintain it can <u>save many lives</u>. It doesn't have to be complicated — sinking a well and adding a pump is often all that's needed.

Who'd have thought there'd be so much to learn about water...

In the UK we're <u>very lucky</u> to have clean water available at the turn of a tap — but it's not a never-ending supply. Fresh water is quite hard to come by at the end of a dry summer. <u>Learn</u> how water is purified and tested in the UK, and what pollutants get through the cleaning process. <u>Cover</u>. <u>Scribble</u>.

Revision Summary for Section Seven

This is a whopper of a section covering loads of different things — they say oil and water don't mix, but they're both included in this section. There's also stuff on rates of reaction, making salts, electrolysis and dry cleaning. Have a go at these questions and see how much you can remember. If you're not too sure about any of them, don't just skulk past them — check back to the relevant page, get it in your head and tackle the question again. It's the best way, I promise.

1) Give an example of a really fast reaction, and an example of a really slow reaction.

2) What are the four factors that affect the rate of a reaction?

3) Describe three different ways of measuring the rate of a reaction.

4) Explain in terms of collisions between particles how temperature affects the rate of a reaction.

5) What is the definition of a catalyst? What does a catalyst do to the activation energy of a reaction?

6) What is an exothermic reaction? Give three examples.

7) The reaction to split ammonium chloride into ammonia and hydrogen chloride is endothermic. It's also a reversible reaction — what can you say for certain about the reverse reaction?

8) What is a reversible reaction? Give one important industrial example of a reversible reaction.

9) Describe the conditions used for the Haber process. What does it produce? What happens to the unused hydrogen and nitrogen in the reaction?

10) Why is ammonium nitrate fertiliser so great? What's not so great about nitrate fertilisers?

11) In industrial chemical production, list 5 factors that can raise the production company's bills.

12) Describe fully the colour of universal indicator for every pH value from 0 to 14.

13) What type of ions are always formed in water by: a) acids, and b) alkalis?

14)* Name the salts formed and write balanced symbol equations for the following reactions:
    a) hydrochloric acid with magnesium,   b) sulfuric acid with aluminium.

15) What type of reaction is "acid + metal oxide", or "acid + metal hydroxide"?

16)* Suggest a suitable acid and a suitable metal oxide/hydroxide to mix to form the following salts. Write out a balanced symbol equation for each reaction.
    a) copper(II) chloride,   b) calcium nitrate,   c) zinc sulfate.

17) Iron chloride can made by mixing iron hydroxide (an insoluble base) with hydrochloric acid. Describe the method you would use to produce pure, solid iron chloride in the lab.

18) What is electrolysis? Explain why only liquids can be electrolysed.

19) Describe the process of purifying copper by electrolysis.

20) Besides fuel, what else is crude oil used for?

21) What's cracking? Why is it done?

22) What's the formula for a 4-carbon alkane? How are alkenes different from alkanes?

23) Are vegetable oils mostly unsaturated or saturated? Which type of oil is runnier? Explain why.

24) Write out the equation for the polymerisation of ethene.

25) Describe some of the problems associated with disposing of plastics.

26) Describe the difference between thermosetting and thermoplastic polymers. Give an example of each.

27) What are the advantages and disadvantages of continuous production and batch production?

28) Explain the advantages of washing clothes at low temperatures.

29) Suggest why you may want to dry-clean some fabrics.

30) Why is it important to preserve water? List four ways to preserve water in the home.

31) A student adds dilute hydrochloric acid and barium chloride to a water sample and a white precipitate is produced. What ions were present in the water?

* Answers on page 140.

Speed and Velocity

Speed and Velocity are Both How Fast You're Going

Speed and velocity are both measured in <u>m/s</u> (or km/h or mph). They both simply say <u>how fast</u> you're going, but there's a <u>subtle difference</u> between them which <u>you need to know</u>:

> <u>Speed</u> is just <u>how fast</u> you're going (e.g. 30 mph or 20 m/s) with no regard to the direction.
> <u>Velocity</u> however must <u>also</u> have the <u>direction</u> specified, e.g. 30 mph north or 20 m/s, 060°.

Seems kinda fussy I know, but they expect you to remember that distinction, so there you go.

Speed, Distance and Time — the Formula:

$$\text{Speed} = \frac{\text{Distance}}{\text{Time}}$$

You'll often be asked to calculate <u>speed</u> rather than velocity (the words 'speed' and 'velocity' tend to be used interchangeably). It's the <u>same formula</u> — since speed is just velocity without direction...

<u>EXAMPLE:</u>   A cat skulks 20 metres in 35 seconds. Find its average speed.

<u>ANSWER:</u>   speed = distance/time = 20/35 = 0.5714 = <u>0.57 m/s</u>

Speed Cameras Measure the Speed of Cars

1) <u>Speed cameras</u> can be used to catch speeding motorists at <u>dangerous accident spots</u>.
2) <u>Lines</u> are painted on the road a <u>certain distance apart</u> to <u>measure</u> the distance travelled by the car.
3) A <u>photo</u> of the car is taken as it passes the first line and a <u>second photo</u> is taken a <u>certain time later</u>.
4) These photos can then be used to measure the <u>distance travelled</u> by the car in this time.

<u>Example:</u> a speed camera takes two photos of a car. The photos are taken <u>0.5 s</u> apart and from the marked lines on the road the distance it travels is measured as <u>5 m</u>. What is the average speed of the car?

Answer: Average speed = $\dfrac{\text{distance}}{\text{time}}$ = $\dfrac{5 \text{ m}}{0.5 \text{ s}}$ = 10 m/s

Distance-Time Graphs

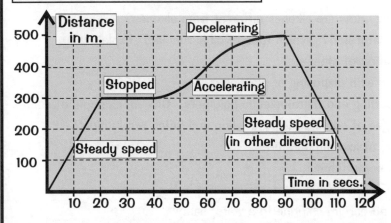

1) <u>Gradient = speed</u>.
2) <u>Flat</u> sections are where it's <u>stopped</u>.
3) The <u>steeper</u> the graph, the <u>faster</u> it's going.
4) <u>'Downhill'</u> sections mean it's <u>going back</u> toward its starting point.
5) <u>Curves</u> represent <u>acceleration</u> or deceleration. A <u>steepening</u> curve means it's <u>speeding up</u> (increasing gradient). A <u>levelling off</u> curve means it's <u>slowing down</u> (decreasing gradient).

Lights, camera, action — science can be so Hollywood...

It's got to be said, speed cameras aren't the most popular of speed measuring devices.
But most drivers do slow down in speed camera areas and this can improve road safety.

Acceleration

Acceleration is How Quickly Velocity is Changing

Acceleration is <u>definitely not</u> the same as <u>velocity</u> or <u>speed</u>.

1) Acceleration is <u>how quickly</u> the velocity is <u>changing</u>.

2) This change in velocity can be a <u>CHANGE IN SPEED</u> or a <u>CHANGE IN DIRECTION</u> or both.
(You only have to worry about the change in speed bit for calculations.)

Velocity is a simple idea. Acceleration is altogether more <u>subtle</u>, which is why it's <u>confusing</u>.

Acceleration — The Formula:

$$\text{Acceleration} = \frac{\text{Change in Velocity}}{\text{Time Taken}}$$

Well, it's <u>just another formula</u>, like all the others. Mind you, there are <u>two</u> tricky things with this one:

1) First you have to work out the "<u>change in velocity</u>", as shown in the example below, rather than just putting a <u>simple value</u> for speed or velocity in.

2) Secondly there's the <u>units</u> of acceleration, which are m/s^2.
<u>Not m/s</u>, which is <u>velocity</u>, but m/s^2. Got it? No? Let's try once more: <u>Not m/s</u>, but m/s^2.

<u>Example:</u> A skulking cat accelerates steadily from 2 m/s to 6 m/s in 5.6 s. Find its acceleration.

<u>Answer:</u> Using the formula:
acceleration = "change in velocity"/time = (6 − 2) / 5.6 = 4 ÷ 5.6 = <u>0.71 m/s^2</u>
All pretty basic stuff I'd say.

You Can Work Out Acceleration from a Velocity-Time Graph

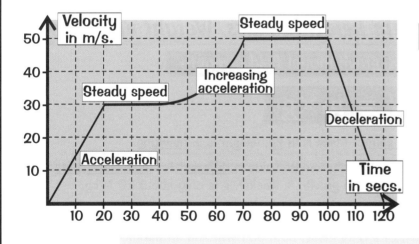

Very Important Notes:

1) <u>GRADIENT = ACCELERATION</u>.

2) <u>Flat sections</u> represent <u>steady speed</u>.

3) The <u>steeper</u> the graph, the <u>greater</u> the <u>acceleration</u> or deceleration.

4) <u>Uphill</u> sections (/) are <u>acceleration</u>.

5) <u>Downhill</u> sections (\) are <u>deceleration</u>.

6) A <u>curve</u> means <u>changing acceleration</u>.

The <u>acceleration</u> represented by the <u>first section</u> of the graph is:

$$\underline{\text{Acceleration}} = \underline{\text{gradient}} = \frac{\text{vertical change}}{\text{horizontal change}} = \frac{30}{20} = 1.5 \ m/s^2$$

Understanding motion graphs — it can be a real uphill struggle...

Make sure you know all there is to know about velocity-time graphs — i.e. <u>learn those numbered points</u>. You work out acceleration from the graph simply by applying the acceleration formula — change in velocity is the change on the vertical axis and time taken is the change on the horizontal axis.

Mass, Weight and Gravity

Gravity is the Force of Attraction Between All Masses

Gravity attracts all masses, but you only notice it when one of the masses is really really big, e.g. a planet. Anything near a planet or star is attracted to it very strongly.

This has three important effects:

1) On the surface of a planet, it makes all things accelerate towards the ground (all with the same acceleration, g, which is about 10 m/s² on Earth).

2) It gives everything a weight.

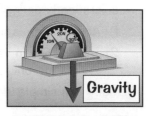

3) It keeps planets, moons and satellites in their orbits. The orbit is a balance between the forward motion of the object and the force of gravity pulling it inwards.

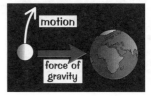

Weight and Mass are Not the Same

To understand this you must learn all these facts about mass and weight:

1) Mass is just the amount of 'stuff' in an object.
For any given object this will have the same value anywhere in the Universe.

2) Weight is caused by the pull of gravity. In most questions the weight of an object is just the force of gravity pulling it towards the centre of the Earth.

3) An object has the same mass whether it's on Earth or on the Moon — but its weight will be different. A 1 kg mass will weigh less on the Moon (about 1.6 N) than it does on Earth (about 10 N), simply because the force of gravity pulling on it is less.

4) Weight is a force measured in newtons. It's measured using a spring balance or newton meter. Mass is not a force. It's measured in kilograms with a mass balance (an old-fashioned pair of balancing scales).

The Very Important Formula Relating Mass, Weight and Gravity

weight = mass × gravitational field strength

$$W = m \times g$$

1) Remember, weight and mass are not the same. Mass is in kg, weight is in newtons.

2) The letter "g" represents the strength of the gravity and its value is different for different planets. On Earth g ≈ 10 N/kg. On the Moon, where the gravity is weaker, g is only about 1.6 N/kg.

3) This formula is hideously easy to use:

Example: What is the weight, in newtons, of a 5 kg mass, both on Earth and on the Moon?

Answer: "W = m × g". On Earth: W = 5 × 10 = 50 N   (The weight of the 5 kg mass is 50 N.)
On the Moon: W = 5 × 1.6 = 8 N   (The weight of the 5 kg mass is 8 N.)

See what I mean. Hideously easy — as long as you've learnt what all the letters mean.

Learn about gravity now — no point in "weighting" around...

Often the only way to "understand" something is to learn all the facts about it. And I certainly think that's true here. "Understanding" the difference between mass and weight is no more than learning all the facts about them. When you've learnt all those facts properly, you'll understand it.

Friction Forces and Terminal Speed

Friction _is Always There to_ Slow things Down

1) If an object has <u>no force</u> propelling it along, it will always slow down and stop because of friction (unless you're out in space where there's no friction).

2) To travel at a <u>steady speed</u>, things always need a <u>driving force</u> to <u>counteract</u> the friction.

3) Friction occurs in <u>three main ways</u>:

   a) <u>FRICTION **BETWEEN** SOLID SURFACES **WHICH ARE** GRIPPING</u> (static friction)

static friction

   b) <u>FRICTION **BETWEEN** SOLID SURFACES **WHICH ARE** SLIDING PAST EACH OTHER</u>

   You can <u>reduce</u> both these types of friction by putting a <u>lubricant</u> like <u>oil</u> or <u>grease</u> between the surfaces.

sliding friction

   c) <u>RESISTANCE **OR** "DRAG" **FROM** FLUIDS (LIQUIDS **OR** GASES, e.g. AIR)</u>

   The most important factor <u>by far</u> in <u>reducing drag in fluids</u> is keeping the shape of the object <u>streamlined</u>, like sports cars or boat hulls.

   Lorries and caravans have '<u>deflectors</u>' (shaped bits of plastic to direct the air flow) on them to make them more streamlined and reduce drag.

   <u>Roof boxes</u> on cars spoil their streamlined shape and so slow them down. For a given thrust, the <u>higher</u> the <u>drag</u> the <u>lower</u> the <u>top speed</u> of the car. The <u>opposite extreme</u> to a sports car is a <u>parachute</u>, which is about as <u>high drag</u> as you can get — which is, of course, <u>the whole idea</u>.

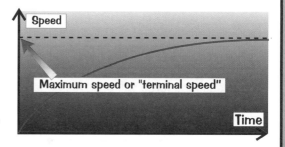

   In a <u>fluid</u>: <u>DRAG ALWAYS INCREASES AS THE SPEED INCREASES</u> — and don't you forget it.

Falling Objects _Reach a Terminal Speed_

1) The accelerating force acting on all falling objects is <u>gravity</u> and it would make them all accelerate at the same rate (about <u>10 m/s^2</u>), if it wasn't for <u>air resistance</u>.

2) To prove this, on the Moon, where there's <u>no air</u>, hamsters and feathers dropped together will <u>hit the ground together</u>. However, on Earth, <u>air resistance</u> causes things to fall at <u>different speeds</u>.

3) When falling objects <u>first set off</u> they have <u>much more</u> force <u>accelerating</u> them than <u>resistance</u> slowing them down. As the <u>speed</u> increases the resistance <u>builds up</u>.

4) This gradually <u>reduces</u> the <u>acceleration</u> until eventually the <u>resistance force</u> is <u>equal</u> to the <u>accelerating force</u> and then it won't be able to accelerate any more. It will have reached its maximum speed or <u>terminal speed</u>.

Speed

Maximum speed or "terminal speed"

Time

An important example is the <u>human skydiver</u>. Without his parachute open he doesn't feel much drag, and reaches a <u>terminal speed</u> of about <u>55 m/s</u>. But with the parachute <u>open</u>, there's much more <u>air resistance</u> (at any given speed) and still only the same force pulling him down. This means his <u>terminal speed</u> comes right down to about <u>7 m/s</u>, which is a <u>safe speed</u> to hit the ground at.

Air resistance — it can be a real drag...

As well as stopping parachutists ending up as nasty messes on the floor, friction's good for <u>other stuff</u> too. Without friction, you wouldn't be able to walk or run or skip or write... hmm, not all bad then.

Forces and Acceleration

Things only accelerate or change direction if you give them a push. Makes sense.

A Balanced Force Means Steady Speed and Direction

> If the forces on an object are all **BALANCED**, then it'll keep moving at the **SAME SPEED** in the **SAME DIRECTION** (so if it starts off still, it'll stay still).

1) When a train or car or bus or anything else is <u>moving</u> at a <u>constant speed</u>, without changing <u>direction</u>, then the <u>forces</u> on it must all be <u>balanced</u>.
2) Never let yourself entertain the <u>ridiculous idea</u> that things need a constant overall force to <u>keep</u> them moving — NO NO NO NO NO NO!
3) To keep going at a <u>steady speed</u>, there must be <u>zero resultant (overall) force</u> — and don't you forget it.

A Resultant Force Means Acceleration

> If there is an **UNBALANCED FORCE**, then the object will **ACCELERATE** in the direction of the force. The size of the acceleration is decided by the formula: **F = ma** (see below).

1) An <u>unbalanced force</u> will always produce <u>acceleration</u> (or deceleration).
2) This 'acceleration' can take <u>five</u> different forms: <u>starting</u>, <u>stopping</u>, <u>speeding up</u>, <u>slowing down</u> and <u>changing direction</u>.
3) On a <u>force diagram</u>, the <u>arrows</u> will be <u>unequal</u>:

The Overall Unbalanced Force is Often Called the Resultant Force

Any <u>resultant force</u> will produce <u>acceleration</u>, and this is the <u>formula</u> for it:

$$F = ma \qquad or \qquad a = F/m$$

m = mass, a = acceleration, F is always the <u>resultant force</u>

Three Points Which Should be Obvious:

1) The bigger the <u>force</u>, the <u>greater</u> the <u>acceleration</u> or <u>deceleration</u>.
2) The bigger the <u>mass</u>, the <u>smaller the acceleration</u>.
3) To get a <u>big mass</u> to accelerate <u>as fast</u> as a <u>small mass</u>, it needs a <u>bigger force</u>. Just think about pushing <u>heavy trolleys</u> and it should all seem <u>fairly obvious</u>, I would hope.

Forces and Acceleration

Calculations Using F = ma — Two Examples

Q1) What force is needed to accelerate a mass of 12 kg at 5 m/s^2 ?

ANS. The question is asking for <u>force</u>

— so you need a formula with "<u>F = something-or-other</u>".
Since they also give you values for <u>mass</u> and <u>acceleration</u>, the
formula "<u>F = ma</u>" really should be a <u>pretty obvious choice</u>, surely.
So just <u>stick in the numbers</u> they give you where the letters are:

<u>m = 12</u>, <u>a = 5</u>, so "<u>F = ma</u>" gives F = 12 × 5 = <u>60 N</u>   (It's <u>newtons</u> because force always is.)
(Notice that you don't really need to <u>fully understand</u> what's going on — you just need to know <u>how to use formulas</u>.)

Q2) The same force acts on another mass and it accelerates at 6 m/s^2. What is its mass?

ANS. The question mentions <u>force</u>, <u>mass</u> and <u>acceleration</u>, so the formula to use is still "F = ma".
But this time you have to find <u>m</u>, which means using the <u>formula triangle</u>.
<u>Cover up m</u> to get: "<u>m = F/a</u>" (m = F ÷ a)
Since <u>F = 60 N</u> and <u>a = 6 m/s^2</u> we stick these in to get: m = 60/6 = <u>10 kg</u>.   Easy innit?

Reaction Forces

> If object A <u>exerts a force</u> on object B then object B
> exerts <u>the exact opposite force</u> on object A.

1) That means if you <u>push</u> something, say a shopping trolley, the trolley will <u>push back</u> against you,
<u>just as hard</u>.

2) And as soon as you <u>stop</u> pushing, <u>so does the trolley</u>. Kinda clever really.

3) So far so good. The slightly tricky thing to get your head round is this — if the forces are always
equal, <u>how does anything ever go anywhere</u>? The important thing to remember is that the two forces
are acting on <u>different objects</u>. Think about a pair of ice skaters:

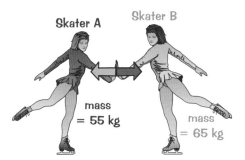

When skater A pushes on skater B (the '<u>action</u>' force),
she feels an equal and opposite force from skater B's
hand (the '<u>reaction</u>' force). Both skaters feel the <u>same
sized force</u>, in <u>opposite directions</u>, and so accelerate
away from each other.

Skater A will be <u>accelerated</u> more than skater B, though,
because she has a smaller mass — remember <u>F = ma</u>.

4) It's the same sort of thing when you go <u>swimming</u>. You <u>push</u> back against the <u>water</u> with your arms
and legs, and the water pushes you forwards with an <u>equal-sized force</u> in the <u>opposite direction</u>.

I have a reaction to forces — they bring me out in a rash...

This is the real deal. Like... proper Physics. It was <u>pretty fantastic</u> at the time — suddenly people
understood how forces and motion worked, they could work out the <u>orbits of planets</u> and everything.
Inspired? No? Shame. Learn them anyway — you're really going to struggle in the exam if you don't.

Stopping Distances

Looking at things simply — if you <u>need to stop</u> in a <u>given distance</u>... then the <u>faster</u> you're going, the <u>bigger braking force</u> you'll need. But in real life it's not quite that simple — if your maximum braking force isn't enough, you'll go further before you stop. There are loads of <u>other factors</u> too...

Many Factors _Affect Your Total Stopping Distance_

The stopping distance of a car is the distance covered in the time between the driver <u>first spotting</u> a hazard and the car coming to a <u>complete stop</u>. They're pretty keen on this for exam questions, so make sure you <u>learn it properly</u>.

The distance it takes to stop a car is divided into the <u>thinking distance</u> and the <u>braking distance</u>.

1) _Thinking Distance_

"The distance the car travels in the time between the driver noticing the hazard and applying the brakes".

It's affected by <u>two main factors</u>:

| **a) How fast you're going** | — obviously. Whatever your reaction time, the <u>faster</u> you're going, the <u>further</u> you'll go.

| **b) How dopey you are** | — This is affected by <u>tiredness</u>, <u>drugs</u>, <u>alcohol</u>, <u>old age</u>, and a <u>careless</u> blasé attitude.

> The figures below for typical stopping distances are from the Highway Code. It's frightening to see just how far it takes to stop when you're going at 70 mph.

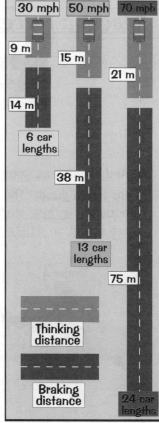

2) _Braking Distance_

"The distance the car travels during its deceleration whilst the brakes are being applied".

It's affected by <u>four main factors</u>:

| **a) How fast you're going** | — The <u>faster</u> you're going the <u>further</u> it takes to stop.

| **b) How heavily loaded the vehicle is** | — with the <u>same</u> brakes, <u>a heavily laden</u> vehicle takes <u>longer to stop</u>. A car won't stop as quick when it's full of people and luggage and towing a caravan.

| **c) How good your brakes are** | — all brakes must be checked and maintained <u>regularly</u>. Worn or faulty brakes will let you down <u>catastrophically</u> just when you need them the <u>most</u>, i.e. in an <u>emergency</u>.

| **d) How good the grip is** | — this depends on <u>three things</u>:

1) <u>road surface</u>, 2) <u>weather</u> conditions, 3) <u>tyres</u>.

So even at <u>30 mph</u>, you should drive no closer than <u>6 or 7 car lengths</u> away from the car in front — just in case. This is why <u>speed limits</u> are so important, and some <u>residential areas</u> are now <u>20 mph zones</u>.

<u>Bad visibility</u> can also be a major factor in accidents — lashing rain, thick fog, bright oncoming lights, etc. might mean that a driver <u>doesn't notice</u> a hazard until they're quite close to it — so they have a much shorter distance available to stop in.

Stop right there — and learn this page...

Leaves and diesel spills and muck on t'road are <u>serious hazards</u> because they're <u>unexpected</u>. <u>Wet</u> or <u>icy roads</u> are always much more <u>slippy</u> than dry roads, but often you only discover this when you try to <u>brake</u> hard. Tyres should have a minimum <u>tread depth</u> of <u>1.6 mm</u>. This is essential for getting rid of the <u>water</u> in wet conditions. Without <u>tread</u>, a tyre will simply <u>ride</u> on a <u>layer of water</u> and skid <u>very easily</u>. This is called "<u>aquaplaning</u>" and isn't nearly as cool as it sounds.

Momentum and Collisions

A <u>large</u> rugby player running very <u>fast</u> is going to be a lot harder to stop than a scrawny one out for a Sunday afternoon stroll — that's momentum for you.

Momentum = Mass × Velocity

1) The <u>greater</u> the <u>mass</u> of an object and the <u>greater</u> its <u>velocity</u>, the <u>more momentum</u> the object has.

2) Momentum is a <u>vector</u> quantity — it has size <u>and</u> direction (like <u>velocity</u>, but not speed).

> **Momentum (kg m/s) = Mass (kg) × Velocity (m/s)**

3) It's measured in kg m/s (<u>kilogram-metres per second</u>).

Momentum Before = Momentum After

When there aren't any <u>external forces</u> acting, <u>momentum is always conserved</u> — i.e. it doesn't change. So, in a <u>collision</u> or <u>explosion</u>, the total momentum <u>after</u> is the <u>same</u> as it was <u>before</u>.

Example:

Two skaters approach each other, collide and move off together as shown. At what velocity do they move after the collision?

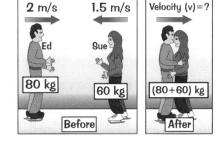

1) Choose which direction is <u>positive</u>. I'll say "<u>positive</u>" means "<u>to the right</u>" — so Ed starts with a positive velocity and Sue starts with a negative velocity.

2) <u>Total momentum before</u> collision
  = momentum of Ed + momentum of Sue
  = [80 × 2] + [60 × (–1.5)] = <u>70 kg m/s</u>

3) <u>Total momentum after</u> collision = momentum of Ed and Sue together = <u>140 × v</u>

4) Momentum is conserved, so:
  <u>total momentum after</u> = <u>total momentum before</u>
  140 × v = 70
  v = <u>0.5 m/s to the right</u>

You know they're moving to the right because the velocity is <u>positive</u>.

You get a similar sort of thing with explosions, except your starting momentum is usually <u>zero</u> (i.e. the thing that explodes starts off sat still). That means that the momentums of <u>all the little bits</u> that fly off in different directions must <u>add up to zero</u>. Weird.

Forces Cause Changes in Momentum

1) When a <u>force</u> acts on an object, it causes a <u>change</u> in momentum.

2) A <u>larger</u> force means a <u>faster</u> change of momentum (and so a greater <u>acceleration</u>).

3) Likewise, if someone's momentum changes <u>very quickly</u> (like in a <u>car crash</u>), the <u>forces</u> on the body will be very <u>large</u>, and more likely to cause <u>injury</u>.

4) This is why cars are designed to slow people down over a <u>longer time</u> when they have a crash — the longer it takes for a change in <u>momentum</u>, the <u>smaller</u> the <u>force</u>.

Learn this stuff — it'll only take a moment... um...

Momentum's a pretty <u>fundamental</u> bit of Physics — so make sure you learn it properly. Right then, <u>momentum</u> is <u>always conserved</u> in <u>collisions</u> and <u>explosions</u> when there are <u>no external forces</u> acting.

Car Safety

Cars are Designed to Convert Kinetic Energy Safely in a Crash

1) If a car crashes, it will slow down very quickly — this means that a lot of kinetic energy is converted into other forms of energy in a short amount of time, which can be dangerous for the people inside.

2) Cars are designed to convert the kinetic energy of the car and its passengers in a way that is safest for the car's occupants.

Seat belts absorb energy by stretching a bit. The seat belt won't be as strong after a crash so it has to be replaced.

3) Crumple zones are parts of the car at the front and back that crumple up in a collision. Some of the car's kinetic energy is converted into other forms of energy by the car body as it changes shape.

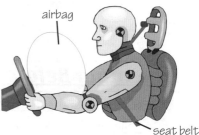

airbag

4) Seat belts and air bags slow the passengers down safely by converting their kinetic energy into other forms of energy over a longer period of time (see below). These safety features also prevent the passengers from hitting hard surfaces inside the car.

seat belt

Some Safety Features Reduce Forces

Cars have many safety features that are designed to reduce the forces acting on people involved in an accident. Smaller forces mean less severe injuries.

1) In a collision the force on the object can be lowered by slowing the object down over a longer time.

2) Safety features in a car increase the collision time to reduce the forces on the passengers — e.g. crumple zones allow the car to slow down more gradually as parts of it change shape.

3) Roads can also be made safer by placing structures like crash barriers and escape lanes in dangerous locations (like on sharp bends or steep hills). These structures increase the time of any collision — which means the collision force is reduced.

Cars Have Active and Passive Safety Features

1) Many cars have active safety features — these are features that interact with the way the car drives to help to avoid a crash, e.g. power assisted steering, traction control etc.

ABS brakes are an active safety feature that prevent skidding. They help the driver to stay in control of the car when braking sharply. They can also give the car a shorter stopping distance.

2) A passive safety feature is any non-interactive feature of a car that helps to keep the occupants of the car safe — e.g. seat belts, air bags, headrests etc.

3) It's important that the driver of a car is not distracted when driving — and there are many features in a car that have been designed to keep the driver's attention firmly focused on the road.

4) Many new cars have controls on the steering wheel or on control paddles near the steering wheel. These features help drivers stay in control while using the stereo, electric windows, cruise control etc.

> Safety features are rigorously tested to see how effective they are.
> Crash tests have shown that wearing a seat belt reduces the number of fatalities (deaths) by about 50% and that airbags reduce the number of fatalities by about 30%.
> In the last 25 years, the number of people killed or seriously injured in road traffic accidents in the UK has halved. This reduction is probably due to the safety features found in modern cars.

Actively learn this — it's the safest way to pass the exam...

The most important thing to learn here is that the forces acting on someone in a crash can be reduced by increasing the collision time — and there are loads of different safety features designed to do this...

Work and Potential Energy

When a force moves an object, ENERGY IS TRANSFERRED and WORK IS DONE.

That statement sounds far more complicated than it needs to. Try this:

1) Whenever something moves, something else is providing some sort of 'effort' to move it.
2) The thing putting the effort in needs a supply of energy (like fuel or food or electricity etc.).
3) It then does 'work' by moving the object — and one way or another it transfers the energy it receives (as fuel) into other forms.
4) Whether this energy is transferred 'usefully' (e.g. by lifting a load) or is 'wasted' (e.g. lost as heat through friction), you can still say that 'work is done'. Just like Batman and Bruce Wayne, 'work done' and 'energy transferred' are indeed 'one and the same'. (And they're both given in joules.)

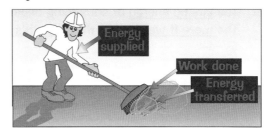

And Another Formula to Learn...

Work Done = Force × Distance

This only works if the force is in the same direction as the movement.

Whether the force is friction or weight or tension in a rope, it's always the same. To find how much work has been done (in joules), you just multiply the force in newtons by the distance moved in metres. Easy as that. I'll show you...

Example: Some hooligan kids drag an old tractor tyre 5 m over flat ground. They pull with a total force of 340 N. Find the work done.

Answer: work done = force × distance = 340 × 5 = 1700 J.   Phew — easy peasy isn't it?

Potential Energy is Energy Due to Height

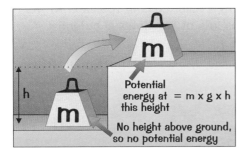

Potential Energy = mass × g × height

The proper name for this kind of 'potential energy' is gravitational potential energy (as opposed to 'elastic potential energy' or 'chemical potential energy' etc.). The proper name for g is 'gravitational field strength'. On Earth, g is approximately 10 N/kg.

EXAMPLE: A sheep of mass 47 kg is slowly raised through 6.3 m. Find the gain in potential energy.

ANSWER: Just plug the numbers into the formula:
P.E. = mgh = 47 × 10 × 6.3 = 2961 J
(joules because it's energy)

Revise work done — what else...

Remember "energy transferred" and "work done" are the same thing. If you need a force to make something speed up (P.101), all that means is that you need to give it a bit of energy. Makes sense.

Kinetic Energy and Roller Coasters

Kinetic Energy is Energy of Movement

1) Anything that's moving has kinetic energy.

2) The kinetic energy of something depends both on mass and speed.
The more it weighs and the faster it's going, the bigger its kinetic energy will be.

small mass, not fast low kinetic energy

big fast lorries Ltd

big mass, real fast high kinetic energy

3) There's a slightly tricky formula for it, so you have to concentrate a little bit harder for this one. But hey, that's life — it can be real tough sometimes:

> Kinetic Energy = ½ × mass × speed²

EXAMPLE: A car of mass 2450 kg is travelling at 38 m/s. Calculate its kinetic energy.

ANSWER: It's pretty easy. You just plug the numbers into the formula — but watch the 'speed²'!
K.E. = ½mv² = ½ × 2450 × 38² = 1 768 900 J (joules because it's energy)

Falling Objects Convert P.E. into K.E.

When something falls, its potential energy is converted into kinetic energy. So the further it falls, the faster it goes.
In practice, some of the P.E. will be dissipated as heat due to air resistance, but in exam questions they'll likely say you can ignore air resistance, in which case you'll just need to remember this simple and really quite obvious formula:

> Kinetic energy gained = Potential Energy lost

Roller Coasters Transfer Energy

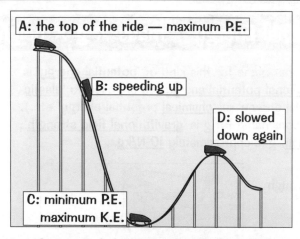

A: the top of the ride — maximum P.E.

B: speeding up

D: slowed down again

C: minimum P.E. maximum K.E.

1) At the top of a roller coaster (position A) the carriage has lots of gravitational potential energy (P.E.).

2) As the carriage descends to position B, P.E. is transferred to kinetic energy (K.E.) and the carriage speeds up.

3) Between positions B and C the carriage keeps accelerating as its P.E. is converted into K.E.

4) If you ignore any air resistance or friction between the carriage and the track, then all the P.E. the carriage had at A will be converted to K.E. by the time it reaches C.

5) A real carriage loses some energy through friction on the way down the hill. It needs to have enough kinetic energy left at point C to carry it up the hill again to D.

Kinetic energy — just get a move on and learn it, OK...

Throwing a ball up in the air and letting it fall again is another good (if a bit more dull) example of transferring K.E. to P.E. and back again. Three chunks to learn, cover, scribble...

Power

Power is the 'Rate of Doing Work' — i.e. How Much per Second

1) <u>POWER</u> is <u>not</u> the same thing as <u>force</u>, nor <u>energy</u>.

2) A <u>powerful</u> machine is not necessarily one which can exert a strong <u>force</u> (though it usually ends up that way).

3) A <u>POWERFUL</u> machine is one which transfers <u>A LOT OF ENERGY IN A SHORT SPACE OF TIME</u>.

This is the <u>very easy formula</u> for power:

$$\text{Power} = \frac{\text{Work done}}{\text{Time taken}}$$

(with work done measured in <u>joules</u>, and time in <u>seconds</u>)

<u>EXAMPLE</u>: A motor transfers 4.8 kJ of useful energy in 2 minutes. Find its power output.

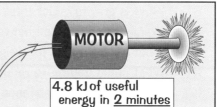

4.8 kJ of useful energy in 2 minutes

<u>ANSWER</u>: First, you need to get everything in the right units, so convert the kJ into J and the minutes into seconds.

So work done = 4800 J and time = 120 s.

Power = work done / time = 4800 / 120 = <u>40 W (or 40 J/s)</u>

Power is Measured in Watts (or J/s)

1) The proper unit of power is the <u>watt</u>.

2) <u>One watt = 1 joule of energy transferred per second</u>.

3) <u>Power</u> means 'how much energy <u>per second</u>', so <u>watts</u> are the same as '<u>joules per second</u>' (J/s). Don't ever say 'watts per second' — it's <u>nonsense</u>.

Cars Have Different Power Ratings

1) The <u>size</u> and <u>design</u> of car engines determine how <u>powerful</u> they are.

2) The more powerful an engine, the more <u>energy</u> it can transfer from its <u>fuel</u> every second, so (usually) the higher the fuel consumption.

3) E.g. the <u>power output</u> of a typical small car will be around 50 kW and a sports car will be about 120 kW (some are <u>much</u> higher).

Sports car power = 120 kW

Small car power = 50 kW

Watt are you waiting for — revise this stuff now...

The power of a car isn't always measured in watts — sometimes you'll see it in a funny unit called brake horsepower. James Watt defined 1 horsepower as the work done when a horse raises a mass of 550 lb (250 kg) through a height of 1 ft (0.3 m) in 1 second... as you do. I'd stick to watts if I were you.

Revision Summary for Section Eight

Yay — revision summary! I <u>know</u> these are your favourite bits of the book, all those jolly questions. There are lots of formulas and laws and picky little details to learn in this section. So, practise these questions till you can do them all standing on one leg with your arms behind your back whilst being tickled on the nose with a purple ostrich feather. Or something.

1) Write down the formula for working out velocity.

2)* Find the speed of a partly chewed mouse which hobbles 3.2 metres in 35 seconds.

3)* A speed camera is set up in a 30 mph (13.4 m/s) zone. It takes two photographs 0.5 s apart. A car travels 6.3 m between the two photographs. Was the car breaking the speed limit?

4) What is acceleration? What's the unit used?

5)* Write down the formula for acceleration. What's the acceleration of a soggy pea flicked from rest to a speed of 14 m/s in 0.4 seconds?

6) Sketch a typical velocity-time graph and point out all the important points.

7) Explain how to find acceleration from a velocity-time graph.

8) What is gravity? List three effects gravity produces.

9) Explain the difference between mass and weight. What units are they measured in?

10) What's the formula for weight? Illustrate it with a worked example of your own.

11) What could you do to reduce the friction between two surfaces?

12) Describe how air resistance is affected by speed.

13) What is "terminal speed"?

14) If an object has zero resultant force on it, can it be moving? Can it be accelerating?

15)* Write down the formula relating resultant force and acceleration. What force is needed to accelerate a 4 kg mass at 7.5 m/s^2?

16) Explain what a reaction force is.

17) What are the two different parts of the overall stopping distance of a car?

18) List three factors that affect each of the two parts of the stopping distance of a car.

19)* Write down the formula for momentum. Find the momentum of a 78 kg sheep moving at 23 m/s.

20) List four car safety features (they could be active or passive), then describe how each one helps to make driving safer.

21)* Write down the formula for work done. A crazy dog drags a big branch 12 m over the next-door neighbour's front lawn, pulling with a force of 535 N. How much work is done?

22)* Write down the formula for gravitational potential energy. Calculate the increase in potential energy when a box of mass 12 kg is raised through 4.5 m.

23)* Write down the formula for kinetic energy. Find the K.E. of a 78 kg sheep moving at 23 m/s.

24)* At the top of a roller coaster ride, a carriage has 150 kJ of gravitational potential energy (P.E.). Ignoring friction, how much kinetic energy must the carriage have at the bottom (when P.E. = 0)?

25)* An electric motor uses 540 kJ of electrical energy in 4.5 minutes. What is its power consumption?

* Answers on page 140.

Static Electricity

Static electricity is all about charges which are <u>NOT</u> free to move. This causes them to build up in one place, and it often ends with a <u>spark</u> or a <u>shock</u> when they do finally move.

1) *Build-Up of Static is Caused by Friction*

1) When two <u>insulating</u> materials are <u>rubbed</u> together, electrons will be <u>scraped off one</u> and <u>dumped</u> on the other.

2) This'll leave a <u>positive</u> static charge on one and a <u>negative</u> static charge on the other.

3) A classic example is a <u>polythene</u> rod being rubbed with a <u>cloth duster</u>, as shown in the diagram.

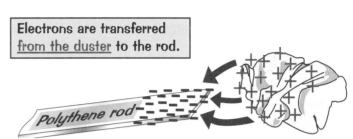

Electrons are transferred <u>from the duster</u> to the rod.

4) Electrically charged objects <u>attract</u> small neutral objects placed near them.
(Try this: rub a balloon on a woolly pully — then put it near tiddly bits of paper and watch them jump.)

5) Some <u>dusting cloths</u> and <u>brushes</u> use static electricity. They become charged as they pass over the dusty surface, and this charge <u>attracts the dust</u> to them.

2) *Only Electrons Move — Never the Positive Charges*

<u>Watch out for this in exams</u>. Both +ve and –ve electrostatic charges are only ever produced by the movement of <u>electrons</u>. The positive charges <u>definitely do not move</u>. A positive static charge is always caused by electrons <u>moving</u> away elsewhere, as shown above. Don't forget!

A charged conductor can be <u>discharged safely</u> by connecting it to earth with a <u>metal strap</u>. The electrons flow <u>down</u> the strap to the ground if the charge is <u>negative</u> and flow <u>up</u> the strap from the ground if the charge is <u>positive</u>.

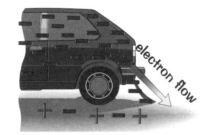

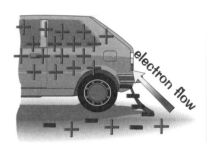

3) *Like Charges Repel, Opposite Charges Attract*

Hopefully this is <u>kind of obvious</u>.
Two things with <u>opposite</u> electric charges are <u>attracted</u> to each other.
Two things with the <u>same</u> electric charge will <u>repel</u> each other.
These forces get <u>weaker</u> the <u>further apart</u> the two things are.

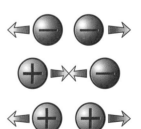

Come on, be +ve — this is the last-but-one section in the book...

Static electricity's great fun. You must have tried it — rubbing a balloon against your clothes and trying to get it to stick to the ceiling. It really works... well, sometimes. And it's all due to the build-up of static. <u>Bad hair days</u> are also caused by static — it builds up on your hair, so your strands of hair repel each other. Conditioners try to decrease this, but they don't always work...

Static Electricity

They like asking you to give quite detailed examples in exams. Make sure you learn all these details.

Static Electricity Being a Little Joker:

1) Attracting Dust

Dust particles are charged and will be attracted to anything with the opposite charge. Unfortunately, many objects around the house are made out of insulators (e.g. TV screen, wood, plastic containers etc.) that get easily charged and attract the dust particles — this makes cleaning a nightmare.

2) Clothing Cling and Crackles

When synthetic clothes are dragged over each other (like in a tumble drier) or over your head, electrons get scraped off, leaving static charges on both parts, and that leads to the inevitable — attraction (they stick together and cling to you) and little sparks / shocks as the charges rearrange themselves.

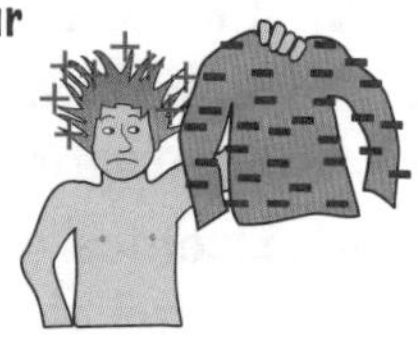

3) Shocks from Water Pipes

If you walk on a nylon carpet wearing shoes with insulating soles, charge builds up on your body. Then if you touch a metal water pipe, the charge flows to the conductor and you get a little shock.

Static Electricity Can be Dangerous:

1) Lightning

Rain drops and ice bump together inside storm clouds, knocking off electrons and leaving the top of the cloud positively charged and the bottom of the cloud negative. This creates a huge voltage and a big spark.

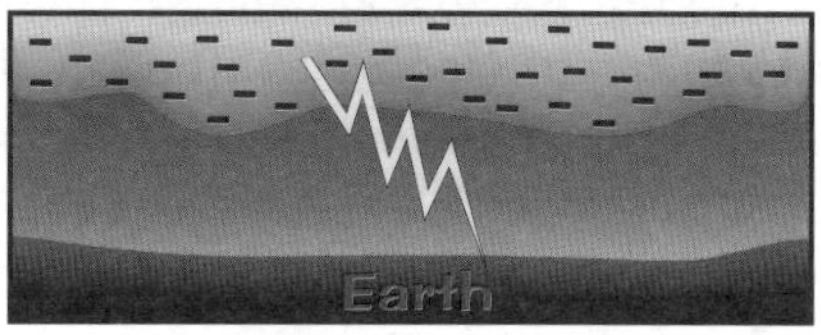

2) A Lot of Charge Can Build Up on Clothes

1) A large amount of static charge can build up on clothes made out of synthetic materials if they rub against other synthetic fabrics — like when wriggling about on a car seat.
2) Eventually, this charge can become large enough to make a spark — which is really bad news if it happens near any inflammable gases or fuel fumes... KABOOM!

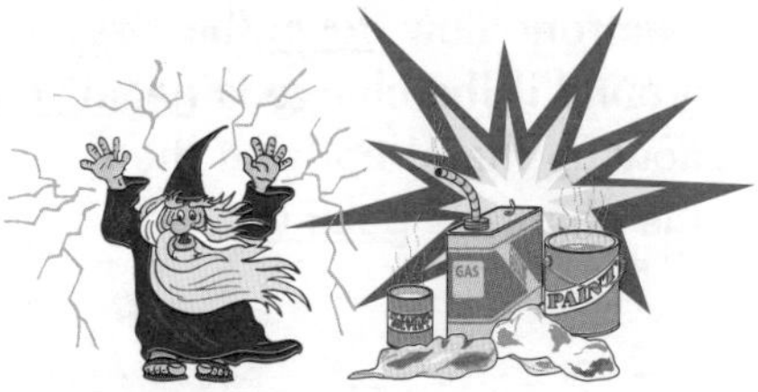

3) Grain Chutes, Paper Rollers and the Fuel Filling Nightmare:

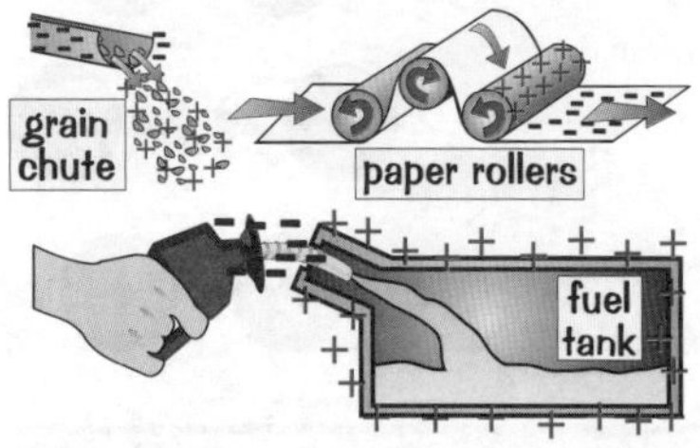

1) As fuel flows out of a filler pipe, or paper drags over rollers, or grain shoots out of pipes, then static can build up.
2) This can easily lead to a spark and might cause an explosion in dusty or fumy places — like when filling up a car with fuel at a petrol station.
3) Static charges are also a big problem in places where there are high concentrations of oxygen (e.g. in a hospital operating theatre) — a spark could cause an explosion.

Static electricity — it's really shocking stuff...

Lightning always chooses the easiest path between the sky and the ground — even if that means going through tall buildings, trees or you. That's why it's never a good idea to fly a kite in a thunderstorm...

Uses of Static Electricity

Static electricity isn't always a nuisance. It's got loads of applications in <u>medicine</u> and <u>industry</u>...

1) Paint Sprayers — Getting an Even Coat

1) Bikes and cars are painted using <u>electrostatic paint sprayers</u>.
2) The spray gun is <u>charged</u>, which charges up the small drops of paint. Each paint drop <u>repels</u> all the others, since they've all got the <u>same charge</u>, so you get a very <u>fine spray</u>.
3) The object to be painted is given an <u>opposite charge</u> to the gun. This <u>attracts</u> the fine spray of paint.
4) This method gives an <u>even coat</u> and hardly any paint is <u>wasted</u>. In addition parts of the bicycle or car pointing <u>away</u> from the spray gun <u>still receive paint</u>, i.e. there are no paint <u>shadows</u>.

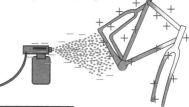

2) Dust Precipitators — Cleaning Up Emissions

<u>Smoke</u> is made up of <u>tiny particles</u>, which can be removed with a precipitator. There are several different designs of precipitator — here's a very simple one:

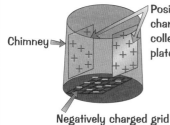

Chimney

Positively charged collection plates

Negatively charged grid

1) As smoke particles reach the bottom of the chimney, they meet a <u>wire grid</u> with a high <u>negative charge</u>, which charges the particles negatively.
2) The charged smoke particles are <u>attracted</u> to <u>positively</u> charged <u>metal plates</u>. The smoke particles <u>stick together</u> to form larger particles.
3) When <u>heavy enough</u>, the particles <u>fall</u> off the plates or are <u>knocked off</u>. The dust falls to the bottom of the chimney and can be removed.
4) The gases coming out of the chimney contain <u>very few smoke particles</u>.

3) Defibrillators — Restarting a Heart

1) Hospitals and ambulances have machines called <u>defibrillators</u> which can be used to shock a stopped heart back into operation.
2) The defibrillator consists of two <u>paddles</u> connected to a power supply.
3) The paddles of the defibrillator are placed <u>firmly</u> on the patient's chest to get a <u>good electrical contact</u> and then the defibrillator is <u>charged up</u>.
4) Everyone moves away from the patient except for the defibrillator operator who holds <u>insulated handles</u>. This means <u>only the patient</u> gets a shock.

4) Photocopiers — er... Copying Stuff

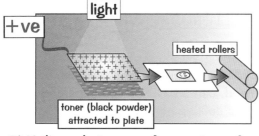

+ve, light, heated rollers, toner (black powder) attracted to plate

1) The <u>image plate</u> is positively charged. An image of what you're copying is projected onto it.
2) Whiter bits of the thing you're copying make <u>light</u> fall on the plate and the charge <u>leaks away</u> in those places.
3) The charged bits attract negatively charged <u>black powder</u>, which is transferred onto positively charged paper.
4) The paper is <u>heated</u> so the powder sticks.

5) Voilà, a photocopy of your piece of paper (or whatever else you've shoved in there).
6) Laserjet printers work in a similar way. Instead of an image plate, the printer has a rotating <u>image drum</u>. And the light comes from a <u>controlled laser beam</u>.

If this doesn't get your heart going — nothing will...

You can get your very <u>own</u> special <u>defibrillator</u> now. One to carry around in your handbag, just in case. No, really, you can (okay, maybe it wouldn't fit in your handbag unless you're Mary Poppins, but still...).

Circuits — The Basics

Isn't electricity great. Mind you it's pretty bad news if the words don't mean anything to you...
Hey, I know — learn them now!

1) **Current** is the flow of electrons round the circuit.
Current will only flow through a component if there is a
voltage across that component.   Unit: ampere, A.

2) **Voltage** is the driving force that pushes the current round.
Kind of like "electrical pressure".   Unit: volt, V.

3) **Resistance** is anything in the circuit which slows the
flow down.   Unit: ohm, Ω.

4) **There's a balance:** the voltage is trying to push the current
round the circuit, and the resistance is opposing it — the
relative sizes of the voltage and resistance decide how big
the current will be:

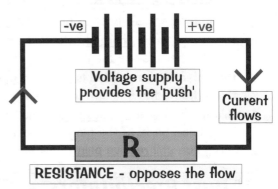

Voltage supply provides the 'push'

Current flows

RESISTANCE - opposes the flow

> If you increase the voltage — then more current will flow.
> If you increase the resistance — then less current will flow
> (or more voltage will be needed to keep the same current flowing).

The Standard Test Circuit

This is without doubt the most totally bog-standard circuit the world has ever known. So know it.

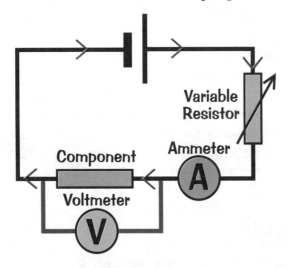

Variable Resistor

Component

Ammeter

Voltmeter

The Ammeter

1) Measures the current (in amps) flowing
through the component.
2) Must be placed in series (see p.116).
3) Can be put anywhere in series in the main
circuit, but never in parallel like the voltmeter.

The Voltmeter

1) Measures the voltage (in volts) across the
component.
2) Must be placed in parallel (see p.117)
around the component under test — **NOT**
around the variable resistor or the battery!
3) The proper name for "voltage" is
"potential difference" or "P.D.".

Five Important Points

1) This very basic circuit is used for testing components, and for getting V-I graphs for them.
2) The component, the ammeter and the variable resistor are all in series, which means they can be put
in any order in the main circuit. The voltmeter, on the other hand, can only be placed in parallel
around the component under test, as shown. Anywhere else is a definite no-no.
3) As you vary the variable resistor it alters the current flowing through the circuit.
4) This allows you to take several pairs of readings from the ammeter and voltmeter.
5) You can then plot these values for current and voltage on a V-I graph (see page 114).

Measure gymnastics — use a vaultmeter...

The funny thing is — the electrons in circuits actually move from –ve to +ve... but scientists always
think of current as flowing from +ve to –ve. Basically it's just because that's how the early physicists
thought of it (before they found out about the electrons), and now it's become convention.

Measuring AC

Mains Supply is AC, Battery Supply is DC

1) The UK mains supply is approximately 230 volts.

2) It is an AC supply (alternating current), which means the current is constantly changing direction.

3) The frequency of the AC mains supply is 50 cycles per second or 50 Hz (50 hertz).

4) By contrast, cells and batteries supply direct current (DC). This just means that the current keeps flowing in the same direction.

AC Can be Shown on an Oscilloscope Screen

1) A cathode ray oscilloscope (CRO) is basically a snazzy voltmeter.

2) If you plug an AC supply into an oscilloscope, you get a 'trace' on the screen that shows how the voltage of the supply changes with time. The trace goes up and down in a regular pattern — some of the time it's positive and some of the time it's negative.

3) The vertical height of the trace at any point shows the input voltage at that point.

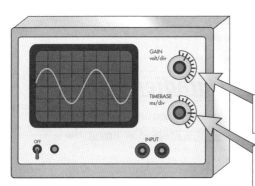

4) There are two dials on the front of the oscilloscope called the TIMEBASE and the GAIN. You can use these to set the scales of the horizontal and vertical axes of the display.

The GAIN dial controls how many volts each centimetre division represents on the vertical axis.

The TIMEBASE dial controls how many milliseconds (1 ms = 0.001 s) each division represents on the horizontal axis.

Learn How to Recognise an Oscilloscope Trace

DC supply

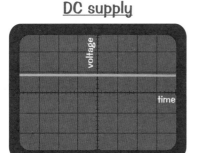

A DC source is always at the same voltage, so you get a straight line.

AC supply

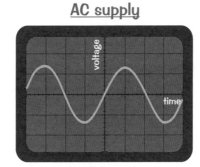

An AC source gives a regularly repeating wave.

I wish my bank account had a gain dial...

Because mains power is AC, its current can be increased or decreased using a device called a transformer. The lower the current in power transmission lines, the less energy is wasted as heat.

Resistance and V = I × R

Three Hideously Important Voltage-Current Graphs

V-I graphs show how the current varies as you change the voltage. Learn these three real well:

Different Resistors
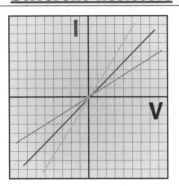

Filament Lamp
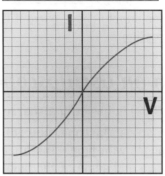

Diode
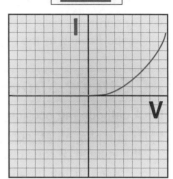

The current through a <u>resistor</u> (at constant temperature) is <u>proportional to voltage</u>. <u>Different resistors</u> have different resistances, hence the different <u>slopes</u>.

As the <u>temperature</u> of the filament <u>increases</u>, the <u>resistance increases</u>, hence the <u>curve</u>.

Current will only flow through a diode <u>in one direction</u>, as shown.

Calculating Resistance: R = V/I, (or R = "1/gradient")

For the <u>straight-line graphs</u> the resistance of the component is <u>steady</u> and is equal to the <u>inverse</u> of the <u>gradient</u> of the line, or "<u>1/gradient</u>". In other words, the <u>steeper</u> the graph the <u>lower</u> the resistance.

If the graph <u>curves</u>, it means the resistance is <u>changing</u>. In that case R can be found for any point by taking the <u>pair of values</u> (V, I) from the graph and sticking them in the formula <u>V = I × R</u>. Easy.

Potential Difference = Current × Resistance

Calculating Resistance — an Example

EXAMPLE. Ammeter A reads 1.5 A and resistor R is 4 Ω. What is the current through voltmeter V?

ANSWER. Use the formula V = I × R.
The answer is then:
   1.5 × 4 = 6 V

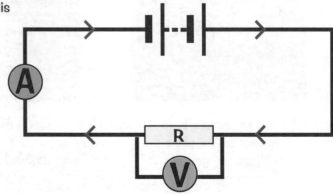

In the end you'll have to learn this — resistance is futile...

You have to be able to <u>interpret</u> voltage-current graphs for your exam. Remember — the <u>steeper</u> the <u>slope</u>, the <u>lower</u> the <u>resistance</u>. And you need to know that equation inside out, back to front, upside down and in Swahili. It's the most important equation in electrics, bar none. (P.S. I might let you off the Swahili.)

Circuit Symbols and Devices

Circuit Symbols You Should Know:

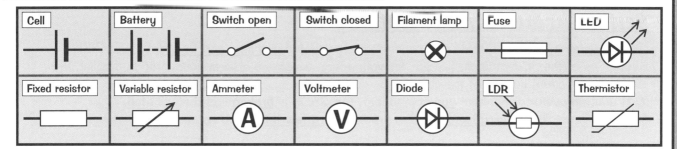

| Cell | Battery | Switch open | Switch closed | Filament lamp | Fuse | LED |
| Fixed resistor | Variable resistor | Ammeter | Voltmeter | Diode | LDR | Thermistor |

1) Variable Resistor

1) A resistor whose resistance can be changed by twiddling a knob or something.
2) The old-fashioned ones are huge coils of wire with a slider on them.
3) They're great for altering the current flowing through a circuit.
   Turn the resistance up, the current drops. Turn the resistance down, the current goes up.

2) "Semiconductor Diode" or Just "Diode"

A special device made from semiconductor material such as silicon. It lets current flow freely through it in one direction, but not in the other (i.e. there's a very high resistance in the reverse direction). This turns out to be real useful in various electronic circuits.

3) Light-Dependent Resistor or "LDR" to You

1) In bright light, the resistance falls.
2) In darkness, the resistance is highest.
3) This makes it a useful device for various electronic circuits, e.g. automatic night lights, burglar detectors.

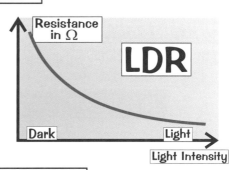

4) Thermistor (Temperature-Dependent Resistor)

1) In hot conditions, the resistance drops.
2) In cool conditions, the resistance goes up.
3) Thermistors make useful temperature detectors, e.g. car engine temperature sensors and electronic thermostats.

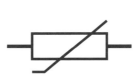

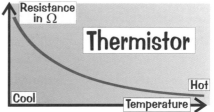

LDRs — Light-Dependent Rabbits...

You have to learn those circuit symbols so you can read circuit diagrams in the exam. It's not too bad remembering how LDRs and thermistors behave — low light/heat means high resistance.

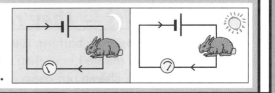

Series Circuits

You need to be able to tell the difference between series and parallel circuits <u>just by looking at them</u>. You also need to know the <u>rules</u> about what happens with both types. Read on.

Series Circuits — All or Nothing

1) In <u>series circuits</u>, the different components are connected <u>in a line</u>, <u>end to end</u>, between the +ve and –ve of the power supply (except for <u>voltmeters</u>, which are always connected <u>in parallel</u>, but they don't count as part of the circuit).
2) If you remove or disconnect <u>one</u> component, the circuit is <u>broken</u> and they all <u>stop</u>.
3) This is generally <u>not very handy</u>, and in practice <u>very few things</u> are connected in series.

1) Potential Difference is Shared:

In series circuits the <u>total P.D.</u> of the <u>supply</u> is <u>shared</u> between the various <u>components</u>. So the <u>voltages</u> round a series circuit <u>always add up</u> to equal the <u>source voltage</u>:

$$V = V_1 + V_2 + V_3$$

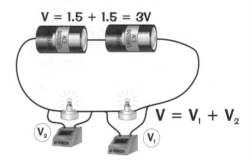

$$V = 1.5 + 1.5 = 3V$$

$$V = V_1 + V_2$$

2) Current is the Same Everywhere:

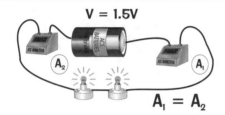

$$V = 1.5V$$
$$A_1 = A_2$$

1) In series circuits the <u>same current</u> flows through <u>all parts</u> of the circuit, i.e:

$$A_1 = A_2$$

2) The <u>size</u> of the current is determined by the <u>total P.D.</u> of the cells and the <u>total resistance</u> of the circuit: i.e. $I = V/R$

3) Resistance Adds Up:

1) In series circuits the <u>total resistance</u> is just the <u>sum</u> of all the resistances:

$$R = R_1 + R_2 + R_3$$

2) The <u>bigger</u> the <u>resistance</u> of a component, the bigger its <u>share</u> of the <u>total P.D.</u>

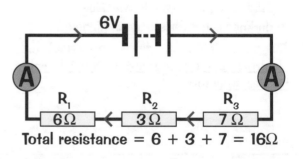

Total resistance = 6 + 3 + 7 = 16Ω

Cell Voltages Add Up:

1) There is a bigger potential difference when more cells are in series, provided the cells are all <u>connected</u> the <u>same way</u>.
2) For example when two batteries of voltage 1.5 V are <u>connected in series</u> they supply 3 V <u>between them</u>.

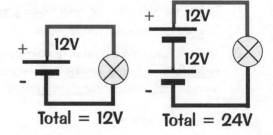

Total = 12V   Total = 24V

Series circuits — they're no laughing matter...

If you connect a lamp to a battery, it lights up with a certain brightness. If you then add more identical lamps in series with the first one, they'll all light up <u>less brightly</u> than before. That's because in a series circuit the voltage is <u>shared out</u> between all the components. That doesn't happen in parallel circuits...

Parallel Circuits

Parallel circuits are much more <u>sensible</u> than series circuits and so they're much more <u>common</u> in <u>real life</u>. All the electrics in your home will be wired in parallel circuits.

Parallel Circuits — Independence and Isolation

1) In <u>parallel circuits</u>, each component is <u>separately</u> connected to the +ve and −ve of the <u>supply</u>.

2) If you remove or disconnect <u>one</u> of them, it will <u>hardly affect</u> the others at all.

3) This is <u>obviously</u> how <u>most</u> things must be connected, for example in <u>cars</u> and in <u>household electrics</u>. You have to be able to switch everything on and off <u>separately</u>.

1) P.D. is the Same Across All Components:

1) In parallel circuits <u>all</u> components get the <u>full source P.D.</u>, so the voltage is the <u>same</u> across all components:

$$V_1 = V_2 = V_3$$

2) This means that <u>identical bulbs</u> connected in parallel will all be at the <u>same brightness</u>.

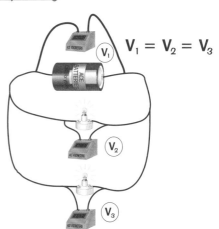

$V_1 = V_2 = V_3$

2) Current is Shared Between Branches:

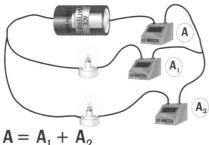

$A = A_1 + A_2$

1) In parallel circuits the <u>total current</u> flowing around the circuit is equal to the <u>total</u> of all the currents in the <u>separate branches</u>.

$$A = A_1 + A_2 + A_3$$

2) In a parallel circuit, there are <u>junctions</u> where the current either <u>splits</u> or <u>rejoins</u>. The total current going <u>into</u> a junction has to equal the total current <u>leaving</u>.

3) If two <u>identical components</u> are connected in parallel then the <u>same current</u> will flow through each component.

3) Resistance is Tricky:

1) The <u>current</u> through each component depends on its <u>resistance</u>. The <u>lower</u> the resistance, the <u>bigger</u> the current that'll flow through it.

2) The <u>total resistance</u> of the circuit is <u>tricky to work out</u>, but it's always <u>less</u> than that of the branch with the <u>smallest</u> resistance.

Voltmeters and Ammeters are Exceptions to the Rule:

1) Ammeters and voltmeters are <u>exceptions</u> to the series and parallel rules.

2) Ammeters are <u>always</u> connected in <u>series</u> even in a parallel circuit.

3) Voltmeters are <u>always</u> connected in <u>parallel with a component</u> even in a series circuit.

A current shared — is a current halved...*

Parallel circuits might look a bit scarier than series ones, but they're much more useful — and you don't have to learn as many equations for them (yay!). Remember: each branch has the <u>same voltage</u> across it, and the overall resistance is lower than that of the least resistant branch.

* Conditions may apply. CGP takes no responsibility for the accuracy of this proverb.

Section Nine — Electricity

Fuses and Safe Plugs

Now then, did you know... electricity is dangerous. It can kill you. Well just watch out for it, that's all.

Plugs and Cables — Learn the Safety Features

Get the Wiring Right:

1) The <u>right coloured wire</u> is connected to each pin, and <u>firmly screwed</u> in.
2) <u>No bare wires</u> are showing inside the plug.
3) The <u>cable grip</u> is tightly fastened over the cable <u>outer layer</u>.

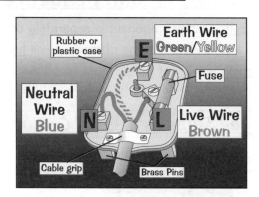

Plug Features:

1) The <u>metal parts</u> are made of copper or brass because these are <u>very good conductors</u>.
2) The case, cable grip and cable insulation are made of <u>rubber</u> or <u>plastic</u> because they're really good <u>insulators</u>, and <u>flexible</u> too.
3) This all keeps the electricity flowing <u>where it should</u>.

Earthing and Fuses Prevent Fires and Shocks

The <u>LIVE WIRE</u> alternates between a <u>HIGH +VE AND −VE VOLTAGE</u> of about <u>230 V</u>.
The <u>NEUTRAL WIRE</u> is always at <u>0 V</u>. Electricity normally flows in through the live wire and out through neutral wire.
The <u>EARTH WIRE</u> and <u>fuse</u> (or circuit breaker) are just for <u>safety</u> and <u>work together</u> like this:

1) If a <u>fault</u> develops in which the <u>live</u> somehow touches the <u>metal case</u>, then because the case is <u>earthed</u>, a <u>big current</u> flows in through the <u>live</u>, through the <u>case</u> and out down the <u>earth wire</u>.

2) This <u>surge</u> in current '<u>blows</u>' the <u>fuse</u> (or trips the circuit breaker), which <u>cuts off</u> the <u>live supply</u>.

3) This <u>isolates</u> the <u>whole appliance</u>, making it <u>impossible</u> to get an electric <u>shock</u> from the case.
It also prevents the risk of <u>fire</u> caused by the heating effect of a large current.

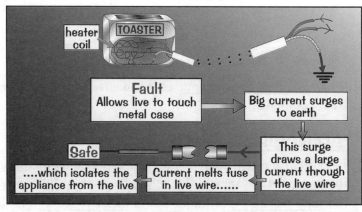

4) <u>Fuses</u> should be <u>rated</u> as near as possible but <u>just higher</u> than the <u>normal operating current</u>.

All appliances with <u>metal cases</u> must be "<u>earthed</u>" to reduce the danger of <u>electric shock</u>. "Earthing" just means the case must be attached to an <u>earth wire</u>. An earthed conductor can <u>never become live</u>. If the appliance has a <u>plastic casing</u> and no metal parts <u>showing</u> then it's said to be <u>double insulated</u>. Anything with <u>double insulation</u> like that <u>doesn't need an earth wire</u> — just a live and neutral.

Why are earth wires green and yellow — when mud's brown...

Have you ever noticed how if anything doesn't work in the house, it's always due to the fuse. The lights, the toaster, the car — always a little annoying, but it makes everything a <u>whole load safer</u>...

Energy and Power in Circuits

You can look at electrical circuits in two ways. The first is in terms of a voltage pushing the current round and the resistances opposing the flow, as on P.112. The other way of looking at circuits is in terms of energy transfer. Learn them both and be ready to tackle questions about either.

Energy is Transferred from Cells and Other Sources

Anything which supplies electricity is also supplying energy.

So cells, batteries, generators, etc. all transfer energy to components in the circuit:

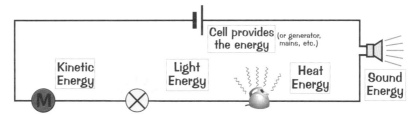

Motion: motors

Light: light bulbs

Heat: Hairdriers/kettles

Sound: speakers

All Resistors Produce Heat When a Current Flows Through Them

1) Whenever a current flows through anything with electrical resistance (which is pretty well everything) then electrical energy is converted into heat energy.

2) The more current that flows, the more heat is produced.

3) A bigger voltage means more heating because it pushes more current through.

4) You can measure the amount of heat produced by putting a resistor in a known amount of water, or inside a solid block, and measuring the increase in temperature.

Power Ratings of Appliances

A light bulb converts electrical energy into light and has a power rating of 100 watts (W), which means it transfers 100 joules/second.

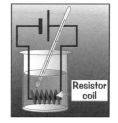

A kettle converts electrical energy into heat and has a power rating of 2.5 kW, transferring 2500 joules/second.

The total energy transferred by an appliance depends on how long the appliance is on and its power rating.

The formula for energy transferred is | **ENERGY = POWER × TIME** | (E = P × t)

For example, if the kettle is on for 5 minutes the energy transferred by the kettle in this time is 300 × 2500 = 750 000 J = 750 kJ. (300 s = 5 minutes)

Electrical Power and Fuse Ratings

1) The formula for electrical power is: | **POWER = VOLTAGE × CURRENT** | (P = V × I)

2) Most electrical goods show their power rating and voltage rating. To work out the fuse needed, you need to work out the current that the item will normally use:

> Example: A hairdrier is rated at 230 V, 1 kW. Find the fuse needed.
>
> ANSWER: I = P/V = 1000/230 = 4.3 A. Normally, the fuse should be rated just a little higher than the normal current, so a 5 amp fuse is ideal for this one.

Current = heat — so eat fruit cake when you're cold...

In the UK, you can usually get fuses rated at 3 A, 5 A or 13 A, and that's about it. You should bear that in mind when you're working out fuse ratings. If you find you need a 10.73 A fuse — tough.

Revision Summary for Section Nine

There's some pretty heavy physics in this section. But just take it one page at a time and it's not so bad. When you think you know it all, try these questions and see how you're getting on. If there are any you can't do, look back at the right bit of the section, then come back here and try again.

1)   What causes the build-up of static electricity? Which particles move when static builds up?

2)   Give two examples each of static electricity being: a) a nuisance, b) dangerous.

3)   Give four examples of how static electricity can be helpful. Write all the details.

4)   Explain what current, voltage and resistance are in an electric circuit.

5)* An oscilloscope is plugged into the mains (50 Hz). Sketch what you would expect to see on the screen if the timebase is set to 2 ms/div.

6)   Sketch typical voltage-current graphs for: a) a resistor, b) a filament lamp, c) a diode. Explain the shape of each graph.

7)* Calculate the resistance of a wire if the voltage across it is 12 V and the current through it is 2.5 A.

8)   Describe how the resistance of an LDR changes with light intensity. Give an application of an LDR.

9)   What is a thermistor? Give an application of a thermistor.

10)* Find each unknown voltage, current or resistance in this circuit.

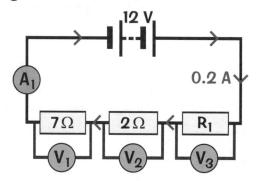

11) Why are parallel circuits often more useful than series ones?

12) Sketch a properly wired three-pin plug.

13) Explain fully how a fuse and earth wire work together.

14) What is double insulation?

15)* Find the appropriate fuse (3 A, 5 A or 13 A) for each of these appliances:
     a) a toaster rated at 230 V, 1100 W,
     b) an electric heater rated at 230 V, 2000 W.

* Answers on page 140.

Atoms and Isotopes

In 1909 Ernest Rutherford and his merry men tried firing alpha particles at thin gold foil. Most of them just went straight through, but the odd one came straight back at them, which was frankly a bit of a shocker for Ernie and his pals. Being a pretty clued-up guy, Rutherford realised this meant that most of the mass of the atom was concentrated at the centre in a tiny nucleus, with a positive charge.

Rutherford Came Up with the Nuclear Model of the Atom

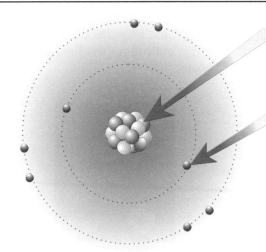

The nucleus is tiny but it makes up most of the mass of the atom. It contains protons (which are positively charged) and neutrons (which are neutral) — which gives it an overall positive charge.

The rest of the atom is mostly empty space. The negative electrons whizz round the outside of the nucleus really fast. They give the atom its overall size.

See Section 5 for a few more details on this.

Learn the relative charges and masses of each particle:

PARTICLE	RELATIVE MASS	RELATIVE CHARGE
Proton	1	+1
Neutron	1	0
Electron	$1/2000$	−1

Isotopes are Different Forms of the Same Element

> Isotopes are: different atomic forms of the same element, which have the SAME number of PROTONS but a DIFFERENT number of NEUTRONS.

1) The upshot is: isotopes must have the same proton number but different mass numbers.

2) If they had different proton numbers, they'd be different elements altogether.

3) A very popular pair of isotopes are carbon-12 and carbon-14, used for carbon dating (see p.129).

Carbon-12

$^{12}_{6}C$

6 PROTONS
6 ELECTRONS
6 NEUTRONS

Carbon-14

$^{14}_{6}C$

6 PROTONS
6 ELECTRONS
8 NEUTRONS

Some isotopes are unstable. Unstable isotopes are radioactive, which means they decay into other elements and give out radiation.

And now it finally IS the last section in the book ☺...

The nuclear model is just one way of thinking about the atom. It works really well for explaining a lot of Chemistry, but it's certainly not the whole story. Other bits of science are explained using different models of the atom. The beauty of it though is that no one model is more right than the others.

Ionising Radiation

Ionisation is where an atom either loses or gains electrons. There are three types of ionising radiation...

Ionising Radiation: Alpha, Beta and Gamma (α, β and γ)

You need to remember three things about each type of radiation:
1) What it actually is.
2) How strongly it ionises a material (i.e. bashes into atoms and knocks electrons off).
3) How well it penetrates materials.

There's a pattern: The more ionising the radiation is, the less penetrating it is. Particles of strongly ionising radiation collide with lots of atoms and knock electrons off. This activity means they give up their kinetic energy more quickly — so don't penetrate far into materials.

Alpha Particles are Helium Nuclei ^4_2He

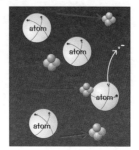

1) They are relatively big and heavy and slow-moving.
2) They have a strong positive charge.
3) Their big mass and charge make them strongly ionising. This just means they bash into lots of atoms and knock electrons off them, which creates lots of ions — hence the term 'ionising'. So they don't penetrate far into materials, but are stopped quickly.

Beta Particles are Electrons $^0_{-1}e$

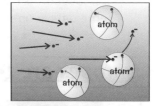

1) These are in between alpha and gamma in terms of their properties.
2) They move quite fast and they are quite small (they're electrons).
3) They have a negative charge.
4) They are moderately ionising and penetrate moderately before colliding.
5) For every β-particle emitted, a neutron turns to a proton in the nucleus.

Gamma Rays are Very Short Wavelength EM Waves

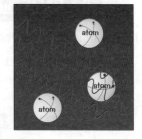

1) They are the opposite of alpha particles in a way.
2) They tend to pass through rather than collide with atoms, so they are weakly ionising and can penetrate a long way into materials. Eventually they hit something and do damage.

> Gamma rays and X-rays are very similar, and have very similar properties. The only real difference between them is in the way they're produced. X-rays can be made by firing electrons at a piece of metal. Gamma rays are released from unstable atomic nuclei when they decay.

Remember What Blocks the Three Types of Radiation...

They really like this for exam questions, so make sure you know what it takes to block each of the three:
Alpha particles are blocked by paper.
Beta particles are blocked by thin aluminium.
Gamma rays are blocked by thick lead.
Of course anything equivalent will also block them, e.g. a thin sheet of any metal will stop beta; and very thick concrete will stop gamma just like lead does.

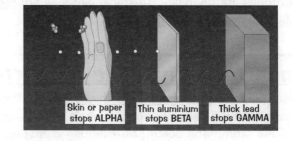

Radioactive Decay

Radioactivity is a Totally Random Process

Unstable nuclei will decay, and in the process give out radiation. This happens entirely at random. This means that if you have 1000 unstable nuclei, you can't say when any one of them is going to decay, and neither can you do anything at all to make a decay happen.

Each nucleus will just decay quite spontaneously in its own good time. It's completely unaffected by physical conditions like temperature, or by any sort of chemical bonding etc.

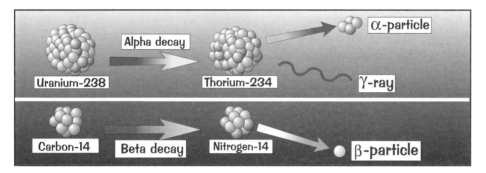

When the nucleus does decay it will spit out one or more of the three types of radiation, alpha, beta and gamma, and in the process the nucleus will often change into a new element.

Nuclear Equations — Not Half As Bad As They Sound

With nuclear equations, it's just a case of making sure the mass numbers and atomic numbers balance up on both sides. The trickiest bit is remembering the mass and atomic numbers for α, β, and γ particles. Make sure you can do all of these easily:

Alpha Emission:

A typical alpha emission:

An α-particle has a mass of 4 and a charge of +2. So when an alpha particle is emitted from a nucleus, the proton number goes down by 2 and the mass number goes down by 4.

Beta Emission:

A typical beta emission:

A β-particle has (virtually) no mass and a charge of –1. When a beta particle is emitted from a nucleus, a neutron in the nucleus is converted to a proton — the proton number goes up by 1 and the mass number stays the same.

Gamma Emission:

A typical combined α and γ emission:

A γ-ray is a photon with no mass and no charge.
After an alpha or beta emission the nucleus sometimes has extra energy to get rid of. It does this by emitting a gamma ray. Gamma emission never changes the proton or mass numbers of the nucleus.

I once beta particle — it cried for ages...

Learn all the details about the three different types of radiation — alpha, beta and gamma. When a nucleus decays by alpha emission, its atomic number goes down by two and its mass number goes down by four. Beta emission increases the atomic number by one (the mass number doesn't change).

Background Radiation

We're constantly exposed to very low levels of radiation — and all without us noticing. Sneaky.

Background Radiation Comes from Many Sources

Background radiation comes from:

1) Radioactivity of naturally occurring unstable isotopes which are all around us — in the air, in food, in building materials and in the rocks under our feet.

2) Radiation from space, which is known as cosmic rays. These come mostly from the Sun. Luckily, the Earth's atmosphere and magnetic field protects us from much of this radiation.

3) Radiation due to human activity, e.g. fallout from nuclear explosions or dumped nuclear waste. But this represents a tiny proportion of the total background radiation.

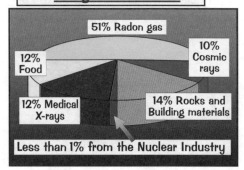

The RELATIVE PROPORTIONS of background radiation:

51% Radon gas
10% Cosmic rays
12% Food
12% Medical X-rays
14% Rocks and Building materials
Less than 1% from the Nuclear Industry

The Level of Background Radiation Changes Depending on Where You Are

1) At high altitudes (e.g. in jet planes) it increases because of more exposure to cosmic rays. That means commercial pilots have an increased risk of getting some types of cancer.

2) Underground in mines, etc. it increases because of the rocks all around.

3) Certain underground rocks (e.g. granite) can cause higher levels at the surface, especially if they release radioactive radon gas, which tends to get trapped inside people's houses.

Radon Gas is the Subject of Scientific Debate

1) The radon concentration in people's houses varies widely across the UK, depending on what type of rock the house is built on.

2) Studies have shown that exposure to high doses of radon gas can cause lung cancer — and the greater the radon concentration, the higher the risk.

3) The scientific community is a bit divided on the effects of lower doses, and there's still a lot of debate over what the highest safe(ish) concentration is.

4) Evidence suggests that the risk of developing lung cancer from radon is much greater for smokers compared to non-smokers.

5) Some medical professionals reckon that about 1 in 20 deaths from lung cancer (about 2000 per year) are caused by radon exposure.

6) New houses in areas where high levels of radon gas might occur must be designed with good ventilation systems. These reduce the concentration of radon in the living space.

7) In existing houses, the Government recommends that ventilation systems are put in wherever the radon concentration is higher than a certain level.

Coloured bits indicate more radiation from rocks

Background radiation — it's like nasty wallpaper...

Did you know that background radiation was first discovered accidentally. Scientists were trying to work out which materials were radioactive, and couldn't understand why their reader still showed radioactivity, when there was no material being tested. They realised it must be natural background radiation.

Section Ten — Nuclear Physics

Radioactivity Safety

Attitudes Towards the Dangers of Radioactivity Have Changed

1) When <u>Marie Curie</u> discovered the radioactive properties of <u>radium</u> in 1898, nobody knew anything about its dangers. People were fascinated by radium — it was used in medicines and luminous paint. You could buy <u>everyday products</u> made using this paint, e.g. <u>glow-in-the-dark watches</u>.

2) By the 1930s people were starting to link health problems to radiation — many <u>watch dial painters</u> developed cancer as a result of radium exposure. More recently, we've learnt a lot from the long-term effects of <u>terrible events</u> like the nuclear attacks on Japan in 1945 and the Chernobyl disaster in 1986.

3) Nowadays there are <u>strict rules</u> governing the use of radioactive materials...

Radiation Harms Living Cells

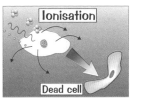

1) <u>Alpha</u>, <u>beta</u> and <u>gamma</u> radiation will cheerfully enter living cells and <u>collide with molecules</u>.

2) These collisions cause <u>ionisation</u>, which <u>damages</u> or <u>destroys</u> the <u>molecules</u>.

3) <u>Lower doses</u> tend to cause <u>minor damage</u> without <u>killing</u> the cell.

4) This can give rise to <u>mutant cells</u> which <u>divide uncontrollably</u>. This is <u>cancer</u>.

5) <u>Higher doses</u> tend to <u>kill cells completely</u>, which causes <u>radiation sickness</u> if a lot of body cells all get <u>blatted</u> at once.

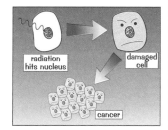

Outside the Body, β– and γ–Sources are the Most Dangerous

This is because <u>beta and gamma</u> can get <u>inside</u> to the delicate <u>organs</u>, whereas alpha is much less dangerous because it <u>can't penetrate the skin</u>.

Inside the Body, an α–Source is the Most Dangerous

Inside the body alpha sources do all their damage in a <u>very localised area</u>. Beta and gamma sources on the other hand are <u>less dangerous</u> inside the body because they mostly <u>pass straight out</u> without doing much damage.

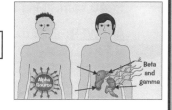

You Need to Learn About These Safety Precautions

Obviously radioactive materials need to be handled <u>carefully</u>. But in the exam they might ask you to <u>list some specific precautions</u> that should be taken when <u>handling radioactive materials</u>. If you want those <u>easy marks</u> you'd better learn all these:

In the School Laboratory:

1) <u>Never</u> allow <u>skin contact</u> with a source. Always handle with <u>tongs</u>.
2) Hold the source at <u>arm's length</u> to keep it <u>as far</u> from the body <u>as possible</u>.
3) Keep the source <u>pointing away</u> from the body and <u>avoid looking directly at it</u>.
4) <u>Always</u> store the source in a <u>lead box</u> and put it back in <u>as soon</u> as the experiment is <u>over</u>.

Radiation sickness — well yes, it does all get a bit tedious...

Sadly, much of our knowledge of the harmful effects of radiation has come as a result of <u>devastating events</u> such as the <u>atomic bombing of Japan</u> in 1945. In the months following the bombs, thousands suffered from <u>radiation sickness</u> — the symptoms of which include nausea, fatigue, skin burns, hair loss and, in serious cases, death. In the <u>long term</u>, the area has experienced increased rates of cancer, particularly <u>leukaemia</u>.

Half-Life

The Radioactivity of a Sample Always Decreases Over Time

1) This is pretty obvious when you think about it. Each time a decay happens and an alpha, beta or gamma is given out, it means one more radioactive nucleus has disappeared.

2) Obviously, as the unstable nuclei all steadily disappear, the activity as a whole will decrease. So the older a sample becomes, the less radiation it will emit.

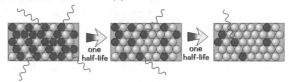

3) How quickly the activity drops off varies a lot. For some isotopes it takes just a few hours before nearly all the unstable nuclei have decayed, whilst for others, it takes millions of years.

4) The problem with trying to measure this is that the activity never reaches zero, which is why we have to use the idea of half-life to measure how quickly the activity drops off.

5) Learn this important definition of half-life:
Another definition of half-life is:
"The time taken for the activity (or count rate) to fall by half". Use either.

> **HALF-LIFE is the TIME TAKEN for HALF of the radioactive atoms now present to DECAY.**

6) A short half-life means the activity falls quickly, because lots of the nuclei decay quickly.

7) A long half-life means the activity falls more slowly because most of the nuclei don't decay for a long time — they just sit there, basically unstable, but kind of biding their time.

Do half-life questions **STEP BY STEP**. Like this one:

A VERY SIMPLE EXAMPLE: The activity of a radioactive isotope is 640 cpm (counts per minute). Two hours later it has fallen to 40 cpm. Find the half-life of the sample.

> You might also see radioactivity measured in becquerels (Bq). 1 Bq is 1 decay per second.

ANSWER: You must go through it in short simple steps like this:

INITIAL count:	(÷2)→	after ONE half-life:	(÷2)→	after TWO half-lives:	(÷2)→	after THREE half-lives:	(÷2)→	after FOUR half-lives:
640		320		160		80		40

Notice the careful step-by-step method, which tells us it takes four half-lives for the activity to fall from 640 to 40. Hence two hours represents four half-lives, so the half-life is 30 minutes.

Measuring the Half-Life of a Sample Using a Graph

1) You first need to take several readings of the count rate, usually using a Geiger counter.

2) The results can then be plotted as a graph, which will always be shaped like this one.

3) The half-life is just the time interval (on the bottom axis) corresponding to a halving of the activity (on the vertical axis). Easy peasy really.

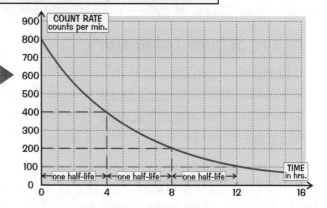

Half-life of a box of chocolates — about five minutes...

You can produce more accurate graphs of half-life by using computer software (see page 129).

Uses of Ionising Radiation

Nuclear radiation has loads of uses in hospitals...

1) Radiotherapy — the Treatment of Cancer Using Gamma Rays

1) Since high doses of gamma rays will kill all living cells, they can be used to treat cancers.
2) The gamma rays have to be directed carefully and at just the right dosage so as to kill the cancer cells without damaging too many normal cells.
3) However, a fair bit of damage is inevitably done to normal cells, which makes the patient feel very ill.
4) But if the cancer is successfully killed off in the end, then it's worth it.

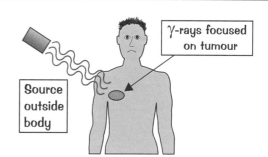

γ-rays focused on tumour

Source outside body

2) Tracers in Medicine — Always Short Half-Life Gamma Emitters

1) Certain radioactive isotopes can be injected into people (or they can just swallow them) and their progress around the body can be followed using an external detector.
2) A computer converts the reading to a display showing where the strongest reading is coming from.
3) A well-known example is the use of iodine-131. It is absorbed by the thyroid gland just like normal iodine-127, but it gives out radiation which can be detected to show whether or not the gland is taking in iodine as it should.
4) All isotopes which are taken into the body must be GAMMA or BETA emitters (never alpha), so that the radiation passes out of the body.
5) They should only last a few hours, so that the radioactivity inside the patient quickly disappears (i.e. they should have a short half-life).

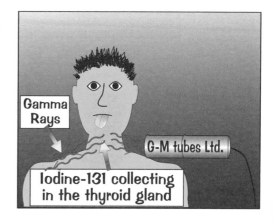

Gamma Rays

G-M tubes Ltd.

Iodine-131 collecting in the thyroid gland

Tracers can be used in industry to find leaks and blockages in pipes. To check a pipe, you just squirt in the tracer, then go along the outside with a detector. If the radioactivity reduces or stops after a certain point, there must be a leak or a blockage there. Saves digging up half the road.

3) Sterilisation of Surgical Instruments

1) Medical instruments can be sterilised by exposing them to a high dose of gamma rays, which will kill all microbes.
2) The great advantage of irradiation over boiling is that it doesn't involve high temperatures, so heat-sensitive things like thermometers and plastic instruments can be totally sterilised without damaging them.

unsterilised | Gamma source | sterilised

Ionising radiation — just what the doctor ordered...

Radiation has many important uses — especially in medicine. Make sure you know why each application uses a particular isotope according to its half-life and the type of radiation it gives out.

Uses of Ionising Radiation

...it's pretty handy in the home and in industry, too.

4) *Irradiation Keeps Food Fresh for Longer*

1) <u>Food</u> can be <u>irradiated</u> with gamma rays to keep it <u>fresh for longer</u>.

2) This is very similar to the method used for sterilising surgical equipment (see previous page).

3) The food is <u>not</u> radioactive afterwards, so it's <u>perfectly safe</u> to eat.

4) The isotope used for this needs to be a <u>very strong</u> emitter of <u>gamma rays</u> and have a <u>reasonably long half-life</u> (at least several months) so that it doesn't need <u>replacing</u> too often.

5) *Smoke Detectors — Use α Radiation*

1) A <u>weak</u> source of alpha radiation is placed in the detector, close to <u>two electrodes</u>.

2) The source causes <u>ionisation</u>, and a <u>current</u> flows.

3) If there is a fire then smoke will <u>absorb</u> the radiation — the current stops and the <u>alarm sounds</u>.

6) *Radioactive Dating of Rocks and Archaeological Specimens*

1) The discovery of radioactivity and the idea of <u>half-life</u> (see p126) gave scientists their <u>first opportunity</u> to <u>accurately</u> work out the <u>age</u> of <u>rocks</u>, <u>fossils</u> and <u>archaeological specimens</u>.

2) By measuring the <u>amount</u> of a <u>radioactive isotope</u> left in a sample, and knowing its <u>half-life</u>, you can work out <u>how long</u> the thing has been around.

3) <u>Igneous</u> rocks contain radioactive uranium which has a ridiculously <u>long half-life</u>. It eventually decays to become <u>stable</u> isotopes of <u>lead</u>, so the big clue to a rock sample's age is the <u>relative proportions</u> of uranium and lead isotopes.

4) Igneous rock also contains the radioisotope <u>potassium-40</u>. It's decay produces stable <u>argon gas</u> and sometimes this gets trapped in the rock. Then it's the same process again — finding the <u>relative proportions</u> of potassium-40 and argon to work out the age.

There's loads more on radioactive dating on the next page →

Will any of that be in your exam? — isotope so...

So radiation isn't all bad, then... Learn the six headings till you can write them down from memory. Then start learning all the details that go with each one of them. The best way to check what you know is to do a mini-essay for each section. Then check back and see what details you missed. Nice.

Radioactive Dating

Carbon-14 Calculations — Carbon Dating

1) Carbon-14 makes up about 1/10 000 000 (one ten-millionth) of the carbon in the air. This level stays fairly constant in the atmosphere.

2) The same proportion of C-14 is also found in living things.

3) However, when they die, the C-14 is trapped inside the wood or wool or whatever, and it gradually decays with a half-life of 5730 years.

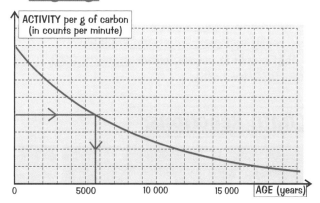

4) So, by measuring the proportion of C-14 found in some old axe handle, burial shroud, etc. you can calculate how long ago the item was living material using the known half-life.

EXAMPLE:	The carbon in an axe handle was found to contain 1 part in 40 000 000 C-14. How old is the axe?
ANSWER:	The C-14 was originally 1 part in 10 000 000. After one half-life it would be down to 1 part in 20 000 000. After two half-lives it would be down to 1 part in 40 000 000. Hence the axe handle is two C-14 half-lives old, i.e. 2 × 5730 = 11 460 years old.

The Results from Radioactive Dating aren't Perfect

Scientific conclusions are often full of uncertainties. This is because they're based on certain assumptions which may not always be true. For example, carbon dating is based on the following assumptions:

1) The level of C-14 in the atmosphere has always been constant.
2) All living things take in the same proportion of their carbon as C-14.
3) Samples haven't been contaminated by a more recent source of carbon (i.e. after they've died).

IN REALITY THOUGH...

1) The level of C-14 hasn't always been constant — cosmic radiation, climate change and human activity have all had an effect. To account for this, scientists adjust their results using calibration tables.

2) Not all living things act as we expect. For example, some plants take up less C-14 than expected — this means they seem older than they really are.

3) Scientists can't be 100% sure that a sample hasn't been contaminated.

MEASURING ERROR also affects the accuracy of results. The proportion of C-14 measured in a sample is unlikely to be exact — either because of the equipment used or human error.

When conducting scientific research, we can use technology to increase the accuracy of results. Measurements of radioactivity can be made more accurately by attaching the counter to a computer. Instead of taking readings and plotting a graph by hand, the computer's software plots the graph for you.

I tried dating rocks — they're not great for conversation...

Carbon dating was developed by Willard Libby in 1949, and the method's still used today. His original figure for the half-life of C-14 has since been altered slightly, but then that's science for you — changes all the time.

Nuclear Fission and Fusion

Nuclear Fission — the Splitting Up of Big Atomic Nuclei

Nuclear power stations and nuclear submarines are both powered by nuclear reactors.

In a nuclear reactor, a controlled chain reaction takes place in which atomic nuclei split up and release energy in the form of heat. This heat is then simply used to heat water to drive a steam turbine. So nuclear reactors are really just glorified steam engines! The "fuel" that's split is usually either uranium-235 or plutonium-239 (or both).

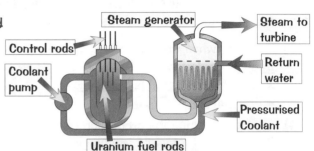

The Chain Reactions:

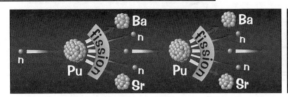 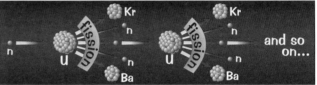

1) If a slow-moving neutron gets absorbed by a uranium or plutonium nucleus, the nucleus can split.

2) Each time a uranium or plutonium nucleus splits up, it spits out two or three neutrons, one of which might hit another nucleus, causing it to split also, and thus keeping the chain reaction going.

3) When a large atom splits in two it will form two new lighter elements. These new nuclei are usually radioactive because they have the "wrong" number of neutrons in them. This is the big problem with nuclear power — it produces huge amounts of radioactive material which is very difficult and expensive to dispose of safely.

4) Each nucleus splitting (called a fission) gives out a lot of energy — a lot more energy than you get with a chemical bond between two atoms. Make sure you remember that. Nuclear processes release much more energy than chemical processes do. That's why nuclear bombs are so much more powerful than ordinary bombs (which rely on chemical reactions).

Nuclear Fusion — the Joining of Small Atomic Nuclei

1) Two light nuclei (e.g. hydrogen) can combine to create a larger nucleus — this is called nuclear fusion.

2) Fusion releases a lot of energy — all the energy released in stars comes from fusion. So people are trying to develop fusion reactors to make electricity.

3) Fusion doesn't leave behind a lot of radioactive waste and there's plenty of hydrogen knocking about to use as fuel.

4) The big problem is that fusion can only happen at really high temperatures — over 10 000 000 °C.

5) No material can stand that kind of temperature without being vaporised, so fusion reactors are really hard to build. You have to contain the hot hydrogen in a magnetic field instead of a physical container.

6) There are a few experimental reactors around, but none of them are generating electricity yet. At the moment it takes more power to get up to temperature than the reactor can produce.

Ten million degrees — that's hot...

In 1989 two scientists, Pons and Fleischmann, claimed to have achieved cold fusion (fusion at room temperature). This caused a lot of excitement — cold fusion would mean lots of very cheap electricity. Many scientists were sceptical, and the results have never been repeated reliably enough to be accepted.

Section Ten — Nuclear Physics

Revision Summary for Section Ten

Hopefully those little radiation facts will have penetrated your brain and stored themselves away — ready to be emitted at high speed in the exam. But there's only one way to find out. And you know what that is, I'll bet. This page isn't full of questions for nothing. So off you go — write down the answers to all the questions, then go back over the section and see if there are any you got wrong. If so, read over the tricky bits and have another go at the questions. It's the best way to check you know your stuff.

1)   Draw a table stating the relative mass and charge of the three basic subatomic particles.

2)   Describe the nature and properties of the three types of ionising radiation: α, β and γ.

3)*   Write down the nuclear equation for the alpha decay of $^{234}_{92}U$ into thorium (Th).

4)*   Write down the nuclear equation for the beta decay of $^{234}_{90}Th$ into protactinium (Pa).

5)   List three places where the level of background radiation is increased and explain why.

6)   What feature must new houses in areas of high radon concentration be designed with?

7)   Explain what kind of damage radiation causes to body cells. What are the effects of high doses? What damage do lower doses do?

8)   Which kinds of radioactive source are most dangerous: a) inside the body, b) outside the body?

9)   List four safety precautions that should be taken whenever radioactive materials are handled in the school lab.

10)   Give a proper definition of half-life.

11)*   The graph shows activity against time for a sample of radioactive material. Use the graph to find the half-life of the sample.

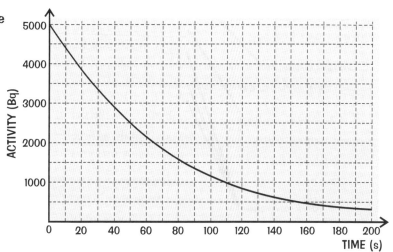

12)   Describe in detail how radioactive sources are used in each of the following:
a) smoke detectors,
b) tracers in medicine,
c) radiotherapy,
d) sterilisation of food.

13)*   An old bit of cloth was found to have 1 atom of C-14 to 80 000 000 atoms of C-12. If C-14 decays with a half-life of 5730 years, and the proportion of C-14 to C-12 in living material is 1 to 10 000 000, find the age of the cloth.

14)   Why might you question your answer to question 13?

15)   Draw a diagram to illustrate the fission of uranium-235 and explain how the chain reaction works.

16)   What is nuclear fusion? Why is it difficult to construct a working fusion reactor?

* Answers on page 140.

Thinking in Exams

In the old days, it was enough to learn a whole bunch of <u>facts</u> while you were revising and just spew them onto the paper come exam day. If you knew the facts, you had a good chance of doing well, even if you didn't really <u>understand</u> what any of those facts actually meant. But those days are over. Rats.

Remember — You Might Have to Think During the Exam

1) Nowadays, the examiners want you to be able to <u>apply</u> your scientific knowledge and <u>understand articles</u> written about science. Eeek.

2) The trick is <u>not</u> to <u>panic</u>. They're <u>not</u> expecting you to show Einstein-like levels of scientific insight (not usually, anyway).

3) They're just expecting you to use the science you <u>know</u> in both <u>familiar</u> and <u>unfamiliar settings</u>. And sometimes they'll give you some <u>extra info</u> too that you should use in your answer.

So to give you an idea of what to expect come exam-time, use the new <u>CGP Exam Simulator</u> (below). Read the article, and have a go at the questions. It's <u>guaranteed</u> to be just as much fun as the real thing.

Underlining or making notes of the main bits as you read is a good idea.

1. Stopping distance divided into distance for thinking and braking

2. Distance varies
→ speed, driver, car

3. Car needs to have good grip on road... to improve stopping distances...

4. Grip on road
→ tyres
→ weather conditions
→ road surface

The distance it takes for a car to stop once the driver has seen a hazard is divided between the <u>thinking distance</u> and the <u>braking distance.</u> These two distances are affected by many factors, such as <u>how fast the car is going</u> and <u>the condition of the driver and the car.</u>

It's important for the car to have a <u>good grip</u> on the road. The better the grip <u>the sooner the car will be able to stop</u>. Tyres should have a <u>minimum tread depth</u> of 1.6 mm to have enough grip in wet conditions. Without any tread the tyre will just ride on the layer of water and skid really easily. Drivers should take extra care when it's w<u>et or icy as</u> the road's slippier than when it's dry. Even the road surf<u>ace can make</u> a difference — gravel, leaves and muck can all cause the car to slip.

Mark Smith, a director of GoodTyres plc, said: "We recommend regularly replacing your tyres for the best control of your car and better road safety."

<u>Questions:</u>
1. Why should a car owner check the tread depth of their car's tyres?
2. In rainy conditions, why should people leave a greater distance between their car and the car in front?
3. Why might some people suspect Mark Smith of being biased?

Clues — don't read unless you need a bit of a hand...
1. Think about what would happen if the tyres didn't have any tread.
2. What happens to the road surface in wet conditions? What effect will this have on the stopping distance?
3. What's his job?

Answers: 3) He's a director of a firm that probably makes tyres — so he'll want to make them sound as important as possible.
2) In wet conditions there is more water on the road, which means the car has less grip. This increases the braking distance and so the overall stopping distance.
1) The tyre tread is important for preventing skidding in wet conditions — so its depth should be checked regularly.

Don't skim read — you might something...

It's so easy to skim read an article given to you in an exam. But don't. Read it really well, underlining or making notes as you go. It's well worth spending some time making sure you understand the article and what the questions are asking for before scribbling down your answers.

Answering Experiment Questions (i)

Science is all (well... a lot) about doing experiments carefully, and interpreting results.
And so that's what they're going to test you on when you do your exam. Among other things.

Read the Question Carefully

Expect at least some questions to describe experiments — a bit like the one below.

Q3 Ellen has three different bottles of citric acid: A, B and C.
The citric acid in each bottle is of a different concentration.

Ellen also has another quantity of citric acid, in the form of kitchen descaler.

Ellen wants to know if any of her three acids are the same concentration as the kitchen descaler. She plans to titrate each of the four citric acid solutions against a solution of sodium hydroxide of a known concentration, as shown.

She repeats the titration 3 times for each acid.

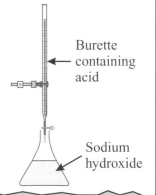

Burette containing acid

Sodium hydroxide

1. What is the independent variable in Ellen's experiment?

   The type of acid used (e.g. A, B or C).

   The independent variable is the thing that the experimenter changes — to see what effect that change has.

   Quite often, experiments involve recording what happens over time, e.g. rate of reaction experiments. In these cases, time is always the independent variable — the experimenter isn't 'changing the time' exactly, but they do want to see what happens as the time changes.

2. What is the dependent variable?

   The quantity of acid required to

   neutralise the sodium hydroxide.

   The dependent variable is the thing that the experimenter measures (every time they change the independent variable).

3. Give two variables that must be kept the same to make it a fair test.

   1. *The amount of NaOH.*

   2. *The type and amount of*

      indicator used.

   To make it a fair test, you've got to keep all the other variables the same (you're only changing the independent variable). That way you know that the only thing affecting the dependent variable is the independent variable.

4. Give one other precaution that Ellen should take to ensure her results are reliable.

   Wash and dry the equipment each

   time (to ensure no contamination).

   If your experiment is being done in a lab, this should be fairly easy (though not always — e.g. you might have to keep temperature constant, which could be tricky). But it's trickier still when you don't have much control over the conditions at all — e.g. if your experiment has to be done outside (where temperature, humidity etc. can vary considerably).

Anything that might affect the results needs to be kept constant, so look at the apparatus, think what Ellen's going to be doing — and you should be able to come up with answers fairly easily.

If the equipment isn't clean, that will definitely affect the results. And if the flask's not dry, the extra water would dilute the sodium hydroxide slightly (which would affect the results). A change in temperature could also be a problem (though probably a small one) — things expand as they get hotter, so Ellen could get a false reading from the burette if the temperature in the lab changes drastically between tests.

Answering Experiment Questions (ii)

5. Why did Ellen repeat the titration 3 times for each acid?

   To check for anomalous results and make

   the results more <u>reliable</u>.

> Sometimes you get <u>unusual results</u> — <u>repeating</u> an experiment gives you a better idea what the <u>correct result</u> should be.

6. The table below shows the amount of acid required in each titration.

	1st result (cm³)	2nd result (cm³)	3rd result (cm³)	Mean (cm³)
Kitchen descaler	24.1	23.9	23.7	
Acid A	23.9	23.5	24.0	23.8
Acid B	33.3	33.7	(38.6)	33.5
Acid C	23.7	23.9	24.1	23.9

> When an experiment is <u>repeated</u>, the results will usually be <u>slightly different</u> each time.
>
> To get a single <u>representative</u> value, you'd usually find the <u>mean</u> (average) of all the results.
>
> The more times the experiment is <u>repeated</u> the <u>more reliable</u> this average will be.
>
> To find the mean:
>
> **ADD TOGETHER all the data values and DIVIDE by the total number of values in the sample.**
>
> The <u>range</u> is how <u>spread out</u> the data is.
>
> You just work out the <u>difference</u> between the <u>highest</u> and <u>lowest</u> numbers.

   a) Calculate the mean amount of kitchen descaler required to neutralise the NaOH.

   Mean = (24.1 + 23.9 + 23.7) ÷ 3 = 23.9 cm³

   b) What is the range of the quantities of kitchen descaler required?

   24.1 – 23.7 = 0.4 cm³

> If one result doesn't seem to fit in — it's <u>wildly out</u> compared to all the others — then it's called an <u>anomalous</u> result. You should usually <u>ignore</u> an anomalous result (or even better — investigate it and try to work out what happened). Here, it's been <u>ignored</u> when the mean was worked out.
>
> This one's a <u>random error</u> — one that only happens occasionally.

7. One of the results on the table is anomalous. Circle the result and suggest why it may have occurred.

   The reading may not have been taken

   correctly, or the wrong quantity of

   NaOH may have been used.

> If you make the same mistake every time, it's a <u>systematic error</u>.
>
> For example, if you measured the volume of a liquid using the <u>top</u> of the meniscus rather than the <u>bottom</u>, all your readings would be a little on the large side.

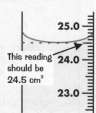

This reading should be 24.5 cm³

8. Using these results, which acid can you conclude is <u>not</u> the same concentration as the kitchen descaler?

   Acid B

> You have to be careful here — both Acids A and C could be the same concentration, since all experiments have a "margin of error" — meaning results are never absolutely spot on.
>
> So you can say that Acid B has a different concentration — but Acids A and C could be the same.

We all make mistakes...

No scientist does an experiment just once — unless they like people to point and laugh when the result turns out to be <u>wrong</u>. It's like weightlifting — the more times you repeat an experiment, the better the results will be (unless you're making <u>systematic</u> errors — you'd just have <u>lots</u> of <u>wrong results</u> then).

Answering Experiment Questions (iii)

Once you've collected all your data together, you need to analyse it to find any relationships between the variables. The easiest way to do this is to draw a graph, then describe what you see...

Graphs Are Used to Show Relationships

These are the results Pu-lin obtained with the King Edward potato.

Number of teaspoons of sugar	0	2	4	6	8	10	12	14	16	18	20
Mass of potato tube (g)	2.50	2.40	2.23	2.10	2.02	1.76	1.66	1.25	1.47	1.3	1.15

4. a) Nine of the points are plotted below.
Plot the remaining **two** points on the graph.

> To plot the points, use a <u>sharp</u> pencil and make a <u>neat</u> little cross.
>
> nice clear mark smudged unclear marks

b) Draw a straight line of best fit for the points.

> A line of best fit is drawn so that it's easy to see the <u>relationship</u> between the variables. You can then use it to <u>estimate</u> other values.

When drawing a line of best fit, try to draw the line through or as near to as many points as possible, ignoring any <u>anomalous</u> results.

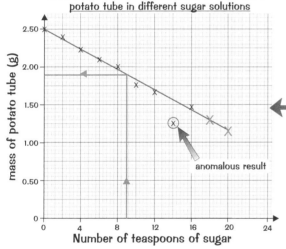

Scattergram to show the mass of a King Edward potato tube in different sugar solutions

anomalous result

> This is a <u>scattergram</u> — they're used to see if two variables are <u>related</u>.

5. Estimate the weight of the potato tube if you added nine teaspoons of sugar.

Estimate of weight = <u>1.90 g (see graph)</u>

> This graph shows a <u>negative correlation</u> between the variables. This is where one variable <u>increases</u> as the other one <u>decreases</u>.

The other correlations you could get are:

> <u>Positive correlation</u> — this is where as one variable <u>increases</u> so does the other one.

> <u>No correlation</u> — this is where there's <u>no obvious relationship</u> between the variables.

6. What can you conclude from these results?

<u>There is a negative correlation between the number of teaspoons of sugar and the mass of potato tube. Each additional teaspoon causes the potato tube to lose mass.</u>

> In lab-based experiments like this one, you can say that one variable <u>causes</u> the other one to change. The extra sugar <u>causes</u> the potato to lose mass. You can say this because everything else has <u>stayed the same</u> — nothing else could be causing the change.

There's a positive correlation between revising and good marks...

...really, it's true. Other ways to improve your marks are to practise plotting graphs, and learning how to read them properly — make sure you're reading off the right axis for a start, and don't worry about drawing lines on the graph if it helps you to read it. Always double-check your answer... just in case.

Exam Skills

Answering Experiment Questions (iv)

A lot of Physics experiments can be done in a <u>nice controlled way</u> in a laboratory. But not all of them. And once you get <u>out of the lab</u> and into the <u>real world</u>, it gets much <u>harder to control</u> all the <u>variables</u>.

Relationships Do NOT Always Tell Us the Cause

On holiday in Scotland, Kate found that mountain streams can be difficult to wade across — the streams flow quite slowly, but there are often many large rocks on the stream bed, which make it difficult to balance.

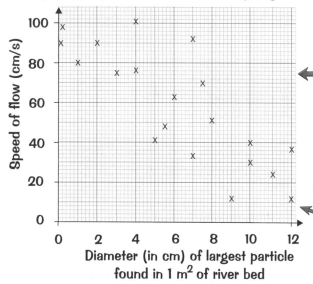

Kate decided to investigate whether the speed of a river and the size of the rocks/pebbles found on the river bed are related.

She measured the speed of flow and the diameter of the biggest rock/pebble that she found, at several points along the length of one river.

> Outside a lab it can be really <u>difficult</u> to keep conditions the same throughout the study — in this example, if there's a sudden rainstorm in the hills, this will affect the flow of the river.

> In this <u>scattergram</u>, each point plotted represents a different place along the length of the river.

1. What conclusion can you draw from these results?

    The bigger the largest particles on the
    river bed are, the slower the river tends
    to be at that point.

> The graph shows a <u>negative correlation</u>. It's not a fantastically <u>strong</u> correlation, but it's definitely there.

> You <u>can't say</u>, just from these results, that <u>bigger particles</u> on the river bed <u>cause</u> the river to slow down. Neither can you say that a <u>slower flow</u> causes bigger particles to collect on the river bed. It could be either way round... or one change might not <u>cause</u> the other at all.

2. Suggest two possible problems with the method Kate has used to describe the size of the particles on the river bed.

    1. Rocks/pebbles aren't usually spherical,
    so it's hard to say what the 'diameter' is.

    2. The one biggest rock/pebble may be
    unrepresentative of the others at that point
    in the river, and so give a misleading result.

> In studies like this where you're unable to control everything, it's possible a <u>third variable</u> is causing the relationship. In this example, the third variable could be something like the width or depth of the river, or the steepness of the slope.

> Try to think of ways the data might be <u>unreliable</u> or the study might be <u>invalid</u>.

Cause and effect — chicken and egg...

It's really hard to prove <u>causation</u>. Think about it — it sounds sensible that a rockier river bed provides more <u>resistance</u> to the flow of water, slowing it down. It sounds just as sensible that as the river slows down, there isn't enough 'oomph' to keep the big rocks bowling along. Which came first? Even if you reckon you <u>know</u> the answer — if your results <u>don't prove it</u>, you <u>can't</u> put it in your conclusion.

Index

A

abortion 15
ABS brakes 104
absorption of oxygen 26
AC (alternating current) 113
acceleration 96-101, 103
acid rain 42, 48
acidity of a lake 50
acids 81-83
    acids reacting with metals 82
activation energy 76, 77
active detergents 92
active safety features 104
active transport 39
adenine 3
adolescence 10
adult stem cells 14
adulthood 10
aerobic respiration 23
aerosols 50
air bags 104
air humidity 37
air movement 37
air pollution 42, 48, 50
air resistance 99, 106
alkali metals 55, 60, 63
alkalis 81, 83
alkanes 87
alkenes 86, 87
alleles 18, 20, 21
alpha radiation 121-123, 125, 128
alternative fuels 86
aluminium 54, 85
    aluminium chloride 82
    aluminium oxide 85
    aluminium sulfate 82
alveoli 6
amino acids 3, 6, 24, 26
ammeters 112, 115, 117
ammonia 61, 79, 83, 84
    ammonium nitrate fertiliser 79
    ammonium salts 83, 84
amps 112
amylase 24, 25
anaerobic respiration 23
anhydrous 78
    anhydrous copper(II) sulfate 78
animal cells 1
anions 59
anodes 85
anomalous results 134
antibiotics 43
antibodies 26
antiseptics 63
antitoxins 26
aorta 28
applying scientific knowledge 132
aquaplaning 102
aqueous 67
A_r, relative atomic mass 68
archaeological specimens 128
arteries 27
artificial hormones 11
artificial insemination 16
artificial selection 16
asexual reproduction 12, 13
astatine 63
athletes 10
atmospheric carbon dioxide 48
atoms 53, 54, 121
    atom economy 71
    atomic number 53-55
    atomic structure 121
atria 28
attraction between masses 98
auxins 11
avian flu 43

B

background radiation 124
bacteria 25, 42, 47
balanced forces 100
balancing equations 67
Banting, Frederick 32
bases (chemical) 81
bases (DNA) 3
    base-pairing 3
batch production 91
batteries 112, 113, 115
battery farming 44
Best, Charles 32
beta radiation 122, 123, 125, 127
beta-carotene 17
big spark 110
bile 24, 25
biodegradable plastics 89
biodiversity 51
biofuels 42
    biogas 42
biological catalysts 4
biological control 45
biological detergents 92
biological washing powders 4, 92
biomass 41, 42
bleaches 63, 92
blindness 32
blood 6, 23, 26
    blood sugar levels 29, 31, 32
    blood vessels 27
body temperature 29
boiling points 58, 62
bonding 54, 57
bonds 88
brain 10
brakes 102
braking distance 102
breathing rate 23
breeding 16
brine 46
bromine 63
bromine water 87
brown stains 63
buckminsterfullerene 65
burglar detectors 115
burning fuels 47, 78
burning splint test 82
by-products 71

C

calcium carbonate 78
calcium ions 84
calculating masses 70
calculating percentage mass 69
calculating resistance 114
calibration 129
cancer 124, 125, 127
canning 46
capillaries 27
car crashes 103, 104
car power ratings 107
car safety 104
carbohydrates 31, 47
carbon 46, 54, 86, 87
    carbon, different forms of 65
carbon cycle 47
carbon dating 121, 129
carbon dioxide 23, 29, 34-36, 47, 54, 83
carbon monoxide 48
carbon-carbon double bonds 88
carbonates 83, 84
care labels for clothes 92
carriers (of genetic disorders) 21
catalysts 4, 74, 77, 79, 80
catalytic converters 48
cathodes 85
cathode ray oscilloscope (CRO) 113

cations 59
cells 1, 4, 6, 12-14, 18, 23, 115, 116, 119, 125
    cell division 12
    cell elongation 11
    cell fibres 12
    cell growth 39
    cell membranes 1, 5, 7, 21, 27, 38
    cell wall 1, 38
CFCs (chlorofluorocarbons) 50
CGP Exam Simulator 132
chain reactions 130
charge 57, 109-111
chemical production 91
    chemical plant costs 80
Chernobyl 125
childhood 10
chlorides 84
    chloride (Cl⁻) ions 85
    chloride salts 82
chlorination 93
chlorine 61, 63, 93
chlorophyll 1, 34-36, 39
chloroplasts 1, 34, 36
cholesterol 27, 88
chromosomes 2, 12, 13
circuit breakers 118
circuits 112, 116, 119
circulatory system 27
circumference 9
clean water sources 94
cleaning fluids 79
climate change 48
clones 2, 18
    cloning 18, 19
clot 26
clothing crackles 110
clotting of blood 26
coding for proteins 3
collision theory 76
collisions 103
    collision force 104
    collision time 104
combustion 47, 78
competition 40
components 112
compost heaps 46
compounds 54
computer software 129
concentration 5, 7, 74, 76
concentration difference (gradient) 5, 39
conductivity, electrical 58, 62, 64
conductors 109, 118
conservation 51
contamination 129
continuous production 91
controlled environment 43
cooling 46
copper 54, 64, 82, 85
    copper carbonate 84
    copper nitrate 84
    copper(II) sulfate 78
coppicing 51
correlation 135, 136
cosmic rays 124
cost of production of chemicals 80
count rate 126
covalent bonding 54, 61, 62
cows 32
cracking hydrocarbons 77, 86
crash barriers 104
crash tests 104
crime scene 2
CRO (cathode ray oscilloscope) traces 113
crop rotation 45
crosslinks 90
crude oil 86

cruelty to animals 43
crumple zones 104
Curie, Marie 125
current, electrical 112, 114-119
cuttings 11, 18
cystic fibrosis 21
cytoplasm 1, 12
cytosine 3

D

dairy cows 16
DC (direct current) 113
DDT 44
decay 46
deceleration 96, 97, 100
decomposers 46, 47
decomposition 46-48
defibrillators 111
deficiency symptoms in plants 39
deforestation 48
deoxygenated blood 27, 28
depression 10
detergents 92
detritivores 46
detritus 46
development 9
diabetes 14, 31, 32
    diabetes (type 1) 31
diamond 62
diet 9
differentiation 14
diffusion 5-7, 36, 37
digestion 24
    digested food 26
    digestive system 25
diodes 114, 115
diploid 12, 19
direct current 113
direction 96, 103
disabilities 15
disease 14, 43, 45
disease-resistance 16
displacement 84
distance-time graphs 96
dividing cells 12
DNA (deoxyribose nucleic acid) 2, 3, 12, 13, 17, 19
    DNA fingerprinting 2
dogs 32
Dolly the sheep 19
dominant alleles 20, 21
double carbon bonds 88
double helix 3
drag 99
drinking water 79, 84, 93, 94
driving force 112
drugs 10, 28, 91
dry weight 9
dry-cleaning solvents 92
drying food 46
dust particles 110
dust precipitators 111

E

earth wire 118
earthing 118
earthworms 46
ecosystems 79
egestion 41
egg cells 13
electric circuits 64, 65
electric shocks 110, 118
electrical conductors 58
electrical energy 119
electrical fires 118
electrical power 119
electrical pressure 112
electrical resistance 64
electricity 64, 85, 109-113, 118

Index

electrolysis 63, 85
electrolytes 85
electromagnetic (EM) waves 122
electromagnets 64
electrons 53, 55, 57, 60, 63, 85,
    109, 112, 121, 122
  electron configuration
    56, 59, 60
  electron shells 55-57, 59, 60
electrostatic paint sprayers 111
elements 54, 55, 121
embryos 14, 15, 18, 21
  embryo transplants in cows 18
  embryonic screening 21
  embryonic stem cells 14
empirical formula 69
emulsification 24
endangered species 51
endothermic reactions 78
energy 23, 34, 41-43, 76, 78,
    105-107, 119
  energy cost 71, 80, 92
  energy flow 41
  energy in circuits 119
  energy of waves 119
  energy saving 92
  energy transfer 41, 78, 105
environment 45, 71, 92
environmental conditions 35
enzymes
    4, 24, 25, 35, 39, 46, 47, 92
  digestive enzymes 24
epidermis 38
equations 67
equilibrium 79
errors 129
escape lanes 104
ethical debates 15, 19, 21
eutrophication 49
evaporation 37, 72, 84
exercise 23
exothermic reactions 78
experiments 82, 133
explosions 74

F

F = ma 100, 101
faeces 25
fair tests 133
falling objects 99
famine 79
farming 16, 18
fats 24, 47
fatty acids 24
faulty cells 14
fermenters 42
fertilisers 49, 79, 84
fertility 10
fertility clinics 15
filament lamps 114, 115
filtration 72, 84, 93
finding formulas from masses or
    percentages 69
fingerprinting, DNA 2
fires, electrical 118
fish dying 79
fish farming 43, 44
fission, nuclear 130
Fleischmann, Martin 130
fluorine 63
foetal abnormalities 15
foetus 6, 15
food 6, 38, 41, 42, 45
  food chains 40, 41, 43, 44
  food preservation methods 46
  food production 42, 43
  food reserves 13
  food shortages 43, 44

food supply 51
food web 51
foot-and-mouth disease 43
force of gravity 98
forces 98-101, 103, 105
forensic science 2
formula mass calculations 69
formulae 67
fossil fuels 43, 47, 48
fossils 128
free electrons 64
free ions 85
freezing food 46
frequency 113
friction 99, 106, 109
frost resistance 17
fructose 34
fruit cake 119
fruits 34
fuel filling 110
fuels 42, 86
full outer shells 61
fullerenes 65
fungi 47
fungicides 44
fuses 118
  fuse ratings 115, 119
fusion 130
  fusion reactors 130

G

gain, on an oscilloscope 113
gall bladder 24, 25
gametes 13
gamma radiation 122, 123, 125, 127,
    128
gangrene 32
gas exchange in the lungs 6
gas syringes 75
Geiger counters 126
genes 3, 9, 13, 17, 20, 21
  gene pool 16, 18
  gene therapy 17
genetic diagrams 20
genetic disorders 17, 21
genetic engineering 17, 32
genetic fingerprinting 2
genetic variation 13
genetically modified (GM) crops 17
gestation 10
giant covalent structures 62
giant ionic structures 58
giant metallic structures 64
glasshouses 44
global warming 48
glorified steam engines! 130
glow-in-the-dark watches 125
glucose 6, 23, 26, 31, 34, 42
glucose-monitoring devices 31
glycerol 24
gold 64
gradient 96, 97, 114
grain chutes 110
graphite 62, 65
graphs 74
gravitational field strength 105
gravitational potential energy 105, 106
gravity 11, 98, 99
greenhouses 43, 44
grip 102
Group 1 elements 55, 59, 60
Group 7 elements 55, 57, 59, 60
groups 55
growth 9-12
  growth factors 10
  growth, humans 10
  growth, plants 39
guanine 3

guard cells 1, 36
gullet 25

H

Haber process 64, 77, 80
habitats 51
haemoglobin 26
half-life 126-128
halogens 55, 60, 63
handling radioactive sources 125
haploid 13, 19
hard water 84
health problems 79
health risks 10
heart 28, 111
  heart attacks 27
  heart disease 10, 14, 88
  heart rate 23
  heart valves 28
heat 78, 119, 130
heating in reactions 72
height 9
helium nuclei 122
herbicides 45
  herbicide resistance 17
hideously important 114
Highway Code 102
homeostasis 29, 30
hooligan kids 105
hormones 9, 11, 26
household electrics 117
household waste 42
human cells 1
human embryos 15
Huntington's disease 21
hydrated 78
hydrated copper sulfate crystals 78
hydrocarbons 86, 87
hydrochloric acid 25, 82-84, 94
hydrogen 61, 79, 82, 85
hydrogen chloride 61
hydrogenation of oils 64, 88
hydroponics 44
hydroxides 83, 84

I

identical twins 2, 18
immunity 43
immunosuppressive drugs 32
in vitro fertilisation (IVF) 21
indicators 81, 84
  indicator species 50
industrial processes 77, 79
infancy 10
inflexible kink 88
insecticides 44
insemination 16
insolubility 34
insoluble bases 84
insoluble salts 84
insulators 110, 118
insulin 14, 17, 31, 32
intensive farming 16, 43, 44
intermolecular forces 62
interdependent species 40
intestines 25
iodine 63
  iodine-131 127
ion content 29
ionic bonding 54, 57, 59
ionic structures 58
ionising radiation 122, 127, 128
ions 54, 57-59, 81
  ions, tests for dissolved 94
iron 54, 64
iron catalyst 77, 79
iron sulfide 54
irradiation 127, 128
isotopes 54, 121, 127

J

joules 105, 107

K

kidneys 30
kilograms 98
kinetic energy 104, 106, 122

L

labels for washing clothes 92
labour costs 80
lactic acid 23
ladybirds 41, 45
landfill sites 51
large intestine 25
lattices 58
lead 49
  lead chloride 84
  lead nitrate 84
  lead sulfate 84
leaves 36
length (as a measure of size) 9
less reactive metals 84
lichen 50
life span 10
light 11, 34-37, 41
light dependent resistors (LDRs) 115
lightning 110
limestone buildings 48
limiting factors 35
lipase 24, 25
lithium 67
live wire 118
liver 24, 25, 30
living indicators 50
loudspeakers 115
low temperature washes 92
lubricants 99
lungs 6, 27

M

maggots 46
magnesium 39, 70, 84
  magnesium chloride 82
  magnesium ions 84
  magnesium oxide 70
  magnesium sulfate 82
mains supply 113
malleability 64
maltose 24
manganese (II) 67
margarine 88
mass 98, 100, 101, 103, 105, 106
  mass balance 98
  change in mass 75
  mass number 53-55, 68
mastitis 16
maturity 10
medical instruments 127
meiosis 13
melting points 58, 62
membranes 7, 12
Mendel, Gregor 20
metals 55, 64, 82
  metal carbonates 84
  metal halides 63
  metal hydroxides 83, 84
  metallic bonds 64
methane 61
microorganisms 26, 42, 46
milk yield 16
minerals 37, 38
miscarriage of a pregnancy 19
mitochondria 1, 13
mitosis 12
mixtures 54
moisture 46
molecules 23

Index

moles 68
momentum 103
money 77
monomers 89
monounsaturated oils 88
moons 98
more reactive metals 84
motor effect 115
M_r, relative formula mass 68
multi-cellular 14
muscles 10, 23
mutations 17
my little MGB 74
mycoprotein 42

N

naming salts 82
nanomaterials 65
   nanoparticles 65
nervous system 21
neutral wire 118
neutralisation 78, 81-84
neutrons 53, 54, 121, 130
newton meter 98
newtons 98
nitinol 65
nitrates 39, 47, 49, 79, 82, 84, 93
   nitrate salts 82
   nitrates in drinking water 79
   nitrates in the soil 47
nitric acid 79, 82, 83, 84, 94
nitrogen 39, 46, 54, 79
   nitrogen cycle 47
   nitrogen oxides 82
noble gases 55, 60
non metals 55
non-living indicators 50
nuclear bombs 130
nuclear equations 123
nuclear fission 130
nuclear fusion 130
nuclear power stations 130
nuclear reactors 130
nuclear waste 124
nucleon number 53
nucleus 1, 2, 12, 13, 53, 121, 123
nutrients 11, 45, 46
nylon carpets 110

O

oil spills 49
oils 88
old age 10
old lead pipes 93
optical brighteners 92
optimum pH for enzymes 4
optimum temperature for enzymes 4
orbits 98
organic acids 92
organic farming 43, 45
organic molecules 47
oscilloscope (CRO) traces 113
osmosis 7, 34, 38
otters 44
Outer Mongolia 42
outer shells 55
over-fishing 51
oxidation reactions 78
oxides 67, 84
oxygen
     23, 26, 27, 34, 36, 46, 54, 61
oxygenated blood 23, 27
ozone layer depletion 50

P

pacemakers 28
pain receptors 15
paint sprayers 111
paired bases, DNA 3

palisade leaf cells 1
pancreas 24, 25, 31
   transplant 32
paper rollers 110
parachute 99
parallel circuits 112, 117
parasites 45
parrot joke 88
partially permeable membranes 7
passive safety features 104
paternity testing 2
pathogenic 17
PCBs 49
pea plant experiments 20
penguins 49
pepsin 4, 24, 25
percentage mass 69
percentage yield 72
periodic table 55, 56, 64
permanent vacuole 1
pesticides 45, 49, 63
pests 45
petrol station 110
pH 25, 46
   pH, optimum value for enzymes 4
   pH scale 81
pharmaceutical drugs, production of 91
phloem tubes 38
phosphates 39, 49
photon 123
photosynthesis 1, 4, 34-37, 39,
      41, 47
pickled onions 46
pigs 32
placenta 6
planets 98
plants 23
   plant cells 1
   plant growth 11
   plant hormones 11
plasma 26
plasticisers 90
plastics 63, 89, 90
platelets 26
'playing God' 19
plugs 118
plutonium-239 130
poisoning (of catalysts) 77
poisonous ions 84
pollution 42, 45, 48-50
polymers 89, 90
polythene rod 109
polyunsaturated oils 88
Pons, Stanley 130
poor metals 55
potassium 39, 63, 84
potassium hydroxides 84
potato cylinders 7
potential difference (PD) 112,
     114, 116, 117
potential energy 105, 106
power 107, 119
   power cables 64
   power output 107
   power ratings 119
   power ratings for cars 107
   power supply 115, 116
precipitate 75
precipitation reactions 75, 84, 94
predators 43, 45
predicted yield 72
pregnancy 15
prejudice 21
premature births 15
preservatives 63, 90
pressure 74, 76, 79
pretty bad news 112
production costs 80
products 67, 70, 72
profits 71

protease 24, 25
proteins 3, 4, 6, 24, 47
protons 53, 54, 121
   proton number 53
puberty 10
pulmonary artery 28
pulmonary vein 28
purifying copper 85
purity 71
pyramids of number and biomass 40

Q

quicklime 78
Quorn 42

R

radiation 122, 123, 125
   penetrating power 122
radiation sickness 125
radioactive dating 128, 129
radioactive isotopes 124
radioactive waste 130
radioactivity 121, 123, 126, 130
   radioactivity safety 125
radiotherapy 127
radium 125
radon gas 124
range (of sizes) 9
rate of production 80
rates of reaction 74-77, 82
raw materials 71, 80, 86
reactants 67, 70, 72
reaction forces 101
reactions of acids 83
reactive metals 55
reactivity 63, 82
   reactivity trends 60
reading in exams 132
real life 117
recessive alleles 20, 21
rectum 25
recycling 46, 51, 89
   recycling carbon 46, 47
   recycling hydrogen 46, 79
   recycling in the Haber process 79
   recycling nitrogen 46, 47, 79
   recycling oxygen 46
red blood cells 26, 48
reforestation 51
refrigerating 46
regeneration of parts of the body 9
relative atomic mass 68, 69
relative charge 121
relative formula mass 68, 69
relative mass 121
relative proportions 128
renewable energy 42
repair 12
replacement planting 51
reproductive cells 13
resistance 112, 114, 116, 117, 119
   resistors 114, 115
resistance forces 99
resistance to disease 17
respiration
     4, 23, 29, 34, 39, 41, 46, 47
resultant forces 100
reversible reactions 72, 78, 79
ribosomes 1
rinse agents 92
rocks 124
   rocks, dating 128
roller coasters 106
roots 37, 38
   root growth 11, 39
   root hairs 38, 39
   rooting powder 11
rusting 74
Rutherford, Ernest 121

S

safety precautions, radioactivity 125
salivary glands 24, 25
salts 46, 63, 81-84, 92
satellites 98
saturated hydrocarbons 87
saturated oils 88
screening embryos 21
sea of free electrons 64
seals 43
seat belts 104
sedimentation 93
seed planting 45
seedless fruits 11
seeds 34
selective breeding 16
semiconductor diodes 115
series circuits 112, 116
sewage 49
   sewage works 46
sex cells 13
sexual reproduction 13
shape memory 65
sheep 16
shells 53, 57
shielding 60
shocks, electric 110, 118
shoot growth 11
sickle cell anaemia 14
silver 64
   silver choride 84
simple molecules 62, 63
simple sugars 24
single-celled organisms 14
size 9
size of particles 74
skidding 104
skin 29
skin cancer 50
skulking cat 96
skydiver 99
small intestine 6, 24, 25
smart materials 65
smog 50
smoke detectors 128
sodium 30, 63, 84
   sodium chloride 57, 63, 85
   sodium hydroxide 84
soil 39, 44, 47
solubility 92
soluble salts 84
solute 92
solutions 92
solvents 92
sparks 110
specialised cells 1, 14
speed 96, 97, 99, 100, 106
speed cameras 96
speed, distance and time formula 96
speed limits 102
speeding up reactions 4, 74-77, 82
sperm 13, 18
spinal injuries 14
sport 10
spring balance 98
squeaky pop 82
stains 92
standard test circuit 112
starch 6, 24, 34
state symbols 67
static electricity 109-111
static friction 99
steady speed 99, 100
stem cells 9, 14, 15, 32
sterilisation 127
sterilising water 63
stillbirth 19
stomach 4, 24, 25
   stomach acid 24

Index and Answers

stomata 36
stopping distances 102
strokes 27
submarines 130
successful collisions 76
suffering 15, 21
sugars 24, 47
sulfates 84
   sulfate salts 82
sulfur 54
sulfur dioxide 48
sulfur impurities 48
sulfuric acid 48, 81-83
sunlight 34
Sun's energy 41
Sun's warmth 43
superconductors 64
surface area 74, 77
surrogate pregnancies 19
sustainable development 77
sweat 30
synthetic detergents 92

T
teenagers 55
temperature 29, 35, 37, 46, 74, 76-79
   temperature detectors 115
   optimum temperature for enzymes 4
tensile strength 64
tension in a rope 105
terminal speed 99
termination 15
test circuit 112
testing components 112
tetrachloroethene, a dry cleaning solvent 92
thermal decompositions 78, 86
thermistors 115
thermoplastic polymers 90

thermoregulatory centre 29
thermosetting polymers 90
thermostats 115
thinking distance 102
third variable 136
thymine 3
time 96, 97, 107, 113
timebase on oscilloscopes 113
timeless mysteries 53
tissue culture 18
tissue fluid 7
top quality food 44
total resistance in circuits 116, 117
toxins 26
tracers 127
trans fats 88
transferring liquids 72
transition metals 55, 56, 64, 77
translocation 38
transpiration 37, 38
transplants 28
tread depth of tyres 102
trees 42, 48
triplets (DNA) 3
trophic levels 40, 41

U
unbalanced forces 100
uncertainties 129
unique DNA 2
universal indicator 81
unpollinated flowers 11
unsaturated hydrocarbons 87, 88
unstable nuclei 123
unsustainable reactions 71
uranium 128, 130
   uranium-235 130
urea 26, 29, 30
urine 30
UV (ultraviolet) radiation 50

V
vacuole 1
valves in the heart 28
variable resistors 112, 115
variables 133
variation 12, 13
vector quantities 103
vegetable oils 88
veins 27
   veins, in leaves 36
velocity 96, 97, 103
   velocity-time graphs 97
vena cava 28
ventricles 28
viability 15
vinegar 46
visibility 50, 102
vitamin deficiencies 17
voltage 110, 112, 113, 116-119
voltage-current graphs 112, 114
voltmeters 112, 115-117
volts 112
volume of gas given off 75

W
washing clothes 92
washing-up liquids 92
waste 46, 51, 71
   waste disposal 49
   waste materials in a reaction 71
   waste products 29, 42
   wasted energy 64
water 7, 34, 37, 38, 61
   water conservation 93
   water content 29, 30
   water impurities 93
   water molecules 7
   water pipes 110
   water pollution 49
   water purification 93

water resources 93
water softeners 92
water uptake 38
water vapour 36
water-borne diseases 94
watts 107
waxy cuticle 36, 38
weathering 50
weeding 45
weeds 44
weight 9, 98, 101, 105
   wet weight 9
white blood cells 26
width (as a measure of size) 9
wires 114
wiring a plug 118
womb 10
woodland conservation 51
woodlice 46
work done 105, 107
world food shortages 43

X
X-rays 122
xylem 37

Y
yeast 42
yield 72

Z
zinc 64
   zinc chloride 82
   zinc sulfate 82
zygote 13

Answers

Revision Summary for Section One (page 8)

15) a) pH1.6   b) stomach

Revision Summary for Section Three (page 33)

3) a) 60 beats per minute
   b) 2 minutes
   c) 70 beats per minute

Revision Summary for Section Four (page 52)

3) a) 40 units   b) temperature and light

Bottom of page 59

1) a) $K [2, 8, 8]^+$ b) $Al [2, 8]^{3+}$
   c) $Be [2]^{2+}$ d) $S [2, 8, 8]^{2-}$
   e) $F [2, 8]^-$

Revision Summary for Section Five (page 66)

16) d)

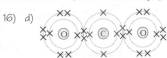

19) sodium fluoride + chlorine

Bottom of page 67

1) $Fe_2O_{3(s)} + 3H_{2(g)} \rightarrow 2Fe_{(s)} + 3H_2O_{(l)}$
2) $6HCl_{(l)} + 2Al_{(s)} \rightarrow 2AlCl_{3(aq)} + 3H_{2(g)}$

Bottom of page 68

1) Cu: 64, K: 39, Kr: 84, Cl: 35.5
2) NaOH: 40, Fe_2O_3: 160,
   C_6H_{14}: 86, $Mg(NO_3)_2$: 148

Bottom of page 69

1) a) 30.0%   b) 88.9%
   c) 48%   d) 65.3%
2) CH_4

Bottom of page 70

21.4 g

Revision Summary for Section Six (page 73)

1) a) $ZnCO_3$, b) NaOH, c)Li_2O, d) $FeCl_3$
2) a) $CaCO_3 + 2HCl \rightarrow CaCl_2 + H_2O + CO_2$
   b) $Ca + 2H_2O \rightarrow Ca(OH)_2 + H_2$
   c) $H_2SO_4 + 2KOH \rightarrow K_2SO_4 + 2H_2O$
   d) $Mg + 2HNO_3 \rightarrow Mg(NO_3)_2 + H_2$
5) a) 40
   b) 108
   c) $12 + (16 \times 2) = 44$
   d) $24 + 12 + (16 \times 3) = 84$
   e) $27 + 3 \times (16 + 1) = 78$
   f) $65 + 16 = 81$
   g) $(23 \times 2) + 12 + (16 \times 3) = 106$
   h) $23 + 35.5 = 58.5$
6) a) 75%, b) 8.7%, c) 27%
7) a) 57%, b) 35%, c) 73%
8) $MgSO_4$
9) a) 186.8 g, b) 80.3 g, c) 20.1 g

Revision Summary for Section Seven (page 95)

14) a) magnesium chloride: $Mg + 2HCl \rightarrow MgCl_2 + H_2$
   b) aluminium sulfate: $2Al + 3H_2SO_4 \rightarrow Al_2(SO_4)_3 + 3H_2$

16) a) e.g. hydrochloric acid and copper(II) oxide
   $2HCl + CuO \rightarrow CuCl_2 + H_2O$
   b) e.g. nitric acid and calcium oxide
   $2HNO_3 + CaO \rightarrow Ca(NO_3)_2 + H_2O$
   c) e.g. sulfuric acid and zinc oxide
   $H_2SO_4 + ZnO \rightarrow ZnSO_4 + H_2O$

Revision Summary for Section Eight (page 108)

2) 0.091 m/s
3) The car was travelling at 12.6 m/s, so it wasn't speeding.
5) $35 \, m/s^2$ 15) 30 N
19) 1170 kgm/s   21) 6420 J
22) 540 J   23) 20 631 J
24) 150 kJ   25) 2000 W

Revision Summary for Section Nine (page 120)

5) The wave should be drawn with one full wavelength (peak to peak) covering ten divisions of the screen.
7) $4.8 \, \Omega$
10) $A_1 = 0.2 \, A$, $V_1 = 1.4 \, V$, $V_2 = 0.4 \, V$, $V_3 = 10.2 \, V$, $R_1 = 51 \, \Omega$
15) a) 5 A, b) 3 A

Revision Summary for Section Ten (page 131)

3) $^{234}_{92}U \rightarrow ^{230}_{90}Th + ^{4}_{2}\alpha$

4) $^{234}_{90}Th \rightarrow ^{234}_{91}Pa + ^{0}_{-1}\beta + ^{0}_{0}\lambda$

11) 50 seconds
13) 17 190 years